Also by Judith Matloff

Fragments of a Forgotten War

HOME GIRL

Judith Matloff

HOME GIRL

Building a Dream House
on a Lawless Block

Random House   New York

Published in the United States by Random House,
an imprint of The Random House Publishing Group,
a division of Random House, Inc., New York.

RANDOM HOUSE and colophon are registered
trademarks of Random House, Inc.

Grateful acknowledgment is made to *The New York Times* for
permission to reprint excerpts from "Whose Neighborhood?"
by Judith Matloff (*The New York Times*, July 14, 2002),
copyright © 2002 by The New York Times Company.
Reprinted by permission.

LIBRARY OF CONGRESS CATALOGING-IN-PUBLICATION DATA
Matloff, Judith.
Home Girl: Building a Dream House on a
Lawless Block / Judith Matloff.
p.   cm.
ISBN 978-1-4000-6526-4
1. City and town life—New York, N.Y.—Harlem.
2. Harlem (New York, N.Y.)—Social life and customs—
21st century.   3. Cosmopolitanism—New York,
N.Y.—Harlem.   I. Title.
HT153.M393 2008
307.7609747'1—dc22   2007040850

Printed in the United States of America
on acid-free paper

www.atrandom.com

2 4 6 8 9 7 5 3 1

First Edition

Book design by Laurie Jewell

This one's for Mom, John, and Anton.

CONTENTS

Author's Note | xiii

Prologue | xv

PART ONE

Chapter 1 Somewhere Uncivilized | 3

Chapter 2 The Decision | 11

Chapter 3 The Hunt | 14

Chapter 4 Surprise! | 22

Chapter 5 "Only God Can Protect Us" | 36

Chapter 6 The Narcotics Wall Street | 46

Chapter 7 Meet the Neighbors | 51

Chapter 8 Abdu | 61

Chapter 9 Peace Talks | 72

PART TWO

Chapter 10 Homeland Insecurity | 89

Chapter 11 Disunited Nations | 100

Chapter 12 Nice Bones, Rotten Organs | 113

Chapter 13 A Parking Space for Mom | 122

Chapter 14 *Quis Custodiet Ipsos Custodes?* | 132

Chapter 15 Pioneer Living | 144

Chapter 16 Ways to Kill a Cat | 154

Chapter 17 The Men from Montenegro | 165

Chapter 18 Charming Apartment, with Doorman | 180

Chapter 19 State of Emergency | 192

Chapter 20 Anton | 205

Chapter 21 Latte Arrives | 215

Chapter 22 Snorting Anthrax | 226

PART THREE

Chapter 23 *Adiós*, Miguel | 243

Chapter 24 A Son of the *Calle* | 259

Chapter 25 Lights Out! | 269

Epilogue | 277

Acknowledgments | 285

Si la pruebas, te quedas.

(If you try it, you'll stay.)

Printed on restaurant flyers
posted along Broadway.

AUTHOR'S NOTE

The events depicted in this book are true, although I often wished they weren't. I compressed a few incidents for narrative expediency, but otherwise they are faithful to life. Masked are the identities of various neighbors, law enforcers, and fugitives from justice, so as not to endanger anyone's safety or privacy. For that reason, I will not openly thank these individuals for sharing their stories.

PROLOGUE

April 2000

I needed to get a second look. After all, I had just pledged our entire savings on a house in Harlem, without informing my husband, who was in Moscow, 5,620 miles away. The decent thing would be to see it again one more time to make sure I had done the right thing.

Leaving the subway platform, I ran up the stairs to the street, where the Mexican vendor cried, "Tamales, tama-ales," like a siren. Wow, that smelled good. Like a linebacker, I pushed my way up Broadway through what seemed like hundreds of men leaning into SUVs and shouting into cell phones in Spanish. What terrific street life! If I closed my eyes and ignored the police sirens—for some reason there were so many—I could imagine myself on a commercial drag in Santo Domingo. I almost bumped into a group playing sidewalk baseball with a broom-stick. They shot me curious looks. No wonder—my battered Russian sheepskin coat stood out here amid the sea of black North Face jackets. This was the realm of luscious *dominicanas* with straightened ponytails; there weren't too many scrawny gringas with unkempt reddish frizz around here.

I swiftly strode the four blocks to the house. It felt like four hundred blocks—I couldn't get there soon enough. Turning the corner of what would soon be my—*my!*—street, I passed a cluster of men who regarded me gravely. *"Buenas tardes!"* I called out cheerily. No one replied. Well, who could blame them for being standoffish to an outsider? I fit in as subtly as a Wal-Mart next to a bodega. Whatever. There would be plenty of time to get acquainted.

When I reached the brick townhouse, I quietly asked a couple of men leaning on the metal gate to please move aside so that I could get past. Heart thumping with anticipation, I trod up the crumbled front steps to the once stately, splintering oak door. This was amazing! Inside, the real estate broker who had sold me the house stood in the empty living room gathering up spare leaflets. He eyed me warily, but I reassured him that I merely wanted another viewing. "Can't wait until we sign the contract!" I told him.

I climbed the central staircase that creaked so romantically, tripping on a loose step. Touring the four floors, I took in all of the space and Victorian woodwork, and counted the various ceilings that were caving in. I tried to call my husband, John, on the cell phone but no one answered. No matter. He would surely love this. He said he was handy. He'd fix everything.

Downstairs, I viewed the ivy-choked garden through the cracked back windows. *"Ah,"* I sighed rapturously. *"This will soon be mine!"*

PART ONE

Chapter 1

SOMEWHERE UNCIVILIZED

The first time I spoke to the man who would become my husband, we talked about another house. It was in 1995, exactly five years earlier, in Johannesburg, and we found ourselves sitting together at a Russian restaurant. We dozen or so members of South Africa's foreign press corps had been convened by Joe, a mutual friend from *Newsweek*, to mark the unusual fact that we were all in town at the same time, in between reporting trips. The mood at the table was variously morose or nonsensical, depending on the state of inebriation.

I was on the lower rungs of glum, having just returned from a trip to Rwanda. I had been covering the first anniversary of the genocide and I was pretty shaken, having witnessed the exhumation of fifteen thousand bodies. It was the most horrendous thing I'd ever seen during fifteen years as a journalist. I had returned to Jo'burg looking forward to some TLC from my photographer boyfriend, only to discover that he had been cheating on me during this absence as well as others. The dinner invitation came just as I broke up with him, and as I drove over to the restaurant I vowed to avoid romance for a long, long while.

Now at the table, though, I couldn't help noticing the handsome Dutchman on my right. The words "newly single" drifted into my ears as he chatted with others. I learned that this manly specimen's name was John, he was my age, and he was a business writer. Joe suggested that we speak; John had recently exposed a diamond-smuggling ring in Angola, a country about which I was writing a book. However, I was more interested in John's tall, athletic body. The debonair way this man with the rugged looks rolled his cigarette was particularly fetching, and I resolved to get his number at the end of the meal.

There was something I wanted from him immediately, though. I was in the process of buying my first piece of real estate ever and needed mortgage advice. Surely John, as a finance maven, had expertise to share.

I introduced myself and prattled on about the airy charms of the house, which had a little pond in front that I could gaze upon while writing. An empty lot in the back provided ample space for my big dog to roam. Two cottages on the property could be rented out to cover the mortgage. All this for $65,000!

John listened intently. His sea-green eyes grew serious. "Interest rates are *twenty percent*. The rand is *collapsing*."

I shrugged.

He persisted. "Judith, only an idiot would buy now."

Never one to mull over inconvenient wisdom, I bought the house the next week. I continually faced danger in my work and was accustomed to weighing consequences when taking risks. This one seemed worth it. Besides, I desired the property with, well, lust.

Lots of people buy real estate at age thirty-seven, but this purchase marked a momentous shift for me. The prosaic phrase "time to settle down" didn't quite convey the violent compulsion I felt to acquire a property deed. While my (mainly) male contemporaries were ditching their first wives or buying vintage Jaguars, my version of a midlife crisis was to obtain a fixed address. For fifteen years I had roamed overseas with an almost adolescent lack of commitment, faithful only to the misguided idealism that my reportage could change the world. From the moment I left college to write about Latin American rebellions I had forfeited most people's notions of safety and comfort. Possessions, lovers, soul mates, relatives—all were sacrificed when I received marching orders for the next assignment, be it in Africa or in Europe. Marriage was a luxury for others. Of course I would have liked a partner to come along, but none was willing to follow me *anywhere.*

The pull to the front lines of history led me to witness the fall of the dictator Mobutu Sese Seko in what was then Zaire, and become an expert at talking my way onto African gun-smuggling planes. I remembered the first time I was shot at, in Guatemala, the way others recalled first kisses.

It was heady stuff. What a privilege! I had visited more than fifty countries, and was soon to be a published author! A rich montage of images flashed when I thought about my years abroad. Nelson Mandela had smiled in recognition when he saw me. UNITA rebels had threatened me with death in Angola. Scorpions had hidden in my boots in Sudan. I had seen the Berlin Wall before it fell and met various presidents. A gorilla had touched my shoulder in the rain forest!

Sometimes, while on long jeep rides past camels in the desert, I had wondered at the fact that people paid me to do this. However, it was beginning to dawn on me that the reality of this life wasn't quite the *National Geographic* spread in my head. I rarely lived in any country for more than three years, and just when I forged a vague idea of what I was writing about and cultivated a nice circle of friends, my editors would send me packing for the next assignment. Over two decades I had moved from Mexico to London to Madrid, back to London, to Lisbon, and then to Johannesburg. These were just bases. Sometimes I visited four countries in one week. More than once I awoke in a dreary hotel and couldn't remember which city I was in.

This geographic fragmentation was particularly bad in Africa, when I was the bureau chief of *The Christian Science Monitor.* My beat covered forty-seven countries, and I spent so much time in airport lounges waiting for delayed planes that I actually managed to write most of my Angola book in between flights. When I met John, I was beginning to get the first twinges of "Surely this cannot be a suitable way for a soon-to-be-middle-aged woman to conduct her life." It was no longer exciting to take cold baths out of buckets, or drive on the shoulders of roads to avoid land mines.

My first step toward nesting was to acquire an abandoned Alaskan sled dog, Khaya, on whom I lavished far too many expensive rump steaks and rambling monologues. Then I found myself spending increasing vacation time with my mother and sister in New York City, where I had grown up, instead of doing something intrepid like diving in Mozambique. I was growing tired of missing the weddings and births of my dearest ten thousand miles away. The agonizing nadir was when I had to leave my father in his hospital bed and fly back to my job in London because my "compassionate" leave was up. The next time I saw him was in an open casket. I tortured myself for missing his final months, and now I was losing out on other major events at home. My sister had given birth and my mother was recovering from serious back surgery. I wanted to be near them for more than two weeks at a time.

Since my work didn't allow for this, I cultivated a substitute: real estate flyers. If I couldn't be at home, I would try to settle where I was instead. All of a sudden, this woman who didn't even own a chair was visiting people's bathrooms just to inspect the wall tiles. When I found myself devoting Sundays in Johannesburg to dropping in on open houses, it was clear: I needed to buy a house.

Yes, brick and mortar. No matter what John thought, a house was more than an investment. It meant growing up, or simply admitting that I was spending so much time on the road that staff at hotels I frequented were becoming close friends. Despite the fact that the house I could afford was in an area notorious for violent break-ins—some neighbors had been tied up at gunpoint during a recent burglary—just owning a home gave me a sense of calm when I drove up to the blue security gate after another trip to Burundi's killing fields.

For the first time in my life I acquired furniture, including a king-size futon on which John—with whom I had been flirting since the dinner—quickly installed himself. Thus began a two-year courtship, during which we tried to coordinate reporting trips, as our assignments roamed among various countries in mayhem. John, unlike previous boyfriends, was pragmatic and grounded and didn't blink when at his first declaration of love I blurted out: "I have to go to Madagascar!" He didn't let my panic and fearsome independence scare him away. John was stubborn, and simply on principle he would not allow geography, or my terror of commitment, to stand in his way. He would surprise me in places like Luanda or Addis Ababa, admittedly not the most romantic of dating spots, especially when I had dysentery. We first discussed a future together on a Sierra Leone airstrip while awaiting a flight to the front line with some mercenaries. We didn't have a ring, though we probably could have secured a blood diamond from the Lebanese smuggler standing close by.

The wedding was planned long distance as well. Over the satellite telephone in Zaire, in between filing stories about atrocities, I argued with my mother over the merits of votive candles versus flowers, raising my voice to shut out the automatic rifles crackling in the background. Safely in Manhattan, John and I made our vows on a rooftop bar behind the famed stone lions of the Midtown public library. Parties followed in an Amsterdam brewery and the house of a writer in Johannesburg. It didn't seem right to celebrate in only one city. Neither of us had the foggiest idea which part of the world was home.

Despite the stability that marriage supposedly promised, further uprooting soon followed. Three months after exchanging rings, we transferred to Moscow, where I was promoted to the head of the *Monitor*'s bureau. I sobbed dramatically when we sold the house in Johannesburg, even though I had known it was a risky investment and, my sensible husband reminded me, a financial liability.

"I told you not to buy," he said dryly, handing me a tissue. "It's amazing you only lost thirty thousand dollars."

The jettisoning of our home came with the delicious discovery that uprooting to another country is much cozier when a man and a dog share the experience. My previous eight moves had been made against a backdrop of loneliness, without even a houseplant to keep me company. The novelty of having a cohort with whom to study a new language and negotiate bribes with movers and so on logically led to another discussion—children. John wanted a family of his own badly, having been a foster child, and it was a source of pain that his previous girl-friend had refused to consider becoming a parent. He was undeterred about this goal and wasn't ruffled, unlike my mother, by my wedding-toast declaration that I wasn't planning to procreate.

"Most people do it, you know. It would be fun," John said.

I wasn't so sure. I had buried the desire to become a parent ages ago. How would I reconcile breastfeeding with my demanding new job? All right, it wasn't an entire continent I was now covering, but it was fifteen former Soviet states spanning eleven time zones. I recalled a colleague who was nursing and contracted mastitis when she got stuck during a bombardment. What if I got trapped somewhere, too? With a baby, I wouldn't be able to fly to Kazakhstan at a moment's no-tice, as my work required. Anyway, I was so nutty—was I really mother material?

John didn't give me a chance to work that one out. One night, after too much whiskey, we got careless. My subsequent euphoria over being pregnant stunned me, although my ecstatic silent monologues—"I'm pregnant! I'm pregnant!"—were disrupted periodically by oceanic ter-ror about what my bosses would think should I dare to impart the news. What if they transferred me to a boring desk back in Boston?

The dilemma was deferred briefly when I lost the baby. Broadsided by grief, all I could think about was getting pregnant again. But when that happened, soon thereafter, the conundrum about work resumed. Without coming clean to my employers, I did only the most essential of travel, but now the editors were clamoring for coverage of Chechnya, and it was hard to say no. Russia had reinvaded the breakaway Muslim territory and egregious abuses were taking place. Soldiers were plun-dering homes and carting men off to secret prisons. Under normal cir-cumstances, I would not have hesitated to go, but these were not normal times, and I wanted to make sure I wasn't endangering the baby. I sought the benediction of my OB/GYN, who reluctantly pro-nounced it safe to travel "if you don't bounce in a jeep longer than three hundred miles."

That seemed reasonable—I was past the dangerous first trimester.

However, when I consulted John, he suspended his normal matter-of-factness about risky assignments. "Is this *really* necessary?" he asked.

"The doctor says it's okay," I assured him. "And it's important for me to go."

Once on the road, I took it easy, or as easy as possible when reporting on a brutal occupation in which a quarter million people had died. The satellite telephone balanced delicately on my knees, far from my abdomen. I declined all offers of vodka—no mean feat anywhere that Russian is spoken—and instead virtuously sipped containers of ultra-pasteurized, long-life milk imported from Italy. To the dismay of my two travel companions, who were frantic to get to the front, I diligently consulted the map to ensure our reporting destinations lay within the stipulated three-hundred-mile limit. I shook my head firmly at offers by a paramilitary unit to travel to the recently occupied capital, Grozny. No matter that *that* was where the story was and we would be among the first to report from there. I wasn't going to get ensnared for weeks in a city just released from a siege, with no running water and few roofs.

None of these precautions made an iota of difference ultimately. Bleeding began on the road back from a village not far from where we were staying. Once back at the house, I curled into my sleeping bag. This being an army town in the middle of nowhere, the only way to get proper medical care was to find a plane and fly to Moscow. A local medic would be great if I had a shrapnel wound but not a miscarriage. I lay awake that night on the warped mattress and stared at the clock, desperately willing it to be time for the first morning flight.

The pain got worse as I boarded the airplane. Back in Moscow, fortunately, John was home to drive me to the hospital—he had the same blood type, A-positive, and it was important to show up with my private blood bank. At the clinic, my fear that we'd lost the baby was confirmed. I begged the attending gynecologist to do the ultrasound again, in case he had missed a faint heartbeat, but he simply looked at me with pity. I couldn't meet John's eyes in case he blamed me, too. Not that it mattered what they thought. I hated myself for having put the baby in jeopardy.

To make matters worse, no anesthesiologist was present, and the gynecologist said he would need to perform the D&C anyway. "You're losing too much blood to wait," he said. As if this ordeal without painkillers were not enough, the doctor berated me for going to Chechnya.

"What were you thinking? You are an old woman. You may never get pregnant again. Is your work that important that you must take such risks?"

I thought I might pass out from the pain. As John massaged my head I had a lucid thought.

"Let's get out of here when this is over," I said. "I want to live somewhere civilized."

Chapter 2

THE DECISION

I quit my job shortly thereafter. Such was my devastation that I couldn't see staying in Russia, or continuing this career that had endangered the baby. The doctor said I probably would have lost it no matter what—I was in my forties, after all, and had suffered a miscarriage before. But I couldn't erase the suspicion, no matter how slight, that the baby would have survived if I hadn't traveled to Chechnya. As well, the brutality of the incident shocked me out of my already waning love affair with the Third World.

Yes, leaving felt right—to me. John had different sentiments, however. He had put his career in jeopardy to follow me to Russia, and only now, after a couple of years, had regained a contract position with his former newspaper. To expect him to give it up was asking a lot.

The endless possibilities of where we might go next became a topic of debate in our noisy kitchen in Moscow, which lay above a nine-lane highway. Shouting over the traffic, the windows and chairs rattling from the noise, we discussed what we wanted in our dream home. What with eight languages between us, we conceivably could go anywhere. We agreed that we didn't want to live in another place like this, an expatriate compound filled with other journalists and diplomats and their retinues of servants. We brainstormed over John's atlas, the dog at our feet. We had enough savings so that we could survive for a few months if we couldn't find new jobs, a likely scenario. John favored leaving the writing life altogether, like some colleagues who had opted for farming in rural France. We briefly discussed a stone grange near the sea that my friend Tony had spotted outside Lisbon. John broached moving to Asmara in Eritrea because he liked the Art Deco architecture, although when pressed he couldn't pinpoint a sound revenue stream to support such a relocation. Or how about a houseboat in Amsterdam?

John had been abroad for only one decade, whereas I had chalked up nearly two. He wanted more travel. We had to find middle ground between his desire for adventure and mine for stability. We drew up lists of what we wanted in a place, which regrettably had little convergence. My bottom line was not difficult to draw: a place where anesthetic preceded surgery. In good Dutch socialist style, John insisted that health care be free. There was another snag: I wanted peace and to be closer to my family. John desired intrigue.

"Light and space," I added to my list of priorities.

John nodded. We had grown accustomed to big living areas, thanks to a strong dollar and corporate housing allowances. At the very least, I wanted an extra bedroom to accommodate all the friends who I imagined would visit from afar.

"That's a must," John agreed.

There was another thing. I was anxious about being able to support myself as a freelance writer, something I had never done before. For twenty years I had enjoyed cushy staff positions. I insisted that the next place be an international news hub.

John suggested Montreal.

"Pleasant but provincial."

"Jerusalem?"

"Too unstable."

"A dining room big enough for the table."

Finally something we could agree upon! Our yellow pine table was more than a mere piece of furniture. It was a symbol! We had dragged this ten-footer to Moscow from Johannesburg, where I had designed it to seat twenty to accommodate our notorious dinner parties. The table was a regular gathering station for all manner of people during our travels. Guests included a neighbor who happened to be a spy, a Siberian shaman, and a doctor who tended cosmonauts. Even my mother from Queens had sat there!

Because The Table, as it was known on two continents, was long and narrow, people were forced to mingle more intimately than was usual. This banquet site produced some of our finest news scoops, as indiscretions were revealed over excessive wine drinking. Of course this storied table had to come with us!

"What else?" I asked.

"At least one shooting a week on the street corner."

"A shooting?" Sometimes I don't get the Dutch sense of humor.

"Judith, lighten up. Of course I don't want people killed. I mean a place that's not dull."

When we tallied all these considerations, my hometown, New York, was at the bottom of the list. Spare bedrooms were highly unlikely without our going into great debt, considering our budget. Forget about affordable, let alone free, health care. Rough and exotic? Hardly. But I had sizable bargaining power in this particular negotiation. After all, I was the one who had endured the horrible experience in Russia and would be the mother of his child.

Naturally, we settled on New York. John wasn't fully sold on the idea, but I did make a convincing case that this was the path of least resistance. In New York, we could live indefinitely with my mother until we got settled. We wouldn't have to worry about work visas once John got a green card. The city was a media capital so we were bound to find jobs, even though neither of us had worked in the United States before.

I adamantly assured John that I could find an abode that met our impossible requirements. At this point, I had even convinced myself.

Chapter 3

THE HUNT

We agreed that I would go ahead to find us a home and John would stay behind in Moscow to wait for his papers and tie up all of our loose ends. This seemed like a good plan, but panic descended the moment I returned to my mother's house and put the sheets on the "guest" bed in the basement. Just what was I doing in this infantile situation? I felt especially pathetic when a friend suggested that I join her at the twentieth anniversary of our Harvard graduation. While my contemporaries were titans of industry or prominent editors, here I was in April 2000, age forty-one, camping in my mother's cellar. Although I was married, my husband was nowhere in sight and I didn't have a job, let alone a child. No way was I going to confront the luminaries of my alma mater at this juncture.

My discomfort at returning to the parental home was compounded by the photographs of my beloved father that Mom had throughout the house. Dad had died twelve years before of a massive heart attack, and these memorials ensured that he remained a presence in Mom's house. While portraits gave her great comfort—a giant one hung over her bed like a Soviet poster warding off unwanted suitors—they had the opposite effect on me. Every time I looked at Dad's jaunty smile my heart shredded in grief.

Then there was the little problem with my mother's boiler. No sooner had I unfolded the sofa bed than the heater burst. Mom quickly installed a new one, but she couldn't figure out how to turn down the thermostat. We broiled in an unseasonable 100-degree sauna.

I *had* to get my own space.

But how? I couldn't qualify for a mortgage, although I had substantial savings and had never been in debt. Since I had just quit my job, I had no liquid income and my sterling foreign credit record didn't mean anything to American banks.

But Mom had some unexpected good news. Although I had worked as a financial journalist with Reuters for eleven years, I had left my social-worker mother to manage my portfolio, so she alone knew my true worth. Thanks to corporate housing and tax breaks, most of my salary had gone straight into Mom's capable investing hands. A quick chat revealed that I had accumulated more than a quarter of a million dollars. While I wrote about the Russian financial crisis, my mother busily shoveled my money into tech stocks, which had soared in value. Wow, I thought. I can pay cash for a house.

I liked cash. Cash was safe. I had grown up with my father's stories about his neighbors in Williamsburg, Brooklyn, who sat on the sidewalk with suitcases after losing their homes in the Great Depression. He nearly wept the day he paid off his mortgage—the bank no longer owned our home! Yes, cash was easy. I routinely traveled throughout Africa with wads of bills stuffed in all sorts of sartorial crevices, because the banking systems had collapsed. Cash was good.

And the amount I had was *amazing*!

Or was it? Upon reflection, it dawned on me that what was a fortune in the ruble economy wouldn't buy much in a sought-after area of Manhattan. If we wanted anything bigger than a studio the size of our Moscow kitchen, we'd have to look in areas that would make most white people tremble.

My cousin Greg suggested that I follow his example: buy a former crack house in what was then one of New York's most troubled areas, Bedford-Stuyvesant in Brooklyn. An abandoned building that needed fixing up would give us our coveted extra space, and we could easily afford it. Greg had paid a pittance for his wrecked brownstone and covered the mortgage by renting out a floor. It seemed foolhardy not to do the same.

I did have a nagging concern: the minor fact that Greg had been stabbed one evening coming home from Manhattan. He was fine now, but had never taken the subway after dark again. Such peril could create problems in the event that I got a job in Manhattan and traveled by train in the evenings. Still, I was sold on the idea of a depressed area with the potential for aesthetic charm. Greedy developers didn't normally venture into ghettos, which meant that block upon block of exquisite nineteenth-century row houses lay untouched. On a previous visit, John had been to Greg's house and loved the old wood floor planks and the trees in the back, as well as the way the soft afternoon light streamed in from both sides of the building. The gabled brick homes reminded John of the Netherlands, if he ignored the torched roofs and addicts lounging out front.

Despite the sinister feel of Greg's street, we both liked the cozy way that people on the block interacted. It reminded me of where I grew up. Mom's house was a humble attached two-family in Queens, identical to the other homes on the surrounding eight blocks. The uniformity created a sense of democracy in our working-class, immigrant neighborhood. In Bed-Stuy, too, children of various backgrounds played softball as the adults enjoyed evenings on the stoops and shouted at the kids to get back on the sidewalk. Bed-Stuy awakened my nostalgia for the small-neighborhood feel of my childhood, although of course I'd never dream of living anywhere near my mother back in Queens.

My sister, Susan, approved of Bed-Stuy, too. She and her fiancé,

Rafael, who were community organizers, had lived for many years in another scorched Brooklyn neighborhood, Bushwick, without undue mishap, unless you counted the times when her car was torched and the junkie upstairs tried to hang himself. For safety, she had adopted a Doberman she found running through the glass-littered streets. It was so protective of Susan that it bit Rafael.

"Just know what you're getting yourself into," Susan advised.

Over the phone, John assured me that he was handy enough to restore a dilapidated house. I believed him. He had built us bookshelves, after all. We agreed that after years of living in nations that were falling apart, it would feel restorative to foster a house back to health. Both of us were exhausted from seventeen-hour workdays. Taking time off for construction would give our addled brains a rest. "It will be fun!" John said.

Yet the more I thought about living in Brooklyn, the more daunting it seemed. From Bed-Stuy, it took at least an hour to get into Manhattan, where I assumed John and I would end up working. While I pondered the possibility of living the rest of my life in my mother's basement, and just how to break this to my husband, a friend offered a fresh idea. Marla was a nurse in Harlem and suggested I look around there. She whispered the magic word: "Cheap."

Marla escorted me through streets filled with brownstones sealed with cinder blocks. There were entire blocks of abandoned buildings sporting the "exposed brick" interiors that New Yorkers so prize, although admittedly the plaster had been stripped by vandals rather than by contractors. I swooned as I read a succession of FOR SALE signs, politely averting my eyes from comatose men lying in the vestibules. These majestic but fire-scarred Victorian relics offered promise. ("Just like Brooklyn," Marla breathed.) The commute from this haven was only fifteen minutes to Times Square on the express train. Danger, schmanger, I thought. Harlem was it!

And moving to Harlem meant coming full circle. After all, I had spent a lot of time there as a teenager, dating my first boyfriend, and I knew the area well, or at least I used to. It was there that I nurtured an interest in Hispanic culture—my black boyfriend was ashamed of being seen with a honky and tried to pass me off as Puerto Rican. The ruse didn't fool anyone, but in the meantime I developed a passion for all things Latino—the people, the food, the music, the literature.

My more cautious, some might say intelligent, friends reminded me that the crack epidemic, although now nonexistent in most of the city for years, had not fully dried up in Harlem. The neighborhood was still a violent place, with lots of homicides. Still, I figured it was tame compared to what it had been when I'd last visited in the bankrupt 1970s. In fact, the entire city was softer now. Back then, I packed mace in my book bag to ward off muggers and often did my algebra home-work standing up on the subway because of all the passed-out junkies monopolizing the seats. Those days were but a quaint memory. The black Mecca of America, Harlem was no longer a violent no-go zone for white people. The gentrification that had taken over much of Manhat-tan while I was living abroad had crept uptown as the middle class was priced out of other areas.

The last time I'd been in Harlem was 1977. I had stopped taking the subway alone to my boyfriend's on 126th Street after looting broke out during the big blackout. I couldn't believe it: Now there was a Starbucks one block from his old apartment. Disney was opening a store. And there was a new, honest-to-goodness suburban-style mall. A mall on 125th Street! Indeed, times had changed.

John and I could deal with Harlem. If worst came to worst, we'd take cabs at night instead of the subway. What was an occasional drug dealer? Hey, we'd lived in South Africa, where one had to drive like James Bond to swerve past carjackers and kidnappers.

I sought John's opinion and he didn't see a problem. After all, he reminded me, in Africa we'd made a practice of flying into places when others fled. We had been shot at numerous times, yet never hit. We were practiced at negotiating roadblocks that were manned by drunks who fired AK-47 rifles if your hello was not quite cheerful enough. In Johannesburg, we had lived behind razor wire in a house where a flak-jacketed guard packing a pistol would rush to our aid at the tap of a panic button. Now *that* was dangerous.

At least in Harlem no one would attack us with a rocket grenade launcher. "We'll manage," John said.

. . .

At the time I was house hunting in Harlem, many medallion taxi drivers found excuses not to go that far north. Some admitted they were scared. Others probably just didn't know their way around. After all, the map posted on the back of the drivers' seats ended at the top of Central Park, at 110th Street. What these drivers overlooked was two square miles north of the park that accounts for about a tenth of the island of Manhattan.

This was a big expanse. I had to narrow my focus. Some places appealed on first glance but not the second. The Senegalese enclave of 116th Street brought back pleasant memories of nightclubs and fish stew in Dakar, but I couldn't see us living in a cramped apartment overlooking that noisy corridor. I quickly established that the Stanford White townhouses of Strivers Row were as spectacularly elegant as the architectural books said—and well beyond our means. So were the homes surrounding Mount Morris, that cute park with the curious watchtower (which, if open, would offer panoramic views of the local prison). Also out of our budget were the museum-quality mansions of Hamilton Heights, named after Alexander Hamilton, the country's first Treasury secretary. He spent his final two years on an estate in the area, which was covered by gum trees when it was still farmland. Sugar Hill was also not possible. In the 1920s, professional blacks settled on this crest, named after the slang word for *money*. Judging from their $600,000 price tags, these houses still had much cachet among the latest generation of sugared families.

Then my sister's fiancé, Rafael, mentioned West Harlem. This was a Dominican outpost on the westernmost fringes of Manhattan that had a reputation for affordable housing. I was unfamiliar with the area, as apparently were most of the real estate agents that I had consulted.

The area is shaped like a plantain, fitting for a community that favors the starchy fruit. If there was one icon of West Harlem, it was the long, green banana-like fruit that fills the wooden racks of the many bodegas on Broadway, the main artery. The enclave stretches from 135th to 155th Streets, between Amsterdam Avenue and the Hudson River. The riverside forms a desolate panorama of meatpacking warehouses and collapsed piers, where the odd fisherman casts for striped bass. This spooky industrial landscape stands in contrast to Broadway and Amsterdam—blurs of yellow Spanish canopies advertising manicures, cash transfers, cell phones, legal advice, plane tickets, and telephone cards. For a gritty urban area, there are a surprising number of green spots, such as the outdated-looking Gothic towers marking the City College campus and the various parks, including one with a giant swimming pool built atop a sewage plant.

Rafael, who was Hispanic and had done some community organizing in the area, gave me a quick tutorial. The district technically belonged to Hamilton Heights, but ethnically it formed an extension of Washington Heights, farther north by the George Washington Bridge, where maybe a quarter of New York's official count of 400,000 Dominicans lived. (Some experts put the number at double that, due to the large number of undocumented immigrants.)

As I later learned, this confused identity reflected a split between the African-American and Latino residents, who lived uneasily next to each other. This ethnic divide was a shame considering how comparatively easily different groups had coexisted there in the last century. Owing to a solid middle-class core that remained over the decades, the once-white area became mainly black without major conflict in the 1930s, when professional African-Americans and West Indians settled in the elegant brownstones and grand apartment buildings. In the 1960s Cubans joined the mix without alienating the status quo.

The ethnic makeup began to change again two decades later, when Dominican immigrants, many of them desperately poor, arrived in large waves to escape poverty and political turmoil on their island. This new Spanish-speaking group quickly outnumbered the English-speaking blacks, with ensuing mutual resentment. Rafael mentioned something about gerrymandering—not one elected official who represented the district actually lived there or spoke decent Spanish. African-American politicians like the powerful congressman Charles Rangel tended to focus on their constituency in the central heartland of 125th Street. Then Rafael said something about the crack epidemic and cocaine wholesale trade. I filed it away but was focusing more on the positives.

If I had done my research like any self-respecting reporter, I might have investigated why there were so many beeper stores on Broadway. I would have asked about the hundreds of men leaning into double-parked Ford Explorers. But my head was too busy spinning at the vibrant street life. John would love this! And to be honest, if I couldn't make this work, I would be without alternatives.

On each of my visits, I felt energized by the broad avenue. It was as jammed as Times Square at rush hour—what with all the people sitting on plastic crates or swiveling to the merengue that blasted out of the beauty salons and ninety-nine-cent shops. The merchandise spilling out of the storefronts congested the streets further. To get to the subway, one had to navigate past manioc, suitcases, Spider-Man balloons, slippers, toothpaste, and cotton nightgowns.

The cold weather on my first visit called for a hat and gloves, but the *bachata* ballads were so evocative that they seemed to raise the temperature. This tropical ambience was further helped by the rotisserie chickens in the windows of restaurants that sported signs with palm trees and the name *Quisqueya*—what Dominicans call their island. *Botánicas* advertised potions to cure heartbreak. Women called out in raspy Caribbean accents that swallowed letters—*Nueva York* became *Nueba Yol.*

Sí, señor. Broadway rekindled my nostalgia for Latin America, a place I had lived for four delightful years. John and I even spent our honeymoon in Cuba. Memories flooded back of my teenage obsession with salsa and peasant revolt and Gabriel García Márquez. I had traveled the length of the region, from Puerto Rico to Argentina. I had rushed to Nicaragua to observe the revolution and volunteered in an orphanage in Peru. I'd always meant to return. How had I lost my way?

I bought a bowl of pozole—chewy hominy-and-pork stew—and felt transported back to Mexico, where I'd launched my journalism career. I made my way to an Ecuadorian man selling roasted corn on a stick. Then I encountered the lady calling, "Tamales, tama-ales!" at the top of the subway station.

This would be as if we were living abroad and at home at the same time, I thought. We'd need to speak Spanish just to buy milk. I pulled the phone from my jacket pocket—just like so many of the men on the street; I'd never seen so many people talking on cell phones. I ignored the fact that it would be much cheaper to call Moscow from my mother's house. I had to get through to John immediately.

"I found the right neighborhood," I reported. "Wait till you see. . . ."

Chapter 4

SURPRISE!

My gushing endorsement got John on board. The house hunt had really, truly begun.

The first lesson I learned was that Harlem didn't follow the norms of most real estate markets. For starters, I needed to pack special equipment just to attend open houses. In Harlem real estate parlance, "Needs TLC" meant the interior walls had fallen down. Because so many of the properties were condemned shells or squatters' dens, I had to bring a flashlight to see and a face mask to block the stench of excrement. I also donned thick boots and construction gloves, for protection against crack vials and rodent dung. My tropical fantasies were such that I didn't contemplate whether any of those crack users still had claims on the houses.

One broker described the Harlem real estate market as the "Wild West," meaning that anything goes: lies, infamy, corruption, theft, and fraud. However, the old American West of the 1800s had probably maintained greater order. At least there were sheriffs. Here I squandered considerable time with shysters offering up buildings that really weren't for sale. Deals withered before I could sign a paper. It seemed every property I looked at had a story: tenants with nowhere else to go, roofs that had caved in, an elderly aunt who laid claims. Just when I thought I'd found one perfect place, federal regulators took it off the market owing to a mortgage scam. A rap singer pushed us out of another deal by slapping down his $50,000 deposit in cash before I could arrange a bank order. The owner of another brownstone raised the asking price as soon as we met it. This happened not just once but three times, until I finally got the message.

Deals proved elusive partly because of what magazines were then dubbing the "New Harlem Renaissance." This had little to do with the flourishing of black writers and musicians in the 1920s and everything to do with money. A handful of modern parlors hosted salons of jazz trios and readings by upcoming African-American authors, but most modern Renaissancers were busy supervising their contractors.

I learned that the Harlem housing revival began under the Clinton presidency, when the so-called Harlem Empowerment Zone attracted $600 million in private investment. Meanwhile, hundreds of abandoned houses in city hands were sold off to developers for one dollar each, to be transformed into middle-class housing. There was a lot of inventory—the city at one point owned 65 percent of Harlem property.

A drop in crime in the early 1990s further reassured black professionals that it was okay to move to Harlem and restore houses. The result was that entire blocks of derelict buildings that had become centers of drug activity were repopulated by homeowners in an area where home ownership had sunk to 10 percent, or half the city average. A tiny cadre of whites were now following suit, having been priced out of digs downtown. Suddenly Harlem's manses were deemed livable by the middle and upward classes. Or some of them, anyway.

The buyers of these homes, who'd taken a leap of faith, could now gloat. Prices were literally rising by the week. I realized that things had gotten out of control when I spotted a blond middle-aged broker with an uncanny resemblance to Joan Rivers roaming Malcolm X Boulevard with a client, asking random elderly black people if they had dying neighbors who would want to sell their houses. "I'll pay you cash to leave," she promised. Having been raised in a politically correct house-hold, I was appalled. I would not buy if it involved displacing people.

Decency aside, it appeared that my dream 'hood, Harlem, was un-affordable, unless I was willing to buy a shell that was truly uninhabit-able. I was adventurous, but not that much. With deep resignation, I renewed my plan to buy in cheaper Bed-Stuy, and one gray Sunday I made an arrangement with Greg to look at some Queen Annes on his block. I consoled myself with the thought that I would be living right near him and his wife. Perhaps John and I would even have savings left over to put in the bank.

Just before leaving for Brooklyn, I drank a final coffee with my mother, who was assiduously studying the finance pages of *The New York Times*. I couldn't resist a last glance at the real estate section. "Just one more look," I told Mom. "Then I'll accept defeat and take the train to Brooklyn." Buried at the bottom of the Houses section, tiny print of-fered a price and size too good to be believed: a twenty-five-foot-wide townhouse within our budget in West Harlem. The asking price was $200,000 below the going rate and the building measured nearly ten feet more across than the average brownstone. "Livable," the ad said.

I called Greg and told him I'd be late.

A cool drizzle sprayed as I emerged from the 145th Street subway station, the area empty except for families heading to church. Com-pared to the women decked out in brimmed hats that matched their white pocketbooks and stockings, I felt scruffy in my never-appropriate Russian coat. Men in suits held the hands of beribboned little ones wearing patent-leather shoes and frilly ankle socks. My trek began in-spiringly at the imposing marble-faced Baptist church where Martin Luther King, Jr., had preached when he visited New York. Just beyond beckoned the grand mansions of Convent Avenue, and, within steps, the familiar signs of ghetto blight. The number of derelict townhouses increased as I headed toward my destination. A broken piano outside a boarded-up house spilled its keys next to a hairy rat writhing in a glue trap. A hulk of a school had been abandoned for so long that a tall ailan-thus tree poked from the roof. In front lay an eclectic mound of refuse:

a dented saxophone, smeared diapers, worn platform shoes. Dirty plastic chairs decorated the community garden, where a picnic table lay splintered among the weeds. I took in the sorry sight, and then stubbornly kept walking.

I crossed Amsterdam Avenue, over that invisible line where black Harlem cedes to Dominican turf. The smells shifted from goat curry to *mofongo*, mashed fried green plantains. More apartment buildings joined the row houses, and signs in English gave way to ENVIOS and PASAJES.

The wide street that was my destination spilled down a hill, framed on either side by tall oaks and maples, which must have been at least a century old. Often row-house blocks are a monotonous repetition of brown sameness, but this street offered a pleasing mélange of red, gray, and tan brick. The hues nicely distracted from the four wrecks that were shuttered up with plywood and gave off a whiff of sewage. Still, the overall impression of the street was of old-age grandeur, albeit faded.

To acquaint myself with the block's illustrious past, I consulted my Harlem history book. It told me that the street was mapped in 1836. Broadway, at the bottom of the slope, was paved only in 1885—after which the house would have been built. An underground spring ran below, which might explain why the houses tilted so. Yes, that must be why.

The playground on the corner was empty except for two men reclining on slides. Candy wrappers swirled in the breeze, joining discarded bottles. Fanta and Hennessy cognac seemed the beverages of choice on this block. I focused on the architecture.

My destination was the third building in from Broadway, a Romanesque revival with a stately stone carving of a leaf above the main entrance. The house was made of rough-hewn limestone, topped by sienna brick. It was the only building on the street that had not been painted over, which lent a refreshingly authentic, albeit splotched, appearance. The structure lay between a red gabled boarded-up house and a double row house that served as a Christian Science church. Both neighboring structures were in a state of serious neglect, and the boarded-up house emitted a foul smell.

I pushed through the oak front door into a buzz of prospective buyers. A pile of sales leaflets from the Douglas Elliman real estate company sat on the rusted hallway radiator. There was honey-colored paneling in the entryway. Yes! Often townhouses have intricate dark woodwork that absorbs the light and creates gloom throughout. But the extraordinary width of this house and the high ceilings—11.6 feet, the leaflet said—created a lofty feel.

As I explored the house, phrases from *Elle Decor* drifted through my head. What patina! What moldings! Here was an architectural *Mary Celeste* that had floated untended since the 1930s as the dove-gray paint slowly peeled off the walls. A period gem of a chandelier cascaded like a crystal waterfall from the living room ceiling. The bathrooms hinted at Art Deco, with salmon and mustard tiles trimmed by black. Separate hot and cold spigots adorned the cast-iron tubs. The generously sized kitchen sported steel cabinets and an enameled Chambers stove from the 1940s.

At what point in history would this house have been inhabited and then neglected? I thought back to an architectural guidebook. The Heights was a favored venue in the eighteenth and nineteenth centuries for wealthy families to establish summer estates. Landowners would ride three hours by carriage from Wall Street to enjoy the breezes and views of the Hudson River. The area later became a suburban retreat for middle-class whites—first American-born Protestants and then Italian, Irish, and German immigrants.

I overheard another prospective buyer say that the house was built in 1888. That was a few years after the elevated trains were extended into Harlem, ushering in the neighborhood's first speculative real estate market. Overbuilding of these magnificent apartments and townhouses led to a bust, and after the Depression landlords began renting out vacant rooms and apartments to blacks, changing the area's complexion. The 1960s saw a chicken-and-egg of landlord flight to the suburbs and poverty. With social unrest and crime came the abandonment of buildings. As Harlem decayed, many houses were carved into "single-room occupancies," or essentially shelters for the indigent.

Judging from the layout, this building had not been so butchered. Although grand by my standards, this was a modest Harlem house for the period, devoid of ornate griffins and curlicue carvings. The geometric designs of the skylights and fireplace mantels were simple enough to be Arts and Crafts.

This property still had a classic row-house flow—two master bedrooms with fireplaces and smaller rooms originally used for dressing or to house servants. The musty basement formed an intimate warren of three rooms and it had a separate patio, a rarity for Harlem townhouses. It occurred to me that this space would be perfect for tenants. The top floor could be a sweet rental, too, perched above the treetops and suffused in light despite the gray weather.

The second floor had a snug room that was ideal for a study. Floor-to-ceiling bookcases covered one wall, and the window overlooked a terrace and the brick backs of nearby houses. This would be the place to wedge a desk and write, glancing during pauses at the crooked crabapple tree outside. Also on that floor were three other rooms—plenty for guests and an office for John. Oh, my goodness—could this actually become our own house?

To be sure, the walls were grotesquely pitted and the parlor-floor ceilings were caving in. Pocket doors and wainscoting had been torn out. Yet it was an unmistakable steal for a 4,860-square-foot building with a 50-by-25-foot garden. The place was so huge that the flyer had neglected to list all six fireplaces and four bathrooms. The formal dining room would amply hold the indispensable South African table.

I returned to the living room on the parlor floor. From there I could see mahogany shutters and a large garden overgrown with a flowering dogwood, three kinds of spruce, wild violets, hibiscus, rosebushes, and forsythia. Whoa, bring on the Smith & Hawken teak benches. Sixty people gathered in the living room—plenty enough space for big parties! The crowd was already bidding by the carved fireplace, and it appeared that the asking price had been met. Business cards fanned the mantel; in a swift glance I noted that one of my competitors was a vice president at Morgan Stanley. A blond fellow in a suede jacket stood in the center; I assumed that he was the real estate broker. I dialed John in Moscow on my cell phone, but he didn't answer. One had to move fast in a seller's market in New York, especially in Harlem. I had already learned that lesson. We would not find another property like this.

Relying on telepathy, I silently told John, "It's right. It's right." I approached the blond man and said firmly, "I'll pay cash."

"This woman said cash," he told the circle.

A man in a black suit raised his hand. Morgan Stanley, I suspected.

"Add another ten thousand dollars," he said.

"Another ten thousand," I replied.

Morgan Stanley raised his hand again.

"Another ten thousand," I said quickly. I wasn't going to let this guy win. "Cash."

My rival looked at the broker and shook his head no.

The broker put his hand on my arm and steered me aside.

"The owner's in a rush. Can you sign a contract in three days?"

I thought about Mom's basement. "The sooner the better."

He extended a palm that felt clammy with sweat, and his handshake was a little too firm, as though he were afraid I would slide away. I felt thrilled at the victory, yet stunned at my impetuousness. What exactly had I done? Had I really just gambled our fortune? It was okay to buy a dress on impulse once in a while. But a house?

I reached John on the telephone that night, fearing that he would yell at me. He can also be prone to recklessness; his motto is "Don't let fear be your guide." Still, John is a practical Dutchman.

"Why is it so cheap?"

"I don't know."

"How many rooms?"

"I'm not sure. There are so many. It's four floors, including the basement."

What direction did it face? Did it have original architectural details? How did it compare with my cousin's place?

I described the interior, adding that the South African table would easily fit.

"*Poyekhali!*" John said, echoing what the first man in space, Yuri Gagarin, cried in Russian upon liftoff. It means "Let's go!"

Generally, finalizing a house sale in New York involves months of paperwork. One has to arrange a mortgage, surveys, transfers, and insurance, and both parties' attorneys go back and forth on all issues. However, paying cash, as we did, speeds up the procedure, and we had to wait only a few weeks to close the deal. I didn't have room for second thoughts. I wanted to complete the purchase quickly, despite lingering suspicions about why the owner was in such a hurry to sell, especially at a below-market price.

"It's an estate sale," the broker explained to assuage my fears. Apparently the executor of the will, the late owner's brother, lived in Washington, D.C., where he worked for President Clinton. The executor didn't want to be saddled with a problematic property in New York.

My one condition of sale was a building engineer's approval. We had set aside a maximum of $50,000 for renovations, which would not pay for a complete gut job. My cousin recommended an inspector, who agreed to look at the property the day before I was to sign the contract that would legally bind me to purchase.

The engineer walked through the house, grunting as he peeked behind pipes and trained his flashlight into holes. He started from the roof down, jumping on floors, flushing toilets, sniffing at the gas stove. The real estate agent looked away politely, like a nurse at a gynecological examination.

Now that I was getting a second look, with the benefit of a professional to point out flaws, I had the opportunity to ponder the truly awful state of the house. For the first time, I noticed that the central staircase was actually on its way to collapsing. And how could I have missed the fact that the entire building leaned ominously to the left, like a flimsy boat? The walls were missing as much plaster as a Roman ruin.

The engineer pursed his lips at the jagged hole in the skylight. I hadn't taken in the broken stained glass the first time around, either.

"Spalding," he said tersely.

"Huh?"

"They throw rubber balls onto the roof from the street. Get that fixed quickly, or the rain will pour in. While you're at it, install a guard so no one can break in."

He pointed out a rectangle of the wall in the living room covered by stucco swirls. The inspector explained that there had once been a window here, so that visitors could peer in from the entrance hallway.

"It's for wakes. People could view the bodies without having to come in." He grew thoughtful. "Imagine how it would have smelled, even with flowers."

I agreed it was not a pleasant thought.

The building engineer spent most of his time in the basement.

"There's some rot, a little asbestos that needs to be removed. It looks like there were termites, but the damage appears superficial." He stuck a penknife into a column and blew wooden dust.

After two hours, we regrouped in the kitchen to await the engineer's judgment. He silently contemplated the garden.

"Poison ivy," he said to no one in particular.

I glanced at the real estate agent, who was checking messages on his cell phone. We waited. I cleared my throat.

"The house has got good bones," the inspector finally said. "You probably need thirty thousand dollars in repairs, mainly cosmetic. You'll need to replaster every wall and put in a new kitchen. Try to avoid touching the plumbing. You replace one pipe and the rest can collapse like dominoes."

He began to button his jacket, indicating that he had finished.

"A work permit shouldn't be necessary," he said. "Except on electrical work, which should be minor. You just have to replace all the wiring and put in new outlets."

I smiled. He regarded me cautiously.

"I can only comment on what I saw." He paused and gave me a weighty look. "You never know what you'll find when you lift the linoleum."

With that pronouncement, the engineer bid me adieu. I resisted the temptation to go down to the basement and lift a small, tiny square from the floor. My mood began a slow drift south.

After the inspection, I stood on the stoop and contemplated my new fiefdom. Looking onto the street, I realized something was odd. This was a completely different scene from that of two hours ago; the pavement was filled with men. I looked at my watch: 11 A.M.

About sixty Dominican youths lined the block at regular intervals, practically in military formation. Then it hit. They must be dealers. Who else would stand in the rain hollering, "Buy," and "Sell," into phones? They must have been sleeping in during the Sunday open house when I first viewed the property. Now, on a Tuesday before lunch, they were out in force. The men wore identical clothes: black puffy North Face jackets over white T-shirts, fitted jeans, and tan Timberland boots. They all had the same close-cropped haircuts and gold chains. The salesmen carried enough walkie-talkies, cell phones, and alphanumeric beepers to fill a wall at RadioShack. Clients—at least that's what I assumed they were—drove up in jeeps and Mercedes sedans with out-of-state licenses spanning the East Coast: North Carolina, Pennsylvania, Florida, Massachusetts, Connecticut, Vermont, and New Jersey—especially New Jersey.

So *that's* why the house was so cheap. The words of Rafael, which I had so conveniently ignored at the time, floated back: "Center for wholesale cocaine." My stomach plummeted. I looked with despair at these men and thought of the hundreds more on Broadway. It was one giant open-air bazaar.

Many cars were double-parked, which made it hard for other vehicles to pass. The resultant honking contributed to an awe-inspiring cacophony: telephone chimes, shouts, merengue, car alarms, cursing, the insistent siren of an ambulance trying to pass. The cloying jingle of a Mister Softee ice cream truck increased the din.

I smelled ammonia and looked down to see one of the young men, practically right under me, urinating on the bottom stair. He shot me a "What are you going to do about it?" look as he shook his penis dry. A comrade joined him, aluminum container of rice in hand, and tossed a gnawed chicken bone onto my future property. Derisive laughter rose from the street. *"Es nuestra calle,"* someone said mockingly. ("It's our street.")

Suddenly, four police cars raced up the one-way street, against traffic. Five beefy men in flak jackets and automatic weapons dashed out and sealed the block with wooden barricades. A helicopter whirled overhead. Undercover police then burst from an unmarked van with battering rams, sledgehammers, and pickaxes, barging into the apartment building that faced my new home. Lightbulb: It's not only *on* my block, it's directly across the street. No, please no, this couldn't possibly be happening. What depths of idiocy had inspired me to choose this block?

The dealers trotted to the traffic island in the middle of Broadway, where they sat on the peeling benches, animatedly talking and gesturing wildly. After an hour, the police emerged empty-handed, peeved. The youths in puffy jackets left the traffic median and stood under the honey locust tree in front of our house, yammering into phones as they casually stripped bark off the trunk. How dare they? That was *my* beautiful tree.

Another commotion erupted in front of El Floridita, the café with a Plexiglas atrium across the way on Broadway. I left the stoop and jogged over to see what the fuss was about. About thirty people had formed a circle around three men who were pushing the face of a fourth into the pavement. His cheek ground into the concrete as the crowd chanted, *"¡Mierda! ¡Mierda!"* ("Shit! Shit!") The spectators clamped cell phones to their ears and gave a running commentary of the events as though the beating were a live soccer game. "They got him! He's down!" An entrepreneurial vendor pushed into the crowd with a grocery cart filled with sculpted fruit on sticks. "Mango, *piña*," he called cheerily, handing out treats to the peanut gallery. I briefly considered buying something but didn't want to lose my great viewing place.

"¿Qué pasó?" I asked a man in a Yankees cap, who was encouraging the trio to commit murder.

"Fue un moreno." ("It was a dark-skinned man.") I looked around. The crowd was mostly dark-skinned Dominicans.

"What did he do?"

"No sé." ("I don't know.")

I was the only white person in the crowd, except for a middle-aged bald man. He sidled over.

"Never boring in the 'hood," he said dryly.

The man introduced himself as Bob and handed over a card that identified him as a real estate broker. He might be useful for tips, I thought.

"You interested in buying around here?" Bob asked pleasantly.

"Actually, I'm buying that house," I replied, pointing to the building in the distance. I noticed with dismay that the muchachos were leaning on the high black gate, which was bending under their weight.

Bob made a face.

"That piece of shit? I looked at that house for two minutes. Fuhgedaboudit. Did you notice how the floors slope? The beams are sagging."

He smiled ruefully. "That house will fall down."

. . .

Bob's grim assessment gave me the jitters. Back at my mother's house that night, I called John in Moscow to discuss my misgivings, as well as the engineer's report. A call-waiting signal interrupted us; it was the real estate broker who had sold us the house. He sounded worried.

"Uh, um, Judith, we have to talk." He inhaled deeply and paused. "The crack addicts from next door broke into the house. They smashed the kitchen transom and stole tools."

I was too shocked to say anything. The broker continued. "The police evicted them. I found a man, a friend of the seller's family, to look after the property. He's nailing boards on the windows to secure the building. He can be there every day. It should be okay for now."

He sounded apologetic. "Do you want to go ahead with the sale? You can wiggle out."

I felt comfortable buying a house without consulting John, but not one occupied, however briefly, by drug fiends. I told John the news, stressing that we could withdraw the offer. I was due to sign the contract the next day and could still pull out.

John wasn't dissuaded. In fact, he thought I was insane for having doubts. This was a bargain, after all.

"So what if there are addicts?" he said dismissively. "We'll put bars on the windows. Close the deal."

I hung up, vaguely reassured. Like any journalist, I wanted as many perspectives as possible, just to make sure we knew what we were getting ourselves into. I called my cousin, figuring he'd have good advice, having been attacked near his former crack den. Greg didn't see a problem.

"Get to know the dealers and they'll look out for you. The dealers will do what they can to keep addicts from hassling you. They want to keep the streets free of petty crime so as not to attract the police," he said.

I then called a friend, Keith, a television sound engineer who had lived in Harlem for fifteen years. Keith liked to tell the story of how he used to find bodies in front of his house on 119th Street when he went to retrieve the morning newspaper. Keith offered now to drive up in his sports car to check out my street. He called back seventeen minutes later.

"It doesn't look half bad," Keith reported. "I saw a bunch of Dominican guys standing around with umbrellas. They don't look menacing. That house is huge, by the way. How much did you say you paid?"

The next day I signed the contract in a lawyer's office near Wall Street. Greg had recommended a savvy attorney to handle the sale. The lawyer had expertise in what real estate agents called "emerging" neighborhoods, otherwise known as blighted urban areas, and had handled Greg's crack house. My cousin assured me he would understand what I was doing.

"You're buying where?" the lawyer asked.

I was flustered enough, signing the biggest check I had ever written, for the $35,000 deposit. The lawyer's pitying look wasn't helping to calm me down.

I rambled on about how it wasn't really that bad, the neighborhood had charms, people were always in the street, and anyway white people tended to have a knee-jerk reaction to the name Harlem, this wasn't a burned-out slum, decent working people lived there . . .

The lawyer interrupted me.

"Get good security," he said, pushing more papers on me to sign. "You don't want stoned crazies breaking into the property and burning it down."

I hesitated, pen in hand.

"I charge by the hour," he said brusquely. "Save your money for the renovation."

After signing the papers, I went back up to the house to make sure it was standing. I turned the corner past the tall fin-de-siècle apartment building with the wedding-cake cornices. (I was hearing the voice of my inner *Metropolitan Home* again.) But I abandoned all thoughts of decorating when I saw that the blue scaffolding outside the building provided perfect cover from the rain for the cocaine dealers, who were out in full force today. As I passed the red vacant house, a frantic limping man with glittering eyes burst forth. Despite his wasted right leg and jerky puppetlike movements, the guy was powerfully, scarily built. He clipped at a nice, fast pace—toward me.

Crack. He must be on crack.

I tried to hide my nervousness. The man approached within a foot of me, close enough so that I could smell the unwashed staleness of his greasy baseball jacket. His eyes were reddened like raspberries.

"They call me Salami," he said, with a sinister jeer. He pointed to his crotch. "Get it? Get it? Because it's long and brown."

I gave him a big, fake smile.

"Are you a fucking broker?" He was missing his bottom two front teeth, which created a hissing effect when he spoke. Like a cobra. "You buying this house?"

My silence was taken as a "yes." Salami's crimson eyes grew angrier.

"It's *my* house," he enunciated slowly, a crusted finger jabbing toward me. "I lived there until the cops kicked me out. I'm gonna get it back." Salami looked intently at me, daring a reply.

I examined him, trying to act macho. Could he discern my trembling? Salami was only a few inches taller than I, but he appeared fit and malevolent enough to attack me at any minute. His hand was in his pocket. Would he pull out a knife and stab me? I stepped back, making sure to maintain eye contact in case he sprang. Salami merely smirked in response.

He hobbled back to the wrecked house next door, kicked the door open with his good foot, and paused at the entrance before disappearing into the darkness.

"You'll be sorry you bought it," he called out behind him. "I'm right next door. It ain't your house, Mama."

Chapter 5

"ONLY GOD CAN PROTECT US"

With my new neighbor's ominous words echoing in my head, that night I asked the broker for permission to install iron security gates before finalizing the house purchase the following month. This was an unusual step in real estate transactions, but we agreed that I needed to ensure that Salami didn't make himself at home before I did. The broker gave me a set of strange, antiquated keys that looked like dental instruments and told me to meet the caretaker at the house. On a cool Tuesday in April, swaddled in the Russian coat and anxiety, I went to the unheated house to take measurements.

Cocaine trading hadn't started for the day, and the street was empty as pages of the *Daily News* fluttered down the hill toward Broadway. Salami was sitting on the stoop of the abandoned house, screwdriver in hand, as he concentrated on the Medusa-like wires of a bent microwave.

As I crept past he sang a 1980s hit by the Police in a mocking falsetto. The song was about a man who threatens to spy on every move a woman makes.

"Every step you take/I'll be watching you."

I ran up the steps and took out the keys, trying not to hyperventilate. I had to get inside the house fast, before that maniac jumped me from behind. I didn't stand a chance if he knocked me down. My head pounded with blood as the large keys stuck. Shit. Salami came closer and screeched, "I'm watching you, Mama!" After what felt like five minutes but was probably seconds, the keys turned and I pushed in to safety.

"Hello," I shouted, walking through to the kitchen. There, a stocky man with a wispy ponytail was nailing plywood onto the shattered transom of the back door. This was Abdu, the custodian hired by the real estate broker.

"Boy, am I glad to see you," he said. "It's spooky being alone in this house."

How reassuring, I thought.

Abdu climbed off the weathered stepladder, his coverall leg catching on a long splinter. He then took me on a tour of the destruction wrought by the invaders. The hempish smell of marijuana wafted off his worn clothes. The back pocket of his coveralls bulged with a Penguin edition of the Koran, which he patted now and again.

"Only God can protect us," he said at regular intervals.

The living room was streaked with brown splotches that resembled excrement, which upon closer inspection turned out to be tar. The addicts, Abdu explained, had tossed the thick slime over the parquet floor and walls. "They were probably high. I can't imagine why else they'd do that," he said. As, with sinking heart, I calculated the cost of removing the tar, Abdu informed me that he had further bad news. We walked upstairs to the top floor, where Abdu was eager to show me the shattered skylight. The hole in the glass had widened so that a slim person could slip through.

"Burglars usually come through skylights," Abdu explained, glancing upward as he plucked up shards with a towel-wrapped hand. "You should get it fixed quickly, before they come back. That gang next door is dangerous."

My heart started to thump harder. Why would the owner of the house next door allow the wicked Salami to remain? I asked. Surely she would want to hire a guard? And by the way, wasn't fixing the skylight Abdu's job?

Abdu explained that the woman who owned the house next door had asked him to keep an eye on the property, but he was too frightened. "She needs someone with a gun."

"So why doesn't she sell the place?"

"Who would buy it?"

I conceded he had a point.

Abdu went on to explain how the owner had lost control of her home. She had been swept away by a short-lived property boom in the 1980s, when common wisdom was that Harlem real estate would rebound. She sank all her life savings—*all*, Abdu repeated with emphasis, looking straight at me—into the house. Her purchase coincided with the onset of the crack epidemic, and her addicted tenants failed to pay their bills and vandalized the property. Fearing for her life, the owner abandoned the house for a small apartment downtown in the East Village.

Periodically she convinced the police to throw out the squatters, but Salami's gang returned with greater force each time. Now, Abdu said, the owner was desperate that the band be evicted within a fortnight.

"Otherwise they could win squatters' rights. Then she might never be able to get them out."

On that reassuring note, Abdu changed the topic to the pile of garbage outside the front gate and led me outside to survey the mess. I saw that the dealers had just started business for the day; the muchachos had set up a domino table in front of the vacant house next door, blocking the sidewalk. Abdu pointed out that the cocaine salesmen ate meals at their workplace—the street—and could not be bothered to walk four feet to the nearest trash bin to throw out the remains. Aluminum plates, foam cups, drumsticks, paper napkins, and plastic forks littered the ground. Adding to the mess, Abdu said, were the residents of the street's three crack houses. They trawled through garbage cans and ripped open bags of trash in the middle of the sidewalk. Then they would remove whatever was of interest: metal for resale, returnable soda bottles, and morsels of discarded food.

This practice created a financial as well as a housekeeping burden for homeowners on the street, Abdu explained. The Sanitation Department would impose a hefty fine if I didn't sweep up litter before 6 A.M.

"You see that?" He pointed to a gum wrapper curled alone in a sidewalk crack. "You'd pay two hundred and fifty dollars just for that."

As though on cue, an elderly black man with a paunch shuffled over from the apartment building directly across the street. He wore a baseball cap and a surly expression. Abdu informed me that this was Clarence, the super of the property the police had raided the other day.

"He used to clean the sidewalk for the previous owner. You should hire him. Otherwise you have to do it yourself."

I did a quick calculation. In order to reach Harlem in time each morning from Queens, I'd have to get up at four o'clock, an unappealing prospect.

Clarence got straight to the point.

"How much did you pay for this old brownstone?" He surveyed me as though I, too, needed a cleaning. "You're rich. You can afford fifty bucks to clean the sidewalk."

I introduced myself.

"I know who you are, girl. You're the fool who bought that house. That's my last offer. Take it or leave it."

Flustered, I said I'd think about it.

Clarence grunted. "Fish oil."

"Fish oil," I repeated, blankly.

Clarence leaned over and inspected my forehead with a sour grimace. He smelled of cheap musk. "You ain't young. Take cod liver oil or you'll get ugly wrinkles." He extended a hand. "Feel it."

With little relish, I gingerly touched his hand. Clarence's skin felt surprisingly soft for a man who made his living taking out garbage cans and minding fuses.

"Fish oil," he said with satisfaction. Clarence lit a Parliament cigarette and inhaled deeply. I wondered if he thought fish oil protected against lung cancer, too.

The dealers loudly slapped down plastic dominoes as they discussed a transaction. *"Oye, loco. ¿Dónde está el dinero?"* ("Hey, crazy. Where's the money?")

"I said the bodega."

"He wasn't there."

"Check again."

A woman tried to pass with a baby carriage. Unable to maneuver around the men, she pushed the pram into the street.

Clarence scowled at the scene. "Punks. The old generation was very respectable. There was a time in the eighties when you couldn't get drugs at three P.M. on Sundays. Good Friday? No way. They didn't do it when people were coming from church."

"What gents," I said sarcastically.

Clarence threw his cigarette butt in front of the gate. I thought about the $250 fine this might incur.

"Then the old guys retired," he continued. "These young punks don't care about anybody. All they want is money and then to go back to the Dominican Republic. Animals, you know what I mean? Animals."

He looked at them scornfully and then turned to me. "Cottage cheese."

I thought I got his drift. "High in calcium!" I said brightly.

Clarence eyed me disdainfully. "No, I mean you folks. White and soft."

He coughed up a wad of yellow phlegm, which landed next to the remains of his cigarette.

"Everything is catching up with us. The storms. God is multicolor. One day he's black, one day he's white. You can't escape. I don't know if I'm going to heaven or hell. A lot of changes have to be done."

With that cryptic pronouncement, Clarence went across the street to his sentry post and leaned against the doorway with arms crossed. He stared ahead with an air of studied indifference as four men whistled loudly, until someone threw down a set of keys from the fourth floor.

I thought aloud. "Maybe I could get Clarence to watch my house. He could chase away the dealers."

Abdu looked alarmed. "No! No! He'd be a liability. The dealers shot him in the butt a few years back. They don't respect him."

.   .   .

Over the following three days, I spent many an hour waiting for the window-bar men to arrive, and then, after they did, awaiting the end of the job. It should have taken just half a day instead of three full ones to complete the task. But it seemed that the welder either was on an extended lunch break or needed to fetch metal from the Bronx, where he invariably got distracted.

When he finally completed the work and left, I continued to hang around the house. After all, I didn't have anything else to do, since I didn't have a proper job. I felt sneaky leaving Queens for my new abode—I still hadn't shared with my mother the news that I had acquired a disaster zone, fearing that she would disapprove. To avoid filling her in, I generally left the house around 6 A.M., before she woke up. In the evenings, when I returned, I'd mumble, "Yeah, everything's fine," when she looked up from her financial reading to inquire after my day. Then I would sneak down to the basement phone and wail to my sister, Susan, about my foolhardiness. The common wisdom in our extended family was that my sister, who was less than two years my senior, was the sensible one. During my rebellious adolescence, Susan served as my lawyer, calmly arguing my case to Mom when I overstayed a curfew or spent time with a particularly wild friend. During my long tenure abroad, I could always count on my tolerant sister to graciously receive my hyperventilating phone calls about the latest crisis—no matter that the eight-hour time difference meant I was waking her at 4 A.M. Susan was my quiet port of call. Admittedly, these days, she was a bit too quiet—she didn't say anything to resassure me about the house purchase. She was no doubt unsure herself about my judgment. But whatever. Her silence was better than what would result if I confided in Mom.

That's right. No way was I going to let my mother in on the secret. At least not now. Maternal censure of this dumb purchase seemed nearly as scary as the possibility that Salami might invade again.

Visiting the house daily also gave me the opportunity to plan our renovation. There were many empty hours waiting for potential workmen to call back, so to pass the time I spent long intervals on the front stoop watching the scene. It was a surprisingly relaxing place to sit. The sun warmed the concrete steps and a fresh zephyr played off the river as the sounds of a basketball game rose from the playground down the hill.

The *bachata* hit that spring was the song "Obsesión," by a group called Aventura. All across Dominican Harlem, the saccharine but nevertheless haunting tune floated from windows and cars, and I'd find myself involuntarily humming along while sitting outside. Salami had adopted "Obsesión" as his personal anthem as well, and he sang the refrain, *"No es amor, no es amor,"* while pushing a navy blue baby stroller full of damaged electronic goods that he was trying to hawk. Salami was a constant fixture on the street, rummaging through garbage cans to collect every discarded hair dryer and television set that he could find. He barely glanced at the items as he piled them into the pram. As he passed me, Salami would shout belligerently, "That's my house, Mama!" Just his voice sent my adrenaline pumping and made my skin clammy. I had to suppress the urge to flee.

Salami often dozed on the steps of his abode next door, propped up against large stereo speakers. He had a regular companion, a hideously emaciated woman missing an eye and much of the waxy hair that she wore in a greasy bob. She followed Salami everywhere, wrapping her arms around him even as he walked. He called her "Bitch," and something else that I couldn't make out. I asked Clarence from across the street what it was.

"'Charm,'" Clarence said. "She ain't got looks so he calls her Charm."

Despite their lack of attention to hygiene, the two were avid launderers and liked to store big bags of freshly washed clothes on the front stairs. There, the socks and T-shirts emitted the soapy smell of Tide. The couple's domesticity extended to taking out the trash, which they did regularly. The problem was that their garbage contained raw sewage (their plumbing didn't work, as the building's owner had long ago stopped paying water bills), and these plastic bags of excrement were thrown into their backyard, from which a putrid stench drifted into my own garden.

But ever the swain, Salami tended to his body. He hung on the corner traffic light to do his workouts, pulling himself up with powerful arms. When he found a discarded treadmill machine, Salami installed it in front of the church on the other side of my house. The treadmill was missing a support, so he propped it up with a gray brick ripped from my tree pit, and ran in place as though the track were plugged in. When Salami tired of jogging, he did stretches and lifted free weights improvised from metal parts.

From my front step, I watched Salami one day as he did push-ups, first ten, and then twenty-five, then fifty. Noticing he had an audience, Salami took off the top of his sweatsuit to show off an upper torso sculpted like a boxer's. The sight of Salami's naked biceps brought home the scary fact of how strapping this man was. Salami was stronger than I had imagined. I had a flashback to Rwanda, to a man with a machete who had chased me to my car. Salami was just as terrifying.

He sauntered over with a smirk and provocatively stretched his bad leg over my metal gate.

"Mind if I make myself comfortable?" It was more of a statement than a question. He rubbed his calf. "Feels like something is pinching or biting," Salami went on. "I got a rod in my leg and an artificial hip. They were shattered. Sometimes it hurts me in the damp weather." He massaged the leg with a grimace.

I was surprised that Salami now wanted to make conversation. He had been so hostile before. Maybe this was a diversionary prelude to jumping me. Or perhaps Salami simply wanted attention. I didn't feel like chatting but didn't want to anger him, either. Salami might lash out if offended. I had locked the front door and mentally mapped an escape route from the stoop if Salami lunged. It was a six-foot drop to the patio below.

"What happened?" My voice went up an unnatural octave.

"I fell out of a four-story window."

"You jumped?"

Salami glared indignantly. "I ain't that stupid, Mama. I got robbed—they pushed me." He pulled up the leg of his grimy sweatpants and rubbed a shin. "I still feel the splinters of bone coming through my feet. They can't vacuum it out."

"Ouch." I shuddered, involuntarily flexing my foot.

"It ain't that bad. I can jump, kick, everything, play basketball and football." Salami mimed a slam dunk, his lopsided frame askew. He bent over and rubbed his bad knee. "My doctor operated for the Knicks. He told me I'd be crippled for life. But I got sick of how the crutches hurt under my arm, so I started to do exercises. You can do anything when you put it in your mind."

I nodded my head at this sage advice.

One of the dealers nosed up behind us. He picked bark off the honey locust tree as he pretended not to be listening. A thought flitted across my brain. *Now they're killing my tree.*

"Get lost. I ain't giving away your secrets," Salami snapped. The man ignored him.

Salami turned to me and patted his leg as though praising a good dog.

"That rod saved my life when I was shot. It was three years ago on 139th Street. My girlfriend stole ninety grams of crack from a dealer. He was stashing it in my house. I hid it inside my speakers. My girl said that I got robbed. So the dealer goes underneath the truck and pulls out a handgun. He followed me into the building. He wanted three thousand dollars. He put the gun to my head. I hit him and he fell onto the floor. I ran out of the building—I was running zigzag and low, like they do in the army. I got shot right in the ass with a nine-millimeter—it hit the rod. I got a Teflon hit. All I felt was a burn. The bullet is still in there. They didn't take it out because that would damage my spine."

I involuntarily glanced at Salami's butt. What was it about this neighborhood and posteriors? Both Salami and Clarence had been shot in the ass. Perhaps I should be worried about mine, too. Though at least my bum was a smaller target than Salami's pumped-up gluteus maximus and Clarence's flabby behind.

Salami interrupted my thoughts to push his right arm up to my face. He rolled up the sleeve to reveal a gnarled scar running from elbow to wrist. The flesh rose like an angry snake.

"Then I got stabbed. I got almost a hundred stitches. I got into an argument with a dealer. The guy owed me money for cleaning the car. He said, 'Wait.' I said I didn't want to wait. So he stabbed me. I was leaking blood. You could see the bone."

Salami went quiet, and his mood suddenly shifted. Leaning on the gate, he leered, his ugly expression showing sore red gums and missing teeth. He swiveled his pelvis suggestively and told me yet again how he got his name.

"You know, Salami." He gestured just in case I didn't get it. "Big hands and feet. Chinese secret. Hey, Mama, wanna see it?"

"Not really." I quickly moved toward the door. That wound him up more.

"Scaredy cat, scaredy cat. Yeah, Mama, you go hide in that fancy house. Just you wait. I'm gonna get it back."

Chapter 6

THE NARCOTICS WALL STREET

Dominicans in the Heights have the reputation among other Hispanic groups of being especially exuberant and loud. There's an expression you often hear among Dominican Yorks, as they're called: *"Haga la bulla."* It translates literally as "to make noise" but as often as not means "Let's party!" Turning up your favorite merengue on the radio is a way of showing the world that you're happy, of announcing your presence, of saying, "I just got paid!" Booming the music of Johnny Ventura until 3 A.M. is accepted, even welcomed, as a sign that the person playing the music is in a good, sociable mood.

Dominicans are also known for their ironic wit. Later, when I visited the island, I was struck by how banter softens the life in shanties and villages in what is one of the poorest places in the Western Hemisphere. Conversation is a well-honed art that takes the edge off joblessness and hurricanes. A common sight across the country is a bunch of guys *chismeando* (gossiping) outside a kiosk or under an almond tree, a circle of Presidente beer bottles on the ground around a blaring stereo. The men trade repartee animatedly as they hip-swivel next to the speakers.

The adaptable Dominican Yorks have imported this outdoors mingling to Upper Manhattan, no matter the northern clime. The mercury might dip to forty-five degrees, but men wearing wool hats will be out in vivacious resilience on the traffic medians, ignoring the fumes of cars. The pavement is treated as an extension of the living room, or as a social club. Anyone with nothing better to do will sit around in the back room of bodegas or in front of apartment buildings and engage in ripe, sharp talk. Throngs appear outdoors in all weather: They'll barbecue by the front door, jiggle babies on the front steps, practice batting. People court on the street and mourn on the street. When someone dies, relatives set up cardboard shrines with tall votive candles, carnations, and photographs of the deceased. Neighbors pay their respects and pass around a cup for donations to bury the body or send it back home. The alfresco life was one of the things that beguiled me about the neighborhood, especially the kids riding their bicycles and playing baseball on the sidewalk even well after dark. This was one of the last neighborhoods in Manhattan where elementary-schoolers played safely in front of their buildings. Any stranger who touched a kid would be lynched by the grannies and uncles watching nearby.

The less appealing part of this sidewalk socializing was that it provided a perfect cover for the dealers. What better way to hide your real activities than hanging out with the middle-aged ladies sitting in lawn chairs? "Officer, I'm not doing anything wrong. I'm just talking with my auntie—she lives here." It dawned on me that some of the men on the traffic island on Broadway whom I had taken to be devoted outdoors domino players were actually awaiting deals. Every now and then a cell phone chimed, and a guy got up off his bench and sauntered to the corner to meet a car. Someone else slipped into his place and pretended to argue over a move if a cop walked by. When police approached they'd whistle loudly in a chain reaction and call, "Five-O!"

The crafty dealers then ducked into apartment buildings or sprinted away.

The muchachos were so barefaced they didn't seem to care that this gringa watching from her front stoop could easily call the police from her cell phone. It was amazing to think that these packages that had been so carefully smuggled in someone's stomach or the false bottom of a suitcase were so brazenly and openly traded here on the street. Under my very eyes, the guys handed over fat wads of cash the height of a brick. Glassine sandwich bags of powder were passed off midstride, relay-race-style. Favored stashing spots included ivy in front yards, or under the stairs of the abandoned house next door. Packages were deposited in telephone booths or fished out of socks. One time I saw a plastic-wrapped cocaine loaf the length of a baguette on top of the wheel of a Land Rover. Meanwhile, at least five moving vans pulled up each week to remove or deliver bedding. The dealers appeared to be smuggling drugs inside these mattresses.

And they were as organized as Wall Street. At 11 A.M. sharp, the muchachos appeared as though to a ringing bell, with the same punctuality as bond traders. The guys slid from Lincoln Mercury sedans driven from the Bronx and took position. They ate, pissed, ordered takeout, and shopped, all on the spot. A brigade of pushcarts brought wares to meet various needs: batteries, jeans, fresh orange juice, crab soup, ices.

The customers also had a distinctive look. Someone drawing a composite picture would sketch a Latino man in his midthirties, a little too puffy from fried food and brandy, and driving an SUV with smoked windows. Loud music broadcast his presence. The younger clients were generally African-Americans who favored hip-hop gangsta fashions such as diamond studs and do-rags. Oversize T-shirts hung to their knees over their equally enormous jeans.

The salesmen broke for lunch at 1 P.M., ordering food on their cell phones. They'd end work around 9 P.M. on weekdays and well after midnight on weekends.

These men crowded together in a small space shouting orders, their electronics chirping. They didn't have Bloomberg terminals, but they instant-messaged as well as any high-tech trader. Their BlackBerry devices and point-to-point cellular radios that no doubt were encrypted evaded detection by the law as well. The muchachos used simpler forms of contact, too, such as whispering into the few pay phones left in the neighborhood.

As Abdu explained it, the process of selling a few ounces of coke was broken down into different stages to minimize the risk of being caught or robbed. The crew might number anywhere from twelve to twenty people. Whatever the gang's size, street dealers preferred to move small amounts of *producto* at a time. This was to avoid keeping too much in the safe houses across the street, which also served as laboratories to cut the powder with lactose or other additives and to manufacture "rock," or crack, the cheaper, smokable variety of coke.

At the top of the hierarchy was the kingpin, who rarely appeared on the street. He was the one who used the narcotics proceeds to build his mansion back on the island. *El jefe* had a street lieutenant who ensured that operations were smoothly run. Customers generally negotiated their orders face-to-face with a "runner," who then passed the order to a "pitcher," who delivered the goods. "Spotters" hung out on the sidewalk, awaiting customers. They rarely carried the product on them. "Hawkers" lined up on Broadway, leaning into cars with out-of-state licenses that would double- or even triple-park. The no-parking spot in front of the church next door to our house was a favored spot for clients, who ran their engines while awaiting deliveries. "Lookers" hung out of windows, sometimes with binoculars, and communicated via cell phones or Nextel two-way radios. Women played supporting roles as street spies. One middle-aged woman, with hoop earrings big enough for a parrot to sit on, acted as a sort of den mother for the street. She clucked over the boys and organized lunch deliveries and hand-overs of keys for the stash apartments.

Salami figured at the bottom of the chain. He did odd jobs for the dealers, such as fetching cigarettes or delivering their jeans to the corner dry cleaner. Salami also washed the clients' Mitsubishis and Hondas with the water buckets and rags that he stored on his baby stroller. This, I realized, was why the dealers sometimes called him "Car Wash."

I often saw Salami locked in a standing embrace with Charm on the corner. While they might have been genuinely romancing, the clinch conveniently disguised his role as sentinel. At the first wail of a police siren they'd separate and Salami would yell, "Five-O!"

Despite his usefulness, Salami served as the village fool, mocked mercilessly by his employers. One day I saw three dealers chase Salami with a spade as he screamed impotently, "Fuck you, bastards!" He spoke passable street Spanish, but the dealers made fun of his every word. They insulted him, imitated his limp, and refused to let him sit on the steps of his house while they worked.

These chipped concrete stairs served as the base of operations for the gang, providing a comfortable perch to wait, watch, and argue about baseball. At least a dozen guys sat there at a given time, and in the afternoon after school their girlfriends and babies joined them. Someone invariably switched on a boom box, and the noise rose as they shouted above the music.

Every couple of days, police raided one of the apartment buildings on the opposite side of the street from our house. Unmarked cars screeched up, doors swung open, and a SWAT team raced past Clarence. It happened so frequently that the beach-chair women simply continued to chat and cuddle infants as cops with assault rifles sprinted by. Clarence was equally deadpan as he leaned against his doorway. "It is what it is," he'd remark.

A few days of observation revealed a pattern. While the dealers evaporated at the sight of police, jeering spectators numbering as many as two hundred instantly materialized to see what was going on. If it was a prolonged raid, people ordered Chinese food on their cell phones, and the deliverymen on bicycles joined the crowd with steaming bags of chicken and fried rice. Then the fracas subsided, and if the raid was successful, the next day Clarence put out steel doors for the recycling truck to pick up.

"It's like Fort Knox," he mumbled. "Some of them apartments have two doors. The police cut them down, and then a new bunch puts them back up."

Chapter 7

MEET THE NEIGHBORS

After Salami's less-than-gracious welcome, I wondered how we would be received by the legitimate
townhouse dwellers. The street was divided along architectural
and social lines. The side across the street was filled with
apartment buildings, most of which were populated by Dominicans of modest means. Our part consisted of nineteen row
houses. Several had been carved up into rooming houses or
had been overtaken by crack addicts. But most of the homes
were still inhabited by single families, sometimes extending
back generations to great-grandparents. Abdu had told me
that the homeowners were mainly middle-class blacks: teachers, musicians, civil servants, office clerks. Many were elderly
people of West Indian descent who had lived in the same

houses for half a century. The former owner of our house, for instance, was a doctor who had practiced out of the basement. Her husband, who died earlier, was a Baptist minister who presided over a nearby church.

We were the first whites on the block in about twenty-five years, and I feared that my pale complexion might provoke strong ambivalence, even hostility, as it did for Salami and the muchachos. We weren't displacing anyone by buying an empty house, but we *were* changing the block's racial makeup. Would our neighbors resent us?

The answer to this question came a few days later. For nearly a week, I had noticed on the street a handsome black woman slightly older than me, with a dapple of freckles adorning her fine features. She wore the classic New York commuter fashion of tailored suits and running shoes, carrying her office pumps in her briefcase. Around dusk, apparently on her way home from work, the woman would slowly make her way up the hill with a briefcase in one hand and empty plastic bags in the other. We nodded hello as she stooped over the tree pits, picking up the slimy litter, before stopping a few doors up from ours. This time she lingered outside my house, gazing at the façade as she put her attaché case down and knotted a plastic bag closed. Three policemen on horses clopped past and told the dealers at Salami's house to move on. The muchachos ignored the cops, and the horses rode on.

"There goes the cavalry," the woman remarked dryly. "They can't do anything. It's legal to loiter. You bought this house?"

"We're in contract."

"I'm glad someone finally bought it." Her eyes swept over my dust-flecked jeans and untamed curls. As she pursed her glossed lips, I got the impression that I wasn't her first choice of a neighbor. "That house has been empty since the doctor died six months ago. It's a blight on the block. I hope you have energy. If you don't mind my saying so, and please don't take this the wrong way, the police will listen to you whites. They don't take us black folks very seriously when we complain about the problem."

"The problem being . . . ?" I nodded in the direction of the dealers. The same fellow who had shadowed my conversation with Salami was back at his listening post at my honey locust tree.

"Them." The woman lowered her voice conspiratorially. "We've been complaining for years to the authorities. We wrote to all the mayors—Koch, Dinkins, Giuliani. None of them did anything. Meetings, meetings, meetings. I'm so tired of it. We need young people with the energy to fight. This is a no-man's-land politically. None of our elected officials live in the neighborhood, not the councilman or assemblyman or senator or congressman. They don't have to deal with this stuff, so they don't give it priority."

My neighbor reached into her purse and offered a business card that indicated that she worked in the human resources department of a major bank. Her name was Leticia. On the back were an address and the words POLICE MEETING. MONDAY 6 P.M.

"We should talk. Come to my house."

I accepted her invitation heartily, maybe a little too keenly, judging from her raised eyebrow. Boy, did I want a peek inside Leticia's house! The same architect had designed my building, and a quick tour could reveal just how much restoration lay ahead. I also might pick up some decorating tips. This was great!

I practically skipped into the parlor. My heart sank at the first glimpse of the polished marble fireplace. Leticia had it all: pocket doors, plaster crown moldings, ceiling medallions, stained glass, brass doorknobs. This was yet *another* reason that our house was so cheap. It had been destroyed. Ruined. Wrecked. Leticia's immaculate abode was the "before" version of my house. Under her well-burnished sconces lay plaster virginally free of layered lead paint. While my walls were cratered to the latticework, Leticia's gleamed warmly with pristine oak wainscoting.

Yes, indeed. Leticia's home was a shrine to Harlem gentility. As she escorted me from room to room, I could easily imagine people shaving for church over the marble washbasins, or brainstorming a literary magazine in the paneled study. Here, upstanding citizens practiced piano in the parlor. Whoever had lived here had doted on this property, and lovingly protected it from tar-throwing maniacs.

In sharp contrast, my dilapidated property was a museum of the crack epidemic. It served as a reminder of all that had destroyed Harlem: crime, looting, despair, poverty, failing schools. My house screamed, "Neglect!"

Leticia sat me down at a teak table in the kitchen ("Danish design, mid-century," she noted) and filled tall crystal glasses with ice cubes and soft drinks as she told her story. Originally from Jamaica, she had moved to this house twenty-five years ago. Leticia showed me photographs of her teenage sons, two attractive boys with open smiles. She gently wiped dust off the glass frames like a caress.

"They've stayed out of trouble," she said. "That's an achievement in this area. It used to be nice here. But it went downhill in the 1980s, when the Dominican drug gangs moved in. I think it was 1983 when they began to appear. For a while they fought for turf. They'd fire out of a car and hit innocent people. I would run from the subway after dark. Yellow taxis stopped coming here.

"We began to organize secretly. We meet with the D.A. and the Three-O—that's the Thirtieth Precinct—to report the dealers. People sit by their front windows and jot down license plate numbers. We have to be careful, though. The dealers heard one man was cooperating with the police and beat him."

Leticia explained that separate meetings were held for the black homeowners and for the Dominican tenants of the drug buildings across the street. A sort of social apartheid existed between the two groups, who sent their kids to different schools and didn't even shop at the same grocery stores. ("We don't trust them," Leticia explained.) Only select people were invited to meet with police, to ensure that the dealers did not plant moles. With the help of these citizen spies, police had wiretapped telephones in the apartment building at the top of the hill in order to break up a gang that was doing interstate sales and harassing residents in the hallways. The leader was arrested in March.

I thought about the throngs on Broadway, and about the arrogance of the muchachos.

"Do the meetings make a difference?"

Leticia ran a fingertip across the rim of her glass. "Not really. As soon as one lot gets arrested, the gangs send more foot soldiers from the Dominican Republic." She paused. "The funny thing is, I think of myself as liberal. I'm black. I'm not racist. I believe in civil liberties. But living here I've grown more, let's say, reactionary. I'm not anti-Dominican, but the authorities should stop every one of these criminals for identity checks and deport them. I pay taxes. I have rights, too. . . ." Her voice trailed off.

I was confused about the picture of race relations that she was painting. I thought the police department was trying to combat an image of racist brutality after two egregious cases of abuses against black immigrants. The first, in 1997, involved a Haitian named Abner Louima, who was sodomized with a broomstick while in police custody. Two years later, police shot dead an unarmed Guinean immigrant, Amadou Diallo, in a fusillade of forty-one bullets. But here, according to Leticia, African-American and West Indian blacks actually wanted the police to get tough on Latino immigrants. Maybe not torture or kill them, but throw them out.

Did I get that right?

"Yes," Leticia said. "We want the National Guard to restore order. The dealers think they own the streets. We can't walk down the block without insults and filth."

I had more questions. Last I heard, the 30th Precinct had earned the sobriquet the "Dirty Thirty" for a scandal in the 1990s, when several officers were caught selling cocaine and protecting drug dealers. The offending policemen ended up in jail. Was the corruption still going on?

"They assure us that they've cleaned up the precinct," she said. "But how do we know? I'm all for those tough Rockefeller drug laws. We're sick and tired of cars being broken into, the noise, people strung out on drugs hanging around Broadway. Lock them up and get them off the streets."

Shouts rang out from the street. Even the thick walls and velvet curtains couldn't keep out the noise. The sound of a crowd droned, punctuated by the odd, shrill *"Oye, heavito"* and *"¡Coño!"*

This woman seemed like a decent neighbor. It was nice knowing she lived a couple of buildings away.

"To our block," I said, lifting my glass.

"Sorry," Leticia said. "I'm selling my house. I can't take it anymore."

Leticia must have put the word out that we were buying the house, because the following day a parade of elderly homeowners came to visit. Experiencing a growing sense of apprehension about committing myself to this property, I felt as if I were being visited at my own funeral.

Our front bell didn't work, so guests had to bang on the door. I grew to recognize the sound of the unoiled gate swinging open as the august visitations got under way. Everyone had a story.

First to drop by that morning was Debbie, a telephone company clerk with waist-long gray dreadlocks. She coped with the tension of living in the neighborhood by praying at a Buddhist shrine. Perhaps I might want to join her one night? Next came Marcia, who was fighting to keep a loan shark from repossessing her house. She was looking for a good lawyer and hoped that I might know one. Then June Hildegarde, an elderly woman bent at the waist from osteoporosis like an upside-down L. She stoically rebuffed my offer to carry her grocery bags up the street.

The afternoon shift began with Mr. and Mrs. Campbell, a formal couple in their eighties whom Leticia had referred to as her "surrogate parents." Leticia had known them in Jamaica as a child and had encouraged them to follow her to New York. The husband was going blind and his wife was increasingly frail, and Leticia felt guilty about leaving them behind. I quickly understood why.

"I used to tell my husband, 'I wish we hadn't come here,'" said Mrs. Campbell, as her husband politely nodded. "At first when we came here it was good. We had a mix of people of different nationalities—Europeans, Orientals, Jewish people, black people, and Hispanics. We had nothing between us. Then in the 1980s these drug people came and it began to get rough. That's when we put up the fence in front of the stoop, but they sit on the stairs anyway. They have no respect for anyone. They won't move if you walk down the sidewalk. And let me tell you some more. The noise outside gets so bad that we can't sleep. It drives us crazy. Three, six o'clock in the morning and they're still blasting. There was this guy in a red Pontiac and he would park outside and blast the music all day. One day my arthritis was hurting me and I went out and gave him a piece of my mind. I won't tell you what he said back!"

The Campbells, as well as everyone else, asked if I had met Mrs. Victoria LaDuke. "She's quite a character. She knows everyone," I was told.

Next came an impish octogenarian with soft brown eyes clouded by cataracts. A diamond stud glittered in his left ear. This, I learned from the offered calling card, was PHILLIP ANDERSON, AAGO, CH.M, FTCL.

I smiled blankly at the acronyms.

"Organist and choirmaster. I studied in the strictly classical tradition at Juilliard. Weren't a lot of us black folks there back then." He stretched his hands, which were gloved in thick padded leather despite the spring warmth. "I have sensitive fingers. Can't let them get cold."

By now I had developed a standard opening line that went something like, "You must have seen a lot of changes around here." The question was meant to be neutral, but it often sparked vitriolic complaints.

Mr. Anderson held forth without hesitation, toying with his gloves all the while.

"I can't understand these Spanish people and they can't understand me. Here I am, born and educated in this country, and I feel like I am living in a foreign land. But back in the 1960s, it was just like Fifth Avenue! The shops on Broadway sold mink coats! My Lord! The block parties we had. We sold hot dogs. We had music. We hung streamers all the way from my house to the playground! Now the police don't let us have parties on the block anymore, because of the drug activity."

His face darkened, but then brightened at the arrival of a curvaceous woman of indeterminate age. She could have been fifty or eighty. This stunning apparition had an unlined caramel-colored face and wore emerald-green sunglasses. Silver waves hung softly in a 1940s side part. Her body formed an hourglass; the ample bosom was encased in a snug T-shirt.

"Our neighbor from around the corner: Mrs. Victoria LaDuke!" Mr. Anderson said, with a performer's bow.

"Phillip, you're too much! Who are you flirting with?" the woman said in a throaty contralto. "Shame on you." Mr. Anderson grinned.

Introductions made, she invited me to peek at the contents of her shopping bag. "The secret is to tighten the elastic. I'm eighty-two. This keeps me firm. I'm getting these fixed at the tailor."

Intimacy established, Mrs. LaDuke felt comfortable dispensing more advice.

"I can see your house from the back of mine. You must be paying a fortune, leaving those lights on all night!"

They're on all night? I thought. *Negligent Abdu. I must bring this up with him.*

Mrs. LaDuke quickly ran through her story. A widow originally from New Jersey, she was still working at the New York University bookstore ("I'm not stopping just because I'm eighty-two!"). She owned three houses around the corner, and shared one with her brother and a pit bull named Thunder. Tenants filled the others.

Like others on the block, Mrs. LaDuke had had travails with the dealers, the latest being that one had just urinated in front of her parlor window.

"I saw a penis right outside. Oh, boy! Can you imagine? So I said to the young man, 'You ought to be ashamed of yourself, that thing is so small. Now go, shoo!' "

Her pet peeve was how the dealers and their clients monopolized parking spots on the street. There were already few enough, owing to another neighbor who stationed a fleet of 1980s Buicks on the block. This caused great inconvenience when Mrs. LaDuke's family from New Jersey dropped by.

"The only place for us to park is by the hydrant. So I have to visit with my relatives in the car, with their motor running. They only get out to use my bathroom."

Our conversation seemed to have run its course. Mrs. LaDuke went off to the tailor. Mr. Anderson spoke about his son, who lived upstate. "He's like a big farmer, cutting down wood and raising animals." Mr. Anderson said his son was raising twenty-five snakes, five dogs, four horses, five cats, fish ("fresh and saltwater"), fifty chickens, forty ducks, geese, and hamsters. "He's the talk of the town," Mr. Anderson chirped.

I asked if he planned to relocate there. It sure sounded nice. Mr. Anderson shook his head no, vigorously.

"I moved here in 1951 and I'll be here until I die. It's very convenient. I don't have to use my car downtown. I'm very satisfied here. Darling, I like people, period."

Good, I thought. *This one is sticking around.*

Mr. Anderson beamed suddenly. "Come—I want to show you my flowers."

He escorted me to his house, which, like mine, lay next to a crack den that smelled of excrement. I jumped back, startled, as a hunchbacked middle-aged man writhed out of the basement window and crawled up to the sidewalk. Mr. Anderson didn't seem to notice. "The hand in the hand," the hunchback mumbled mysteriously as he went up the hill.

Mr. Anderson led me to his ground-floor entrance. There, two window boxes filled with plastic purple and yellow pansies cheerily greeted us.

I wasn't sure what to say. "Upkeep must be easy."

Mr. Anderson flashed me a radiant smile. "You got it! I don't have to water them. They never die!" He steered me to the neighbors' front yards, where withered dandelions poked sadly out of the ground. "It's impossible to grow anything around here. Those boys pick them or trample on them or throw garbage. But these, these will never die!"

Leticia gave me a fat handbook that a local historian had drawn up about the immediate neighborhood. The booklet formed part of a failed bid to landmark our street. I read that our block was a fraction of a four-hundred-acre parcel granted to the first settler of the area, Jochem Pieterson Kuyter, following the incorporation of the Dutch village of Nieuw Haarlem in 1658. A good tidbit to pass on to John, I thought. Maybe the Dutch connection would help divert his attention from the drug problem.

The street entailed a series of almosts. It had just missed forming part of the Sugar Hill district. Lots of Harlem luminaries had lived in Hamilton Heights: Duke Ellington, Supreme Court Justice Thurgood Marshall, W.E.B. Du Bois, pianist Mary Lou Williams, novelist Ralph Ellison, the Reverend Adam Clayton Powell Sr., painter Aaron Davis.

But no one famous had resided on our block. It figured.

The general vicinity boasted an important victory in the Revolutionary War, when the American colonists won the 1776 Battle of Harlem Heights. However, I couldn't decisively say, "George Washington was here." He had been headquartered twenty blocks uptown, and as far as I could gather, no decisive fighting had occurred on what was now our street.

Even West Harlem's one national landmark—a yellow federal house known as the Grange that was Alexander Hamilton's final abode—lay a couple of blocks away. The red double-decker buses carrying white tourists (locals called them "safari buses") never rumbled down our block.

In keeping with the lack of prestige, the architect who designed our house was no one of note. Search as I did in the records, I couldn't find anything spectacular that Michael J. Fitz Mahony had built.

If that wasn't enough, our street lay just yards outside the land-marked district. The brown street sign at the top of the hill teasingly signaled that we had just missed being protected against ruthless de-velopers. They could come charging in at any moment and tear down the pretty row houses and put up ugly high-rises in their stead. This lack of protection had another practical implication. Landmarked houses have higher property values and therefore the owners tend to take good care of them. You rarely saw abandoned properties or crack-heads like Salami on such blocks.

My friend Keith, who lived in a landmarked section of Harlem, tried to console me. "It costs a fortune to maintain those façades," he said, describing the expensive wooden window frames that would have to be installed if our building was landmarked. "They control what color you can paint the stoop." But I couldn't help noticing that the buildings on the other side of the landmark sign were fetching a quar-ter of a million dollars more than ours, even though we were more con-veniently situated to shops and the subway.

However, our block had one great distinction that the historians left out: the cocaine wholesale business. "Location, location, location," real estate agents like to say. Well, we were ideally placed for drug traf-fickers who drove up and down Interstate 95 to satisfy habits in Boston, Baltimore, Newark, Richmond, and Washington, D.C. We were close to the George Washington Bridge, which ideally met the snorting de-mands of New Jersey and Pennsylvania. For salesmen who preferred to fly, our block was an easy ride to La Guardia Airport. Ours was one of the few streets in this corner of Manhattan that had drive-through ac-cess from east to west. In fact, according to Leticia, the cops said it was the epicenter of narcotics trafficking on the entire northeastern seaboard. They called it "Ground Zero."

Chapter 8

ABDU

The fact that I was craving cigarettes for the first time in fourteen years was an ominous sign. I also desired whiskey, sleep, canoeing on a river, grenade attacks, malaria—anything but home ownership. No doubt I had made a terrible mistake. My legs cramped as I paced my mother's basement at 4 A.M. I wanted to call my sister for reassurance, but it was too late at night. Not that she would have put me at ease, of course. I carried on a silent conversation with an army photograph of my father. He looked particularly dashing in his uniform, leaning on the doorway of a train with a rakish smile. Dad often recalled his perilous army days with nostalgia, and transmitted the message that stifling domestic life should be avoided. He took vicarious pleasure in my adventures, even the time when he called the State Department because I went incommunicado for a few weeks in Brazil. Dad sent me off at sixteen to be an exchange student in India, and advised me what type of cocktail to order on my first date with a much older man. After he fell ill, he encouraged me to go on a trip to China rather than visit home.

I looked more closely at his picture. "You'd approve of this venture, right, Dad?" I asked. His soldier's face simply smirked.

If only I could get out of the purchase. Only a moron would buy that house. I tried to read a magazine but couldn't sit still. Salami's crude leer intruded, and his falsetto echoed.

Amid many chimeras hovered one enormous anxiety. If I went through with the house deal, could I find a contractor before John arrived? I felt guilty about strong-arming my accommodating husband to move to New York, seeing that all our savings would soon be invested in a former crack house that he hadn't seen. I had unfairly left John with the arduous task of packing our belongings in Moscow and explaining to our large circle of friends and associates why I had suddenly left town without saying good-bye. He was making an exceptional professional sacrifice for an uncertain future in New York. So far John had been a good sport. The least I could do was pay him back by getting the construction started.

I frenetically consulted everyone I knew, and quite a few strangers, for references of contractors. I cold-called hardware shops. I scanned ads in newspapers. I telephoned people I hadn't spoken to in years. In this desperate search for workmen, I even initiated conversations with strange men in coveralls on the subway.

Despite my best efforts, not one individual was available to start work in less than six months, when our savings would likely run out. I wanted to start as soon as we closed on the house, if not before. However, it seemed that the legions of people enriched by the dot-com boom had contracted all the city's workmen to install Sub-Zero refrigerators and green slate counters.

Rather than remain idle, I dutifully reported to the house each day to ensure that Abdu was, if nothing else, keeping Salami at bay. We got to talking about ourselves, as people do who spend hours together in tense, claustrophobic settings, and in a moment of vulnerability I confessed my despair about the contractor situation. What was I to do? I practically wailed: John was due home in a few weeks.

Abdu's brown eyes glistened. His normally scared look softened. For the first time, I saw him smile.

"Hire me," he said.

I was stunned. Surely it couldn't be that easy. "You know about this construction stuff?"

"Trust me."

I had a fleeting thought about the boards, which seemed so poorly fastened onto the kitchen door that breaking in would be a snap for the crack-fueled Salami. I momentarily considered the ceiling hole—wasn't Abdu supposed to fix that, too? But then he gave his quote for the painting job. Even a novice could tell that painting and skim-coating—I had just learned that meant adding a smooth layer of plaster—four floors for $2,000 over two weeks was an unbelievable steal. Besides, who else would do the job?

"Let's put that in writing," I blurted out, lest he withdrew the offer.

"No need for a contract," Abdu replied, his soft brown eyes welling with hurt. (Or, I fleetingly wondered, with greed? But then my wonderful powers of denial banished that thought posthaste.)

The next morning I pushed through a phalanx of muchachos leaning on the gate and descended to the basement, where Abdu was sweeping with an expression of raw dread. He was shaking so hard that he dropped the broom when I came up behind him. "Oh," he moaned. Abdu pointed to the two back windows that faced the garden. They were smashed, and shards lay scattered across the muddy linoleum.

"Salami," he whispered. "He broke in again."

The adrenaline rush kicked in, a surge of fight-or-flight hormones released during combat and traumatic situations. With speedy heartbeat, I tracked two sets of sneakered footprints on the stairs leading up to the kitchen.

"Did you check upstairs?" I whispered to Abdu. Whispering seemed the appropriate way to communicate. What if Salami still lurked in the house?

"No one there," Abdu whispered back.

I must have smiled with relief.

"I bet they're coming back," Abdu said. He mumbled, "If Allah wills it," and patted the Koran in his back pocket as he fastened plywood boards onto the empty window frame. His hands shook so hard that he hit his left index finger with the hammer. Moving to the kitchen, Abdu struggled to attach a piece of Sheetrock over the hole in the ceiling. After an hour of failing to secure it, he muttered something about a demanding wife and went home. I sat in the kitchen, fretting under the Sheetrock, which angled off the ceiling like a taut sail.

For lack of anything better to do, I toured my battered estate. Abdu had been talking about the past owner's ghost—he was convinced that it took the form of the white flowers on the dogwood tree in back, which he insisted had never blossomed before. Certainly her remains, if not her spirit, hovered throughout in the form of left-behind furniture and intimate stains on the toilet. I saw that the doctor liked a firm mattress, a Sealy orthopedic bed of considerable bulk that remained in the living room. (Abdu told me that she had died there.) Her taste in artwork verged on kitsch; the one wall painting, hanging crookedly in the second-floor master bedroom, was a cheap rendition of a saint praying on his knees. The doctor had a flirtation with 1970s decor, judging from the settee with flower-power upholstery and the disco-ball lamp hanging in the entrance corridor.

The doctor's relationship with her husband was particularly intriguing. Abdu described it as "not very tight." The couple had no children and maintained separate surnames, an unusual step for a Baptist minister and his wife born in the early 1900s. The couple's differences apparently extended to their worldviews as well. While the doctor collected Soviet literature and the complete works of Karl Marx, her husband's taste leaned toward theological tomes on virtuous behavior. He also chose to live closer to God and farther from her. This explained why the decay, otherwise rampant throughout the house, stopped at the third floor. The minister had installed himself up there alone, with freshly painted walls and a characterless modern bathroom of the Holiday Inn variety.

I felt haunted—by the dead doctor, by Abdu's fear, by Salami outside. I heard him shouting, "I know you're in there, Mama!" It was only noon, but I thought it best to call it a day and go back to Mom's house. *There'll be more time to sort this out,* I thought out loud. I repeated it again and again. The mantra got me down into the subway and to safety in Queens.

On the way from the train to Mom's, I stopped at an Internet café. I hadn't consulted my e-mails since I had returned from Russia—my laptop was still in Moscow and, despite having made a fortune in tech stocks, my mother didn't own a computer.

I trawled through the mere twenty messages that had accumulated over the past few weeks—a sad statement on how quickly my allegedly good friends in Russia had forgotten me. It was a stark contrast to my not-so-distant days as bureau chief, when two hundred e-mails snowed the inbox each day. Since I had already paid for the computer time, I decided to do an Internet search on cocaine trafficking. Just for the heck of it.

To quickly paraphrase a long and violent history, the Colombian cocaine cartels that dominated international smuggling worked with Mexican middlemen, who took care of distributing much of the product within the United States until the early 1990s. At this juncture, the kingpins in Medellín and Cali came to the conclusion that the Mexicans had become too greedy and were pocketing too much of the drugs for resale.

No problema. If not by land, then by sea. The Caribbean route was ripe for exploitation in the 1980s, and the mass Dominican immigration to New York created a new distribution network on the East Coast. The island lay conveniently halfway between Colombia and Manhattan, and served as both a transit point for drugs and a steady supplier of foot soldiers, many of whom made a treacherous journey on rickety boats called *yolas* to Puerto Rico. From there, the relatively unpoliced domestic flights made it easy for undocumented Dominicans and their illicit cargoes to sneak into New York. Once in Manhattan, these new partners of the Colombians easily sold the drugs along the northeastern seaboard, where demand for smokable crack was soaring.

The Dominican distributors provided a perfect cover. Amid the bustle of honking gypsy cabs and hoarse-voiced vendors selling CDs, narcotics gangs established operations in storefronts and apartments. Common strategies were to bankroll tenants or offer a loan to a struggling bodega owner and then use the back of the store for storage and rendezvous.

Uh-oh. I didn't like what I read next. Although originally coke activity was concentrated in Washington Heights, a mile or two north of our new home, it slipped down to West Harlem after July 1992. That's when police shot a young man named "Kiko" García on West 162nd Street. The incident prompted riots and, in response, a saturation of three thousand police. Uncomfortable with so many cops around, the dealers went south.

Plenty of young Dominicans were happy to oblige the Colombians, seeing that as much as half the population was living below the poverty line in New York. Things were even worse in their native country, where youth unemployment was perhaps 25 percent. Although I was no fan of the cocaine bazaar on my street, I couldn't blame enterprising young men for going to New York to support their parents back home. In fact, as someone who hoped one day to be a mother, I appreciated such devotion to Mama. Back on the island the average per capita income was $2,000 a year, but muchachos could make that amount in one week here simply by steering customers to the corner. In five weeks of *narcotraficando*, one could buy a couple of acres of land and build a small cinder-block home in the Dominican Republic. It wasn't fancy, but the family could live off the chickens and goats in back. Even if you were jailed, the retirement home would be waiting when you got out. For a large number of young men, it certainly beat doing twelve-hour shifts in gypsy cabs. And New York girls liked men with money who took them to salsa clubs and bought Nikes for the toddlers.

Curious to learn more about business trends in my adoptive neighborhood, I went to the website of the Drug Enforcement Agency. It described the American drug market as one of the most profitable in the world, attracting the "most ruthless, sophisticated and aggressive drug dealers." The DEA warned that the crack market was particularly bloody, "accompanied by homicides, armed robberies and assaults."

Mysteriously, the NYPD statistics for the 30th Precinct were tame, although this neighborhood led the city in narcotics arrests—some three thousand so far this year. I was flabbergasted to read that the fancy Upper East Side had 307 burglaries, compared to a mere 145 here. Robberies there likewise outpaced us—215 versus 188.

The news that I would not be moving into a hub of violent crime served to enliven my mood, and I felt exuberant riding the train back to Queens. The sun had never glinted so vibrantly on the Chrysler Building, I thought, as the subway left the tunnel and the skyline of Manhattan came into view. Somewhere buried in the northern canyons of concrete was my new street, full of drugs, perhaps, but not murdered bodies.

A few days later, I got a better sense of things as I passed a cop reading Miranda rights to a handcuffed youth on my way to the house. The officer was awaiting backup from the precinct and welcomed the opportunity to shoot the breeze with someone who wasn't shouting "*mierda*," or "shit," at him. This quick lecture on the paradoxes of organized crime revealed that underworld cocaine syndicates didn't need to pick pockets.

"A successful street dealer can make as much as a corporate lawyer," the policeman explained. "The Dominican gangs will pay the Colombians twenty-two thousand dollars per kilo and then 'step on it,' or add substances like baking soda. If they do that, they could get up to forty-five thousand dollars." The cop nudged the perp, whose cheek was mashed against the car. "This guy is probably from a midlevel gang that moves one kilo every two weeks. They're making about 1.8 to 2.6 million dollars a year spread out over eight to twelve people."

The detainee mumbled something and the cop prodded him again. "Shaddup, will ya?"

I asked about the drive-by shootings that were so notorious in the 1980s and 1990s. The cop assured me that they were rare these days, as the gangs had carved up turf. (*A silver lining*, I thought. *No drive-by shootings.*)

If I did get hit, it would be purely by accident. "They're aiming for rivals or someone who stole their stash. Not some Joe off the street." I shouldn't be worried by too much crack activity, either. The dealers were profit-oriented salesmen who didn't use the "product." They didn't like petty criminals attracting the police.

"These guys are businessmen," he explained, prodding the detainee again. "Police are bad for business."

The day of the closing, May 19, arrived three days later. I put on my finest gray suit, the one that I used to wear to interviews with government officials and CEOs, to give the impression of a responsible adult who routinely signed six-digit checks. A button fell off as I fastened the jacket, spoiling the grown-up effect. The driving rain intensified my anxiety, as it reminded me of the hole in the skylight. What would John think of this? I sloshed through puddles to the Greenwich Village townhouse where the seller's contingent awaited me. I couldn't help noticing the Federal-style buildings, tidy and brick, with nary a crack house in sight. No one like Salami camped on *this* block.

I entered a living room warmed by the aroma of coffee and shook off water like a bedraggled dog. Another button dangled loose. The seller's lawyer led me to an elegant black gentleman who looked to be in his seventies. He rose from the sofa and made a slight bow. This was the late owner's brother, who had arrived that morning from Ethiopia, where he was assessing reports of a new famine for President Clinton.

I chatted with the gentleman about prospects for peace in Africa as the lawyers handed around documents to sign. Talk arose about liens, something about a cracked sidewalk that carried a hefty fine.

"Okay, okay," I cut in hastily. Having spent three weeks panicking about buying the house, now all I wanted was to end the process before more surprises arose. I had gone this far; I wanted to just close it. This was not a time to be asking questions. "Where do I sign?"

The seller was equally eager to finalize the deal, explaining that he no longer wanted to be saddled with this "disgusting wreck." He also needed money to pay taxes on the three-million-dollar estate of his sister and her late husband. Three million? The man must have read my thoughts.

"She had so much money. How could she live in that squalor?" He signed the last paper with a satisfied sigh. "That's that. I'm glad to be rid of it."

My left eye began to twitch.

The lawyer neatly slid the signed documents into a manila envelope. We sipped our final coffees and exchanged business cards, knowing full well that he would want to sever every last tie with this burdensome property. Then I headed into the rainstorm to take proud ownership of our new home.

I had agreed with Abdu that he would commence reconstruction work the moment I closed on the house. I arrived there to find him drinking tea with someone named Raul, who resembled a short Abraham Lincoln if the sixteenth president had been a diminutive bodybuilder. In fact, it was those canteloupe-size biceps that had inspired Abdu to approach Raul, as he hung around the hardware shop on Broadway. Abdu reported that Raul was perfect for us: While he knew nothing about construction, he had won a karate championship of minor distinction in his native Dominican Republic.

To demonstrate the strength of his executive decision, Abdu barked, "Now!" and Raul went up to the third floor and carried an old washing machine down on his shoulders, breathing easily, as if it were merely a light bag of laundry.

Raul's other qualification, Abdu confided, was his prison record.

"That's a plus?"

"He really needs a job."

Terrific. Outside was Salami, who wanted to invade, and a club of narcotics salesmen, who collectively would face one hundred life sentences. Now an ex-con was renovating my house.

"What was he in for?" I asked sourly.

"Some minor offense," Abdu said. "Drugs, I think. Don't worry. He's not mixed up with that stuff anymore. They said at the hardware shop that he's decent."

My face no doubt registered anxious skepticism. Abdu grew defensive. "What do you think I am? I wouldn't hire a thug." He got up and put his tea mug in the sink and mumbled something about neurotic New York women.

As it turned out, I didn't need to worry about Raul. He was punctual and honest. If I gave him money to fetch supplies, he returned with receipts and exact change to the penny. A family man devoted to his two small boys, Raul was no problem.

The problem was Abdu. Perhaps it was a fear of Salami, but Abdu tried to spend as little time as possible in the house. And when he did show up, it was clear even to me that his workmanship left something to be desired. The walls were taking on the texture of hardened tapioca pudding, and Abdu was well behind schedule.

Any doubts about his handiwork were confirmed by Clarence, who had developed a habit of knocking on the door throughout the day to inspect our progress.

"You pay him to do that shit? Girl, I thought you were dumb buying this house. You're even dumber than I thought."

The next morning, I arrived to find Abdu passed out on the stained mattress where the former owner had died. On the floor were his Koran and a 1970s blown-glass ashtray filled with marijuana roaches. Abdu groaned when I poked him. "Who are you?" he moaned, startled, fixing dilated pupils on me. "Please, don't hurt me!"

Over the next ten days, he showed up for a total of four hours. When the two-week deadline had passed, only six of the fifty-six walls were "finished," and they looked worse than when he had started.

Meanwhile, I sat around directionlessly with Raul, trying to dream up tasks to do. As neither of us had rehabbed a house before, I bought a do-it-yourself book from Home Depot. The book advised us to scrape the old paint to ready the walls for a fresh coat. Clarence warned that previous layers certainly contained lead, so we wore face masks and vacuumed the flakes immediately after they fell. When we had made sufficient progress in smoothing the walls, we readied the basement for demolition. I whacked at the wood paneling with a crowbar, and then Raul pulled it off with his bare hands.

Raul was pleasant company with whom to smash walls. We talked about a number of things—his childhood in the Dominican Republic, how he came here seeking a better life and got a little sidetracked by that drug situation, and concerns that his boys might be tempted by the street. Raul's dreams were to open a karate school and steer his sons safely into college.

"I don't need a space too big to teach karate," he said. "About . . . well . . . actually, this basement would be perfect."

Raul's desire to live the straight life moved me. I felt comfortable making a confession of my own. "I don't know what to do about Abdu."

"I think he's scared," said Raul.

"That's charitable."

Raul concentrated on tearing a plank from the wall. It took some effort, before he reeled back with the wood. He inhaled slowly. "There's something I need to tell you."

I steeled myself. Now he confesses that he jumped bail, or violated parole. Now I find out that he's a murderer. "Yes?" I asked warily.

"I've seen Abdu buying weed from the guys on the corner."

I processed this in silence.

"He doesn't buy coke," Raul hastily added.

"How reassuring," I said sarcastically. This was rich. I'm telling the muchachos not to deal in front of my house, and then this moron who can't paint a wall properly is scoring on the corner.

"The jerk," I spurted. "He's fired."

"Er," Raul said. "That was the other thing I wanted to tell you. Abdu said he wasn't coming back." Raul held out the Penguin edition of the Koran. "He left this for you. Said you might need it."

Chapter 9

PEACE TALKS

R aul stayed on. I didn't want to be alone in the house while Salami lurked outside. The sight of Raul's giant biceps had a soothing effect on my nerves, and I felt further protected by the fact that he was on nodding terms with the drug crew on the block. Surely no one would attack me with Raul nearby. With security in mind, I conjured up a few tasks for us to muddle through until John got to New York.

We launched our partnership at El Floridita, the rowdy café across the street that the muchachos used as their indoor office when they needed a bathroom or a retreat from the rain. Men chattered animatedly over mashed plantains and gave slapping handshakes as they circulated among the tables by the mirrored walls. They eyed me suspiciously as we walked in. I was the only female except for the waitresses spilling out of their tight pink uniforms. All the tables in the atrium were taken, so Raul and I sat on the vinyl swivel chairs at the counter under the plastic hanging ferns.

Raul highly recommended the *cubano* sandwiches, a house specialty that involved piling ham, pickles, roast pork, and cheese on plushy submarine rolls. Indeed they were tasty, although unlike anything I had ever eaten in Cuba, perhaps because of the shortage of ingredients there. As we chomped on our food, I proposed a rough game plan, shouting over the loud merengue, "We'll work until John comes. Then we'll see."

That was fine with Raul. He didn't have anything to do other than hang out with his kids, and of course he had to support them. Raul stretched out his hand for a high five.

"*Hecho* (deal)."

The restaurant afforded a perfect view of my block, and with dismay I saw Salami hanging on my gate as though it were a swing. About twenty men walked in and out of Clarence's building in quick succession.

"What goes on there?" I asked Raul. I recounted how once I'd gone inside looking to borrow a tool from Clarence. Guys slunk around a corridor that stank of piss, outside an apartment secured by a thick iron gate. The men had fallen silent as I walked past.

Raul lowered his voice as he spoke, spearing an errant pickle with a toothpick. "Those were probably guards. They have an apartment where their customers go and wait, like in a dentist's office. A guy sits there with a forty-five pistol."

I raised an eyebrow.

"Guns are rare," Raul hastened to assure me. "The security wants to keep customers from robbing one another. Other than that, if you stuck someone up, the whole community would chase you. I've heard that customers go to another apartment to pick up the goods. That's where they cut the stuff, and it has scales and things. The dealers won't stash large amounts in the same place in case of raids. The dealers pay off the landlords. If the apartment costs three hundred dollars, they'll pay fifteen hundred. If the police close it up, another associate moves in. A common practice is to set up a grandmother or aunt in an apartment. Cops don't like harassing old ladies. What if she gets a heart attack?"

I listened with rapt attention. So great was my admiration for this entrepreneurial acumen that I momentarily forgot that these were the same oafs who used my steps as a urinal.

"Don't legit residents rat to the police?"

Raul looked around shiftily. He spoke again when he was reassured that no one was eavesdropping. "People are scared. The dealers could hurt them or their families back home. Mind you, this building isn't as rough as others. There's a gang on 146th Street that holds the tenants virtual hostage in two apartment buildings. The gang rules the hallways. They strut around drinking beer and harassing the women. They extort money from residents and threaten anyone suspected of working with the police."

The men behind us were speaking loudly on their cell phones. One said, "I got the chicken dish." My eyes strayed to his table. He was eating tripe.

Raul read my thoughts. "Everything is spoken in code," he murmured softly. "Something like, 'I'm bringing a box of diapers,' or, 'I'm getting McDonald's.' There's also, 'The sugar has arrived.' That one is pretty obvious. I haven't heard it for a while."

I asked for the check and got up to use the toilet. Even that wasn't straightforward here. Raul explained that I needed to ask permission, "like in school." Sure enough, I had to inform the manager about my needs. He scrutinized me hard and then hit a button under the counter. The buzzer noise followed as I walked to the back, where the sign on the toilet door advised that only one person was allowed in at a time.

"That was weird," I said, upon returning to my seat and picking up the check.

"I don't know why they make such a fuss about drug dealing in the bathroom," said Raul. "It happens right here at the tables."

After lunch, our next stop was the Mercedes grocery. Raul suggested that I befriend the owner, who was "clean." The bodega was reminiscent of a village *colmado*—simple stores in the Dominican Republic that sell basics, from canned goods to toilet paper. *Colmados* double as gathering places for playing dominoes or discussing baseball scores. In good Dominican tradition, Mercedes's was a place to meet people and pick up gossip, Raul said. It smelled of wet cardboard and cat piss. Men came and used the back storage room for energetic conversation with other hombres sitting on plastic chairs. Mercedes was cordial but wary as I bought some bottles of water. Her eyes drifted to the muchachos standing behind us.

"She has to be careful," Raul explained as we made our way out. "She's from the same town as them back home."

Raul and I quickly got into a cozy routine: I'd pick up coffee and *cubanos* on the way from the subway station, we'd puzzle over the how-to book, then we'd smash walls. The tedium was broken in the afternoon by his sons, who joined us when school let out. One of their pet games was to load up a dolly with old Sheetrock and wheel it around the garden in a convincing imitation of us bumbling adults. The clowning lightened my gloom about the house and sent me into swooning fantasies of filling the yard with my own offspring, should John ever join me here.

But first things first: getting rid of the building debris that had created a six-foot pyre in the basement. Clarence advised me not to rent a Dumpster to dispose of the detritus, as the dealers could use it to store drugs. The best option, Clarence said, was to hire a van to cart off the rubbish. The cheapest company I could find in the newspaper classifieds was named "2-3-4 MEN With TRUCKS." It actually consisted of one man with a small van. Chester was a refugee of the civil war in Liberia, which had left him nervous about dangerous places. The name Harlem made him jumpy—"I hear it's a rough place," he told me on the phone—and I had to cajole him to venture here with promises of extra money. I assured him our corner had nothing on his native country, where fourteen-year-olds high on amphetamines and wearing Halloween masks had contributed to the massacre of 150,000 people. However, Chester's flashbacks of violence set in after just one look at our relatively tame drug crew and he demanded to be paid an extra bonus, to compensate for the trauma that the visit reignited. "I didn't leave Liberia to see this kind of shit," he said.

While I was dealing with Chester's psychological baggage, I found that our disposal of the former owner's furniture had attracted Salami, certainly not my intention. I thought I had seen the last of the leaking fridge when Raul carried it outside—single-handedly, of course. Salami plugged the appliance into the lamppost to see if it worked. It did.

"You got anything you want fixed? A washing machine? CD player?" he called to me.

"No."

"You sure? I can fix anything." Salami switched the fridge on and off. "I used to be a radio operator in the army. I was stationed on the aviation post in Germany. That's how I learned about electronics. It's not hard. If you break down or dissect something like a TV, you can diagnose the problem."

"That's impressive."

"I'm no fool. I guarded the pope."

This provoked guffaws from the dealers. Two of the noisier ones waved Raul over to help them carry the fridge to the front of their steps. I was pleased to see the apparatus gone, but then I realized that it was going to cause bigger problems. The muchachos laid the fridge on its side like a park bench, and someone went to fetch cushions to convert it into a divan. I had just made their life more comfortable.

After we tore out the basement's wood paneling and flimsy room partitions, we moved on to smashing the Sheetrock to expose the brickwork and pipes behind. The more we threw out, the more superstitious Raul became. Abdu's talk about the doctor's ghost was contagious, and Raul was convinced that we were displeasing her by shaking up her quarters. He was particularly spooked about a creepy corner under the stairs, which was jammed with boxes of X-rays of people long dead. Next to the pile rose a pyramid of balled-up chewing gum, hardened to the consistency of stone. I conjured up an image of the doctor's secretary sitting in the airless spot, chomping with boredom.

While the secretary was tossing masticated Wrigley's over her shoulder, the doctor apparently prepared for the apocalypse. In another section of the basement we found twenty five-gallon buckets filled with food: barley, lentils, millet, corn, three kinds of beans, oats, rice. The stuff, sadly, was inedible. Water had leaked in and dark mold had spread throughout.

Raul summoned his formidable strength to carry the buckets out for rubbish pickup. Clarence ambled over to examine the pile.

"I heard she was slowly losing it over the years," he commented.

Clarence looked toward the house. "Come. I want to show you something." He led me to the second-floor study and knelt at a twelve-inch hole where a plank of the floor had been removed. Sticking in his arm, Clarence rummaged around, about elbow-deep.

"This was her safe," he said, squinting in concentration while he moved his hand about. "The family found seventy thousand dollars in here. She didn't trust the banks."

He pulled his arm out with a disappointed look.

"Maybe there's a stash somewhere else," I mused.

That was the cue Clarence was waiting for. A hint of a smile glimmered; Clarence wasn't capable of a full smile. He stood up quickly. "Let's go!" He charged downstairs.

Clarence had lots of ideas about potential hiding spots, which made me wonder what else he knew about the house. He showed me holes in the floor in the living room where Salami and others had torn out a radiator. Clarence introduced me to the passageway that had housed the dumbwaiter. The tunnel began in the basement and went up vertically to the third floor, with the worn pulleys still hanging in the crawl space in the kitchen and second-floor study. We looked in every small crevice at the foot of radiators. Alas, no cash. Actually, that came as a source of relief. If we *had* found anything, Clarence might expect to keep some of the bounty—or worse, he could tell others on the street about the discovery. If Salami found out that he had missed the treasure, he might invade with renewed vigor.

Raul not only provided easy company to pass the drifting days but also served as a useful ambassador on the street. I needed protection—or what Russian mobsters call a *krysha*, or "roof." Instinct said to trust Raul. He seemed sincere about breaking with his criminal past and earning an honest living. He was a dutiful father. He carried a Bible and spurned alcohol. This surely indicated a clean outlook toward life.

Whatever his spirituality, Raul dutifully conveyed to the muchachos that I desired coexistence and was not, contrary to common perception, working for the police.

"They think I'm a cop?" I asked incredulously. I thought I had established some kind of street cred with these guys, even if we never spoke. Surely they couldn't possibly think that someone like me would work for the NYPD. This hurt my vanity. "Do I look like a cop?"

Raul admitted that I didn't look like a cop. He explained the skewed logic. "The mentality of these people is that if you're white, you're police. If you're an American black, you're a user. If you're selling, you're selling to American blacks. American blacks are not to be trusted."

We sat on the stoop, eating take-out *cubanos* and watching an undercover cop push a detainee against a wall. Another cop whipped a kilo of cocaine from under the perp's jacket. He held it up as though it were a trophy trout.

"You're bringing down the neighborhood," the cop snarled at the youth.

"*No es mío, no es mío*, it's not mine," the suspect whined, as he was led to an unmarked car.

An African-American guy with dreadlocks walked by. One of the muchachos called out, "Yo, money, I got fikale."

Raul translated. " 'Fish scale.' Dominicans have trouble pronouncing the 'sh.' The cut glistens like a silver fish because of what they add to the coke."

What balls! The guy was trying to make a connection directly across the street from the undercovers' bust. "He must be making good money to take that risk," I said.

Raul nodded. "These guys can get paid a hundred dollars for walking one block with two kilos on them."

I thought about how hard Raul worked for me, at a much lower rate. "Surely you're tempted?"

"No way." Raul's eyes flared anxiously. "Anyway, they don't trust me. I'm not from San Francisco de Macorís. Everyone in the gang is from there."

. . .

This revelation—that each block was run by guys from the same town in the Dominican Republic—prompted my call to Ric Curtis, an anthropologist at Manhattan's John Jay College of Criminal Justice. While his fellow academics specialized in policing tactics and history, Professor Curtis devoted his studies to New York's drug gangs.

The professor explained that boyhood ties meant that members of a given drug crew were less likely to betray one another than if they had been randomly thrown together in the name of business. "Anyone who breaks rank knows there could be reprisals against the family back home," he said.

The guys on my street weren't the only ones from San Francisco de Macorís, according to Professor Curtis. So were some of the most infamous Dominican kingpins, as well as ordinary residents and shopkeepers on Broadway who had nothing to do with drug traffic. One only needed to look at the travel agents on the avenue advertising two-hundred-dollar passages home to see that there was a lot of going back and forth. Dominicans jokingly call the soulless market town of 122,000, set on a baking plateau in the Cibao breadbasket, the "American consulate" for all the immigrants who have left for the United States. San Francisco is notorious for laundering drug money, too, much of it poured into the monstrous arriviste mansions and condos that ring the outskirts of town.

San Franciscans have a reputation for entrepreneurship and rebellion, handy traits in the drug industry. Over two centuries, San Franciscans had risen up against Spanish rule, American invading troops, and dictator Leónidas Trujillo as well as his crafty successor, Joaquín Balaguer.

The fertile land grows cereals. The main official industry is a dairy-product company. But the true source of wealth is described on the town's official website: "The injection of dollars sent in large quantity by absentees."

Working on the assumption that anything this corporate probably had a top-down structure, my best protection against Salami and the muchachos would be to woo the director of the local drug crew. Indeed, my cousin Greg had suggested that the main honcho would be my best ally in keeping the boys off my property. The underlings would treat me with greater respect if given the right sign from above. That's what you did in Angola if a militiaman stuck his rifle into your car window and wouldn't let you pass. You pulled rank and demanded to speak to his boss.

The right man here was easy to identify. He was older than the others, maybe in his late thirties, and dressed more formally, in a soft brown leather jacket instead of the standard parka on the cooler days. Around his neck hung a thick gold chain with a medallion of the Virgin of Altagracia, the patron saint of the Dominican Republic.

Everyone else was addressed by a nickname, or *apodo*, generally taken from a distinguishing characteristic such as "Puma," "Goatee," or "Forehead." This guy was simply called Miguel.

He could have been dubbed "Panther," what with his sleek body and feline cheekbones. Like a feral cat, Miguel quietly observed his hunting ground, coiled up tensely, and then leaped when the quarry—Ford Explorers filled with drug customers—drove up to the curb. Miguel commanded authority. All he needed to do was call softly in his velvety voice and the muchachos scurried to the steps of Salami's house. *El comandante* then sent them into formation on the street, and strutted up and down giving orders.

My first overtures to this narcotics lieutenant consisted of bland comments on the weather and baseball. The game normally bored me, but I was making an effort to follow the sport that was a national obsession of my Dominican neighbors.

"The Yankees are doing very well this year," I commented in Spanish, wanting to show off the fluency of which I was so proud.

Judging from his baffled expression, Miguel didn't understand me. "*¿Perdón?*"

Damn, and I had thought that my accent was so good. I repeated the phrase in English.

The following day I spotted an opening for negotiations as I went out to buy some coffee at El Floridita. Miguel held the gate open, probably less out of gallantry than as an apology for leaning on it, something I had requested that he refrain from doing on numerous occasions.

Just to show that he was a nice guy, Miguel leaned down with a clean paper napkin and plucked up a hairy mango pit, with a fastidious snivel of disgust. Then he asked if I was Italian.

"¿Perdón?"

"You speak good Spanish but with an accent. I can't place it."

"It must be Portuguese."

"What?"

"Portuguese."

"Portuguese?"

"I used to live in Africa."

"Africa? What were you doing there?" Miguel regarded me suspiciously.

"Oh, you know, things." I changed the subject back to the old conversational chestnut, baseball. "What do you think of A-Rod?"

Miguel had a lot to say.

Having broken the proverbial ice, I commenced peace talks. I thought back to the sophisticated negotiations that had ended the Cold War and apartheid. Playing tough always helped to win the advantage. Did I have a trump card? My only bargaining chip was that I could call the cops, which admittedly wouldn't achieve much. Chances were, the muchachos would have handed over their glassine bags and evaporated before any cop drove up, thanks to *Radio Bemba*—Dominican slang for word of mouth. Nonetheless, Miguel struck me as a fussy man who probably didn't want to be inconvenienced. To win his sympathy, I portrayed myself as a tolerant liberal who believed in freedom of expression, even when it came to drug use. But I expected respect and didn't like the idea of paying hundreds of dollars in sanitation fines for his employees' mess.

"I also don't like crap on my stairs," I said huffily. Miguel followed my pointing finger to the steps leading to the basement entrance. There lay a dark turd that had been deposited the previous day. (Clarence wouldn't sweep it up, so it sat there, growing hard.)

Miguel wrinkled his nose. "It must have been Salami. My boys wouldn't do that."

"How do you know? You're not here all day."

Miguel tilted his head as he considered this, and conceded the point affably. "Yes, they can be pigs. Some of them are not well educated—you know, in the countryside people do things differently. Country people throw things on the ground. But, *Mami*, they're not bad people, simply poorly educated." Miguel sighed companionably. "This generation is so different from ours. Men my age"—he paused for emphasis—"*our* age, are gentlemen."

I smiled at the thought that Miguel had taken me into his confidence to talk about personnel problems. This was progress.

He offered an arrangement: I would come to him with problems and he would "train" the boys not to defile my steps. We hauled a metal trash container from the basement to the front of the derelict house. Miguel firmly instructed the muchachos to throw their rubbish there instead of on my property. They sulked but didn't protest.

I paced the boundaries, under Miguel's watchful eye. I explained to his associates that they were to keep at least two feet from either side of my gate. Miguel stood beside me for ostensible support, although his expression indicated that he wasn't completely on board. "*Mami*, any problems and you come to me. Miguel will sort it out," he said, as his sullen protégés looked on. "Don't go to anyone else."

We shook hands formally.

What a coup! I had won over *el jefe*!

My alliance with Miguel went only so far, I soon learned. If he was not around, which was annoyingly often, the muchachos leaned on my gate or sat on the steps.

I bestowed my own *apodos* upon the two nastier ones. "Penknife" was a muscular guy with short pinwheels of curls and a tendency to pull out a switchblade when irritated. The others would hold him back as he waved his arms and shouted expletives at whoever was getting on his nerves. I wondered why Miguel hired such a volatile liability. Maybe they had attended the same elementary school. Then there was the light-skinned one I dubbed "Nose" because of his prominent white schnoz, which turned red from being in the sun all day. He was mean—to me, to Mrs. Campbell, to the kids playing baseball on the street. With a cruel laugh, Nose scooped up errant balls and threw them into the middle of Broadway, his goal being to send the kids running into traffic.

A few days later, after my clever nicknaming blitz, I discovered that I had received one, too. As I walked past, Penknife said derisively, *"Cuidado. Viene la carpintera."* (Watch out. Here comes the lady carpenter.) I flushed at the compliment.

But wait a minute. Was it really a compliment? *Cuidado* meant they didn't trust me. Hmm. On second thought, *la carpintera* was more likely a sarcastic moniker.

While I had had a breakthrough of sorts with Miguel, Clarence remained a cipher. Even after our bonding treasure hunt, his idea of conversation was still a mumbled, "It is what it is." Dialogue was not helped by Clarence's verbal evasion. Everything was top secret as far as the super was concerned: his age, what time the garbage truck came, the price of Pine-Sol. If I pressed him, he'd say, "Don't you give me that smile. I know what you're getting at." (He said it so many times that I was beginning to wonder, *What exactly am I getting at?*)

Oddly, the one area Clarence was forthcoming about was something intimate: where he got shot. One day, after giving me another lecture on diet (I should eat avocados for that weak hair or else it would fall out), he told me he wanted to show me something.

He took my hand in his, softened by Vitamin E. At the entrance of his building he pointed to a chip in the limestone masonry. It took some time for him to locate the exact spot; the surface was so pitted that he had to trace his hand over it to find the match for his bullet.

"Wait a minute, I think it's here," he said, groping the wall. He patted another place, face contorted in concentration. Then he relaxed. "I found it. *That's* where the bullet went." He stood back and showed me a small hole.

"I thought it went through you, your . . ." I waved in the general direction of his body. I didn't want to say the word *butt*.

"Hip," Clarence said. "One bullet hit the wall. The other got my hip."

"What did they have against you?"

"Nothin'. There was a shoot-out on Broadway. It was an accident. It was around lunchtime." He tapped his head. "Maybe it was 1989."

Clarence made a harsh hacking noise that was meant to be a laugh. "And where were the police when I was shot? Nowhere. Ha. That's what the police are for—protection, right? Ha. Some protection."

The police would not have appreciated Clarence's cynicism. By now I had gotten to know a few of the officers on the beat, and they seemed well intentioned, albeit beleaguered. All I had to do was sit on the stoop and watch a raid, and a cop would stroll over, lean on the gate, and spill his guts. The complaints were always the same: They had too little backup, and the justice system served as a revolving door that would send the perps back onto the street.

"You see that movie *Groundhog Day*?" griped one of the officers, known as Pat. He had just loaded up the police van with handcuffed young men and was waiting for someone to book them in. "It's like that weather guy, you know, the actor, Bill Murray. We relive the same scene every day. The punks get picked up, get a small fine, and are back on the streets in no time. The ones who do get locked up are replaced within days. It's like Darwinism. The lazy, stupid ones get caught. The smarter ones stay on.

"The guys are constantly refining their tactics. They're clever. When undercovers bust a stash apartment, they simply set up another one. Every thirty days they get rid of their cell phones so we can't trace the calls. They rent rooms with an old couple as a cover. The money is so good that even if they get locked away for seven years, they have their retirement money and a house built for Mama back on the island."

Pat was on a roll. I got the impression that he didn't often have an audience. "Many people in the community are complicit, or too scared to report the dealers to the police. Some landlords help them. There are some places where the scaffolding has been up for five and a half years. You know what—I could have built the Pyramids in five and a half years. That scaffolding isn't there for construction. If it's raining and storming, it's a great place to sell drugs."

A teenage girl passed by. Pat, an outgoing Irishman with an avuncular manner, seemed to greet every kid on the beat, which he had worked for more than a decade. He knew which of the girls had just taken Communion and the names of their cousins. He pointed at his wristwatch.

"Shouldn't you be in school, young lady?"

The girl shook her head sassily. Her hair was so slicked down that it didn't move. "I already been."

"What? It's only noon." Pat turned to me and continued his rant. "The government is spending millions of dollars to destroy cocaine fields in Colombia and they can't dispatch enough officers to police a street corner in Harlem. You see any white people? Mayor Giuliani doesn't give a fuck about blacks and Latinos. He only cares about tourists in Times Square and rich people. The problem isn't just man-power. We get no cooperation from the INS and IRS. The feds won't get involved. We could clean up this area in no time if we could search people for immigration documents. Half the guys we pick up are repeat offenders who overstayed their visas. But immigration, whoa, that's a political hot potato. No mayor's gonna touch that."

PART TWO

Chapter 10

HOMELAND INSECURITY

I fretted over what Pat said on the way to the subway station. His bleak assessment of botched law enforcement added to my general dread about the house endeavor. Why, oh why, hadn't I done research before buying? I was a reporter, after all. How could I forget to make inquiries about this most crucial matter? My colleagues would mock me if they heard. Part of the point of moving to New York was to live in a place where the government kept the peace. I had witnessed enough breakdown of order elsewhere and wanted some calm. However, the picture emerging of West Harlem was of criminals running the streets. The police were under siege and the federal government wasn't doing much to help them. As the cop said, what was the point of pouring resources into stopping *coca* production in Colombia when a stream of snorters converged on West Harlem every day? Fumigate one crop and another will be grown elsewhere. One didn't have to be an economist to know that supply met demand.

Upset as I was, my formidable reserves of denial kicked in. It was a bit late to dwell on failed narcotics policy. I couldn't change it, at least for now. Better to focus on matters within my control. The house! I could make it nicer! Then we could resell and move elsewhere—provided anyone would want to buy it. So onward with the house!

Through my cousin Greg, I cobbled together a motley construction team that had saved his former crack house from caving in many years before. Raul was fine for demolition, but he didn't know how to rehaul plumbing or electricity. A procession of men in coveralls streamed through our building to give quotes, wincing at the corroded pipes and burned wires. Hopefully they could restore the house to minimal functionality with our remaining $50,000.

After the experience with Abdu, I wondered why these subcontractors were available right away. My cousin assured me that a series of coincidences had freed up all the men this week. He could testify that they were competent, more or less.

The first to sign up were painters. These were an ornery Russian named Boris and his partner, Clayon, a former reggae singer who hailed from one of the few black Jewish families in Jamaica. They bickered about everything: the weather, the music channel, politics, soccer, painting technique. A typical conversation went like this:

"You did it."

"No, you did it."

"You don't do it this way."

"Yes you do."

"That's my brush."

"No, it's mine."

Next on the list was an electrician. My cousin recommended Alex, a hyper Honduran whose business card not so reassuringly promised "adequate" lighting. Alex punctuated every spoken guarantee with "Trust me!" After Abdu, this had the reverse effect.

Greg also recommended Mr. Kamal, a Bengali mason. The plumbers were found on the yellowed label on the boiler. The next challenge was locating a carpenter to bolster the beams and other sundry matters. Greg had a friend, Jorge, who had a friend, a Dominican yoga master named Manuel. Manuel was not only spiritually sound, he had salvaged Jorge's splintered house in Brooklyn. "This guy could build you a home from scratch," Jorge reassured me.

I had a mental image of a hulk who could carry beams on his shoulders, much like the mighty Raul. Instead, a tiny man weighing no more than a hundred pounds arrived at the house with a yoga mat and the serene expression of the newly meditated. I couldn't imagine this diminutive fellow building houses from scratch. I couldn't picture him lifting anything heavier than a bottle of water. I didn't know if he could plane a door, let alone install a concrete-filled support.

But Manuel's rates were astoundingly cheap. He was free to start the next day. Most important, he was shorter than I was. I could boss him around.

"You're hired," I said, looking down from my great height of five feet three inches.

The city grew balmy as the men set to work. The muchachos shed their puffy jackets for the summer uniform: white T-shirts and running shoes. The multicolors of Salami's discarded crack vials matched the spring leaves and daylilies that poked defiantly from the soil under the honey locust tree.

Now that I had a full-time crew, I spent even more time in the house. The irony did not escape me that the all-engrossing reconstruction project was keeping me from normal social life. This removal from reality was not unlike being a foreign correspondent, where one's existence often feels like a big fantasy. As I withdrew into the building cocoon, I wondered about the previous logic that having a house in New York would bring me closer to friends and family. Because I worked so late, I never went out. Greg and his wife visited the house at an early stage ("Good choice," they said approvingly) and my sister's fiancé, Rafael, occasionally dropped by when he had meetings in nearby Washington Heights. But Mom showed little interest in coming by while the house was in dusty construction, and I barely saw my sister, who worked long hours in Queens and lived in deep Brooklyn. We spoke often, though—my nocturnal panicked calls were increasing in frequency.

I finally got to see her in person on the day of her wedding, in a charming wooded park in Queens. Susan and Rafael had been together long enough to have a five-year-old child, and the refrain at the celebration was *"¡Por fin!"* or "Finally!" Mom was ecstatic that her elder daughter was finally legally hitched, and even joined in dancing when the salsa music struck up.

Many of Rafael's activist friends were in attendance, and I circulated widely, seeking contacts in the neighborhood. Tired of getting nowhere— a lot of people were familiar with Washington Heights but not West Harlem—I consoled myself with a large helping of cake. Rafael sat down next to me.

"How's the house?"

I proudly told him about the progress I had made with Clarence and Miguel. I thought he'd be impressed with my negotiating skills.

Rafael was shocked. "Judith, you have to be careful. You can't trust anyone."

"Aw." I shrugged.

Rafael continued, his normally soft brown eyes stern. "These drug dealers can be dangerous. Be careful whom you speak to."

Some well-wishers approached. As Rafael rose to receive their embraces, he gave me one last warning. "Be careful. This isn't like being abroad. No embassy is going to help you get out."

In early June, the long-awaited call came from Moscow: John had obtained his visa. He and the dog would come "home" the following week.

Since I didn't have much progress to show on said home, I decided to at least look attractive myself. Special attention was needed for my fingernails, which had cracked from scraping the walls.

There was a choice of sixteen nail parlors on an eight-block stretch on Broadway. In most of the salons, men sat around talking animatedly into cell phones and were decidedly not getting their cuticles trimmed. Despite the rows of varnish in the window at Rosa Nails Unisex, the sulky proprietor shook her head no when I asked for a manicure. At the next nail place, the grumpy woman filing her own index finger said no one was on duty. In other joints, the story was the same: We don't do nails, there's no one here—always accompanied by wary looks.

I settled on Princess Nails, which also styled hair, amused by the sign in the window that said in misspelled Spanish, PLEASE DO NOT OCCUPY SEATS IF YOU ARE NOT DOING ANYTHING OR GETTING A HAIRCUT. The barber's chairs were empty, and a dozen men sat on the aquamarine vinyl seats by the window doing nothing except looking at the police car parked outside.

However, Princess did do nails, after a fashion. I sat down on a chair and the manicurist used the wrong side of the file to buff, and sliced a hangnail so hard that it bled.

As she polished the final thumb, a teenager came through the door and plucked from his baggy jeans a wad of money four inches high. With a hard glance toward me, the barber shoved him toward the door.

"Come back later," he said. "Go play basketball or something."

Back at the house, Raul smiled knowingly at my adventure. He explained that while beauty salons were popular socializing spots here as well as in the Dominican Republic, the true nature of some establishments—particularly the ones open twenty-four hours a day— was to launder drug money. Serving the same purpose were several of the thirty-eight money-wiring envío shops that doubled as purveyors of beepers. The money-laundering industry also explained the preponderance of virtually empty upscale sneaker boutiques.

Through a colleague who covered crime, I met an undercover agent, Gino, who used to investigate these establishments. He explained that the biggest challenge for drug syndicates was not, as one might think, sneaking the drugs into the country. Rather, it was moving the huge profits out. The traffickers were making millions of dollars a week, and they set up business fronts to obscure narcotics profits. These Laundromats, beauty salons, and clothing stores sometimes also doubled as storage spots for drug deliveries.

"There is no reason for someone to get a haircut at three-thirty in the morning," Gino pointed out. "I know what a second-floor barbershop is for. It's to deal drugs. No one is going to buy a four-hundred-and-fifteen-dollar pair of shoes on 139th Street."

To smuggle the money, the drug organizations hired "Smurfs"—named after the tiny blue Belgian cartoon creatures. Smurfs divided cash money transfers into amounts less than $10,000 to avoid American reporting requirements, and then sent them to Latin America through the small remittance parlors on Broadway.

A friend or relative of a dealer would walk into a couple of remittance shops and send, say, parcels of $1,000 each to thirty names. Sometimes the dealers wired the cash to associates or family. The dealers could get false receipts once a personal relationship was struck up with the cashier sitting behind the bulletproof glass.

According to the undercover, it was easy to set up a remittance business. All you needed was a storefront, a deposit ticket to the account of a company such as Western Union, and proof that you paid taxes and didn't have a criminal record. The fifty-odd licensed companies in New York City issued deposit tickets to up to five thousand sub-agents.

The remitters were supposed to exercise due diligence to ensure that fraud was not committed. But in reality all the authorities usually got was a *"No sé"* when they pointed out misdeeds.

"No one is going to rat on customers that keep their business alive," Gino noted.

He suggested that I consider the gross domestic product of the Dominican Republic to get a sense of the scope. The GDP was about $19 billion, of which $1 billion came from remittances sent yearly from the United States. Half of that amount came from the small wiring shops.

"Most of that has to be drug money," Gino said. "Do the math. The average Dominican working-class household in New York makes about twenty-five thousand dollars a year and sends home installments of three hundred dollars a month. That doesn't add up to the fortune wired."

My nails were done. A work crew was set up. John and the dog's flight was booked. All I needed was a car to pick up the "family" at the airport.

I spent half a day telephoning taxi companies, which successively turned me down once I explained that our party would include a large animal passenger. ("You gotta be crazy, lady. What if it pees in the car?") Still in the Moscow frame of mind, where anything is possible for a price, I found a dispatcher with a Slavic name. Sure enough, a vehicle could be arranged for a price, a very large one. We bargained a bit, in good post-Soviet fashion, and on the required day, an hour late, an Azerbaijani driver in a van with a prominent American flag hanging over the dashboard arrived to pick me up.

The ride to Kennedy Airport was consumed by the driver's monologue about the evils of American materialism. Once at the arrival hall, we were in for a surprise. Contrary to expectations, it proved easier to get the dog through immigration than my weary husband, whose new green card offered no special privileges.

I had steeled myself for a repeat of our arrival in Moscow from Johannesburg in 1997. Khaya had howled in a dark crate while Russian customs men in leather jackets thrust poles at him through the slats. John and Yasha, my new office manager, ran from desk to desk with offerings of bonbons to obtain the requisite thirteen stamps to liberate the miserable animal. Meanwhile, I sat on a stool in the hangar, trying to think of how to stop the men from tormenting the dog. Suddenly, I had an inspiration.

"Laika," I bellowed, pointing to the cage. "Eto laika."

The thugs put down their sticks and regarded the crate with respect.

For those unfamiliar with Soviet cosmonaut history, Laika was the first dog in space. Even today, he is held in celebrity regard in Russia. Laika means "Siberian husky," a breed that vaguely resembled Khaya's. To the cries of "Eto nash!" ("He's ours!"), the men at customs pried open the cage and offered the befuddled creature mineral water and smoked salmon.

That was then. This time Khaya waltzed into the arrival hall before the human passengers, escorted by none other than the pilot and a blond stewardess who resembled the supermodel Elle Macpherson. "Nice doggie," the flight attendant cooed, as Khaya rubbed against her long legs. The dog licked my hand casually as though we routinely met in airports after long flights.

While I was joyfully reunited with our pet, a surly immigration official held John captive. The man insisted that my husband was Russian, despite his Dutch passport. The official eyed John's American visa skeptically as though it were fake. The immigration thug also failed to notice that my husband spoke better English than most New Yorkers, and interrogated him with careful enunciation:

"You . . . speak . . . English?"

"Yes."

"Do . . . you . . . understand . . . me?"

"Yes."

"Do . . . you . . . understand . . . me?"

"Yes," said John, unsure now that he did.

This went on for some time, until John was finally able to convince his warden that he was neither a criminal nor a Russian. John then went into a holding area, where a planeload of people from Guyana looked abject as the immigration official barked at them to sit down.

After a while, the official abruptly ordered John to leave, and my husband emerged in the arrival hall muttering foully about racism and moral bankruptcy. As I got up on my toes to kiss him, John only offered a cheek so he could continue his diatribe against American hypocrisy. "This country loves dogs more than people. Hypocrites. This is a country of immigrants but they're harsh to new arrivals. They're denying their own heritage. Hypocrisy, that's what it is."

I tried to interrupt, pointing to the Azerbaijani taxi driver, who had been nodding his head energetically in agreement with my husband. "John, this man is our taxi driver."

"And they have the balls to say that this is the land of the free . . ."

The Azerbaijani taxi driver interjected as he pumped the air with an angry fist: "Mister, you are right. All Americans care about is money. This is an economy, not a society." He grumbled something in Azerbaijani, no doubt a curse on Western capitalism.

We walked toward the taxi, both men glowering about their adopted country. Khaya lifted his leg and anointed the back wheel with his first American piss. The driver let out a yelp.

"Hey! Filthy animal! That's going to cost you an extra hundred bucks! I'm doubling the price!"

. . .

The next day, after a fitful sleep in Mom's basement and far too much coffee, I shepherded John uptown to inspect his new home. "Nervous" did not adequately describe my mood. What if he didn't like it? Would he hate me? I pictured him silently withdrawing from me in that big house as our marriage withered. We rode the train in silence, and the rain outside added to my gloom.

As we left the subway and rounded the corner, I was relieved to see no sign of Salami. I wasn't ready to introduce him to John. Not today.

Penknife stood under the scaffolding, muttering curses. His black folding umbrella had been blown inside-out by the wind, and he was smashing it against the metal support rods of the scaffolding to bend it back into shape.

"That's one of the locals," I explained helpfully.

John studied him carefully. "Is that the Baloney guy?"

"Salami. No, this is one of the more benign ones." Penknife scowled darkly and smacked the umbrella against the scaffolding again. I waved at him cheerily. "¡Buenos días!"

Penknife glared in our direction. "¡Qué coño!" ("What the hell!")

The apprehension returned. Oh, no. We owned the building. We were stuck with it. There was no wiggling out now. My chest tightened and I could barely breathe.

Miguel was leaning on the gate and waved me aside with a sour expression. "Who's the guy? Your brother?"

"Husband."

Miguel swept John with his eyes. His face lengthened into a sulk. "You didn't tell me you were married." I wasn't in the right frame of mind to discuss my private life with the local drug lieutenant, and turned my attention to opening the door of the house. I fumbled with the keys. John took them from me, and the front door swung open.

I tried to see the faded gray walls through John's eyes as we entered the building and moved silently from room to room. His face revealed nothing. Uh-oh. This was ominous. Why was he so quiet? He must be upset. What was bothering him? Did he notice the stairs separating from the wall? John went up alone. I perched tensely on the dead woman's bed in the living room, thumbing through Abdu's abandoned Koran.

The book advised me to fear my Lord. "The catastrophe of the

House of Doom shall be terrible indeed. When that day comes, every suckling mother shall forsake her infant, every pregnant female shall cast her burden, and you shall see mankind reeling like drunkards although not drunk."

John's footsteps echoed upstairs. He jumped a couple of times. Was he testing the strength of the floors? What if they broke? The jumping stopped. What had he seen? *He hates it,* I thought.

The footsteps descended slowly. John softly walked behind me and put his arms on my shoulders. He squeezed them and kissed my neck. "The table will fit. Now what did you say about the shooting on the corner?"

A celebration was in order, and I suggested that we toast our new life in our local café, El Floridita. The rain was by now coming down in torrents, and we sprinted across Broadway to the warm confines of the atrium. As men at the nearby tables made drug deals, we knocked back Presidente beers and fantasized about decorating the house. Much to my relief, John was amused by the activities around us, and he rekindled his knowledge of Spanish by eavesdropping on the conversations about kilos. After a pleasant meal, we paid the bill and splashed back to the house through the puddles.

The muchachos were at their usual work station and eyed my husband guardedly. The presence of a fit white man with good posture apparently made them think *cop,* and they shouted "Five-O" as we passed.

John led the way as he once more toured our new estate. He reached the top floor and halted abruptly at the landing. A wet trail of what looked like blood seeped down the red-carpeted corridor.

My first instinct was to run. Had Salami gotten in again? Whom had he killed? I thought I heard a muffled giggle from the kitchen. *So this is how it ends,* I thought. I had survived land mines and mortars for this? A rangy crack addict was about to kill me in my own home.

John broke my macabre reverie. "Don't just stand there!" he snapped. "Rain's pouring in. Get a bucket or something!"

Oh, so a *flood* had caused the wet on the carpet. Not blood. Whew! Scurrying to the kitchen, I found a dented aluminum pot. John put it under the broken skylight. Then we went downstairs to the tar-streaked living room and sat quietly on the dead woman's mattress, listening to the rain drip into the kitchen. After about ten minutes of this uplifting scene, John got up and put on his jacket. "Let's go back to Mom's," he said.

Chapter 11

DISUNITED NATIONS

Like many couples who marry fairly late in life, John and I were still adjusting to each other's eccentricities. In our five years together, we had gotten along just fine in terms of values and lifestyle—we shared a fondness for nightclubs and tidy kitchens, and we both became journalists out of a sense of social mission. We were the same age, had the same taste in friends, and my dog liked him. John was the only man I knew who wasn't fazed by my impulsivity and long absences. In fact, he seemed to appreciate the challenges that these taxing traits presented. However, we clashed over one major thing: danger. Granted, I had taken some idiotic risks in Africa, such as walking through an ammunition dump after it was blown up, and traveling to Chechnya while pregnant wasn't so smart. But John upped the ante further: He argued with armed men.

This pigheadedness so alarmed me that I threatened to call off our engagement one time in Sierra Leone, when John refused to hand over his baggage for inspection by a soldier who stuck an AK-47 into our car window on the way from the airport. After twenty long minutes, John was vindicated when the man finally withdrew the barrel and waved us on without shooting us.

Still, in the comparatively calmer waters of West Harlem I worried about John's first encounter with the volatile Salami. My husband had agreed to leave the negotiations with the muchachos to me. It made sense; after all, I spoke fluent Spanish and as a woman was deemed less threatening. I wasn't sure, though, that John would refrain from provoking our resident crack addict.

Adding to my distress were the pyrotechnics. It was still mid-June, but already the muchachos were gearing up for July Fourth. They set off illegal fireworks in the middle of the block, in the path of speeding cars. Clearly new to explosives, many of the guys didn't realize that they should hold them at arm's length to avoid catching sparks in their hair. "Straight up, *mano*, straight up!" someone would shout at the smell of burned hair. I walked quickly through the battle zone. The more experienced guys planted cherry bombs inside trash cans and laughed uproariously when the fireworks exploded as I passed.

A common reaction after exposure to sustained gunfire is to shudder uncontrollably whenever you hear a boom. In West Harlem, my combat mind-set returned in full force with the sounds of fireworks. I jumped at the whoosh of M-80s.

In Africa, many of us had suffered from what used to be quaintly called "shell shock." We'd nod indulgently if a colleague dived to the floor when a car backfired. "He's seen a lot of bang-bang," you'd say sympathetically over your strong alcoholic drink.

This tic, however, was embarrassing in New York, where most people have not encountered major artillery. And the last thing I wanted was to lose my composure in front of Salami. Until now, or so I thought, I had masked my fear. I had to maintain this macho charade and not flinch at the sizzle of a sparkler.

The moment of truth came two days after John returned from Russia. As we approached our future home, planning to introduce John to the workmen, Salami popped out of his lair like a jack-in-the-box. His massive arm was draped over Charm. John stopped and stared, his hand on the gate and his mouth gaping open a quarter of an inch.

"Salami?" John asked.

"The one and only," I said.

"Holy cow! Those are some muscles for a junkie." He adopted a confrontational posture and I withered.

Boom! A firecracker went off in a trash can. I winced and squeezed John's hand hard, managing to remain upright. Salami didn't seem to notice my alarm, so intent was he on making John's acquaintance.

"You her man?" Salami snarled, puffing his chest out. His left hand slithered disturbingly into the pocket of his track suit. I noticed that he had lost another fang. I hoped he wouldn't bite us, and even more I hoped John wouldn't inflame him.

John regarded Salami with bemusement. This wound up Salami several notches. He sneered. "Don't be getting ideas about that house."

John said nothing.

"You got ripped off. No one pays that on a street like this."

John grinned broadly, showing *his* teeth.

"Fuck you, man," Salami said, frustrated that John wasn't taking the bait. Salami put his arm back around Charm's shoulders and steered her to their hovel. "We're outta here. These folks got a problem with black people."

I expelled a huge breath as the couple retreated. So far, so good! We heard a call—"Well, if it isn't . . ."—and saw Mrs. LaDuke strolling toward us. She smoothed her spotless size-six white trousers and lowered her green sunglasses to get a better look at John. Much to my irritation, most women find my husband irresistible. John enchants all manner of females with his urbane smile and toned physique, on which they like to drape themselves. No matter where we go, it's always the same story: Women find pretexts to run their hands through his luxurious silver hair, while purring seductive endearments. One Barbie-doll type in Moscow had the audacity to stick her tongue in his mouth, right in front of me! John's vaguely British accent has a particularly intoxicating effect on American women of a certain age (myself included) who were weaned on the Beatles.

Mrs. LaDuke was no different, despite her eighty-two years.

"You got a good one, dear," she enthused. "Does he have a brother?"

"Yes, but he's not as good-looking as I am." John offered his most captivating smile.

"They're both married," I butted in, much too quickly. What was this? Had my perspective become so warped during the weeks of cloistered construction that I now felt threatened by an octogenarian?

"We can all share." John's sea-green eyes fixed on Mrs. LaDuke.

She hooted with laughter. "Oh, you're too much! You're so bad! You'll never make it up there to heaven!"

They beamed at each other.

The spell was broken as Clarence shuffled over from across the street, displaying his customary upbeat attitude. "Morning, all. It's gonna be a terrible day. Evil breeze coming in from the west." Clarence nodded politely to Mrs. LaDuke. Then he scowled at John.

"You the husband? What took you so long? I told her, that man has dumped you. Give him up for a goner."

"She knew I'd return," John said. "For the house."

Clarence grimaced disdainfully. "That house ain't worth shit. It's her killer smile. I bet she's got you wrapped around her finger."

I sparkled what I thought was a dazzling smile. No one seemed to notice.

We went into the house and waited for the workmen to arrive. When all had assembled—by then it was noon; Alex, the electrician, had run late owing to an "emergency" in Queens—they lined up in the living room with expectant expressions that said, "Thank God—finally a *man* for a boss." Within minutes, John was fluently talking in several languages about Allen wrenches and 220-grit sandpaper, while I stood by dumbly. John knew absolutely nothing about American building codes and needed to consult conversion tables just to buy paint, but that went unnoticed.

"*Khoroshy chelovek* (a good man)," Boris said. The others nodded, even though they didn't understand Russian. Clearly Boris was saying something positive about John, who was able-bodied as well as male.

"He is very, *very* good," added Mr. Kamal, the mason. They all agreed with energetic head nods and grunts. I stood there feeling superfluous. Being a sensitive fellow who noticed that I was left out of the male-bonding experience, Mr. Kamal turned to me kindly. "You are okay, Mrs. Judith. But you don't know anything. Mr. John, he is smart."

I had to admit John had managerial vision. Right then and there he drew up a master plan, something that had not occurred to me. Our new steward sat with clipboard and mapped out precisely what we needed to do floor by floor, complete with diagrams.

A good boss knows to make everyone feel important, even weak members of the team. The "important" responsibility assigned to me, John told his wards, was to handle the bills, order supplies, and sit on the stoop. Lest the men think that this was a piddling task, John stressed the importance of guard duty. We needed to prevent Salami from barging in, something he had tried to do on several occasions.

Another of my jobs, John said, was to ensure parking for the workmen. The dealers' customers tended to snap up all available spaces even before drug trading started. I was to get there first and line up plastic buckets to reserve the spots.

And I was to deal with Charm if she stole the workers' hubcaps or supplies. Manuel had reported parts of his van missing, and early in the construction I'd had an unfortunate experience with a gardener. Despite my best efforts, I could not protect his truck while he was in the backyard unloading forty pounds of soil. Charm made off with two bags of gravel, leaving behind a trail of stone chips leading to her house, but I was too scared to confront her.

"Any questions?" John asked expectantly at the end of the meeting. Of course, this was rhetorical. Everything was fine. The men got up and went to work, enthusing in various languages about our new commander. We were like the whistling Seven Dwarfs. Things were going to be okay. Finally, everything was under control.

The next day, I wasn't so sure.

Alex made a big hole in the wall with his pneumatic drill in order to drape cables. This enraged Boris, who had just spent an entire week repairing the very same surface. When John demanded that he fix it, Alex slopped plaster over the holes and then poured the excess down the kitchen sink. He then enraged the mason and his crew by blaming his misdeed on them. Mr. Kamal was feeling bad enough, having been chastised for tracking in tar from the roof. And being Bengali, he didn't appreciate being called a "Paki."

This melee was before lunchtime. John and I went on a run to El Floridita and came back with a mollifying stack of *cubanos* that no one but the voracious plumber would touch. Of course the Muslim masons didn't eat pork. What had we been thinking? Raul and Manuel were shunning meat like good Buddhists. Boris the painter didn't eat "that Spanish shit." The electrician didn't stay for lunch. He shouted something about an emergency in New Jersey and took off for the turnpike.

After lunch, the plumber tried to unblock the old galvanized steel piping that had become stopped up with Alex's concrete. The pipes crumbled. This meant installing new copper ones.

As the plumber worked, I heard the sound of irreplaceable tiles cascading off an upstairs wall. I ran up to the bathroom to find the shattered remains of what was once a fine specimen of 1940s design.

"Shitty tile work." The plumber kicked a broken shard.

Boris ran in, enraged. "Someone ruined my wall," he growled.

"Wasn't me," the plumber said with a straight face. "It was that dirty Honduran."

Just then Clarence barged in for one of his routine inspections. For a super who worked with toxic cleaning solvents, Clarence had surprisingly little appreciation for their combustible potential. He held his cigarette dangerously aloft a can of paint remover that Raul was planning to apply to the metal bathroom cabinet.

"You paid this joker to do this?" Clarence said. The plumber glared.

Clarence shrugged. "See ya later. I've got chicken marinating. Ginger. Good for the blood pressure."

I assertively escorted Clarence to the stoop, sulking as I watched Miguel direct his efficient crew. They huddled at the abandoned house, and then took up positions on the street. It occurred to me that the dealers ran an enviously cohesive team, unlike our workers, who more resembled a dysfunctional family of rebellious adolescents. Miguel's tight control over his staff was, dare I say, highly professional.

Miguel glanced at me and, noticing my distressed expression, padded softly over. He cocked his head with concern.

"¿Qué pasa?" ("What's up?")

I studied his disciplined troops. In the shadows of my house, men yelled at one another over the whine of the pneumatic drill.

"Agh," I blurted out. "I'm having staff problems."

"¿Qué?" Miguel asked politely.

"They fight all the time. They don't listen to me. They break things."

Oh, no. What was I doing venting? Admitting weakness to the narcotics lieutenant was unwise. What would I reveal after this? Childhood slights I'd never gotten over?

Unaware of my inner thoughts about his untrustworthy nature, Miguel nodded respectfully and contemplated his men.

"It is not easy to manage people. I, too, sometimes have trouble managing the muchachos. They run off with money. They don't always follow instructions." He eyed me intently. "At least you can fire your people. It is more complicated for me."

Just then, a gigantic glistening SUV pulled up to the curb. Penknife leaned his body against the passenger door and shouted into the tinted window, his hands pounding on the door. *"Tiene sangre de maco"* ("You're cold-blooded"), he yelled at the customer.

Miguel got up reluctantly. "See what I mean? *Te veo en la bajadita.*" ("Catch you on the rebound.") He stalked over to Penknife, who backed off from the customer and returned to the steps.

I watched with envy. If only I could direct the plumber as easily.

Things continued on this chaotic tilt for the next six weeks. The house took on the appearance of Home Depot, what with all the cables, buckets, and sacks stacked in various rooms.

Only the Dominican workmen, Manuel and Raul, remained beacons of principled calm, no doubt spiritually fortified by their meditation routines. Everyone else engaged in verbal abuse fueled by racism. Nationalities, skin color, religion: All were cited in ricocheting name-calling. Men of rival groups "borrowed" or broke one another's tools.

The degree of hatred among our "staff" was directly proportionate to the geographical proximity of their orgins. The Bengali masons argued worst with the Sri Lankan door refinisher. As for the Hispanics, Che Guevara would have despaired over their lack of Latino solidarity. The light-skinned Mexican plumber mocked the mestizo Honduran, who looked down on the even darker Dominicans.

A characteristic household exchange went like this:

"It was the Ecuadorian's fault."

"You mean the Mexican?"

"Whatever. That Spanish asshole."

"Hey, what you darkies got against Latinos? We had calendars when you were living in trees."

"Cut it out, guys." (This from me.)

"He started it."

"Hey, who the fuck stole my wrench?"

Being a white Jewish liberal, I couldn't allow this naked racism under my cratered roof. This was disgusting! My grandparents came to this country to escape pogroms, which my social-worker parents reminded us of as they drilled us in politically correct behavior. My gentle father was a community figure in Queens who had mediated in racially tense situations when we were young. Talk at the family dinner table—the rare times he was home from saving society or working his two jobs to save money for our college educations—was about civil rights or Johnson's New Deal. Dad's philosophy was that young children should learn ethnic tolerance at a tender age, and my earliest memories were of sampling pickled jellyfish legs prepared by Dad's Chinese friend Alvin Lee and watching footage of corpses at Auschwitz. These childhood experiences might explain why my sister and I chose poor-paying careers that purported to provide public service. Dad would be proud of us! We made sacrifices for social justice! And we appreciated other cultures, as evidenced by our choice of husbands. Not only that, I had spent twenty-five years trying to adapt to foreign countries. So what exactly was I doing here, hiring some of the most prejudiced people in New York?

Usually I would simply snap, "Stop that!" if I heard an insult. But once I was so fed up that I convened a meeting of the various crews to deliver a high-and-mighty lecture. I thundered on about the Rwandan genocide and apartheid, with my most smoldering hell-and-brimstone look. "People die from words!" I yelled, shaking my finger. But as soon as I left the room, it was back to work, and the plumber called Raul "a fucking nigger."

There was one upside to all this nastiness. I had heard about renovations tearing couples apart, and yes, John and I had the odd squabbles, generally over his desire to do something himself that I thought we should pay someone else to do. Mostly, though, the infighting among the crews drew us closer together. We were so busy trying to persuade them to get along that we barely had time to argue over each other's taste. I was beginning to see John's point, too, that we should not give these warring extortionists further tasks. Our focus must be trained on one goal: getting them to finish and take leave of our house.

I had meant July Fourth to be a day of rest. We gave the workers time off, less because it was a national holiday than because they feared the firecrackers on the street. The pyrotechnics had intensified, and the day before one of the rockets had gone off under Manuel's van, nearly setting the tires aflame.

"Fucking Dominicans," the Mexican plumber said to him. "Why are you guys so loud?"

John remained in the house to take stock. Raul suggested that I join him and his sons to see the ships sail up the Hudson River. This was a fine opportunity to get acquainted with Riverbank State Park. Community activists had fought hard to get it built atop a sewage treatment plant and, minus the occasional whiff of gas, it was a pleasant refuge with a commanding view of the Hudson River. State police patrolled in cars to ensure that troublemakers stayed away from the empty tennis courts and Olympic-size pool.

By the time I arrived, a cluster of kids were craning their heads toward the bottom curve of Manhattan. They waited for the ships. And waited. And waited another hour.

Finally, a shout went out. Tall masts were glimpsed in the distance. The kids let out kittenish mews of excitement as they strained on the railing. *"Mira, mira, ya viene."* ("Look, they're coming.")

"It was worth the wait," one boy said.

Suddenly, the flotilla turned around and headed back downtown.

"What the fuck . . . ?"

A child cried. Then another. A rumor rippled through the crowd that the ships were behind schedule and had to dock in time for the evening's festivities.

The kids stared, disappointed, at the water.

"Harlem. We always get shortchanged," a teenage boy said.

"Yeah, they don't care about us black folks uptown."

The kids looked at the water. They stared for a long time, as though willing the ships to come.

Back on the block, the smells of lighter fluid floated through the air as the Dominican supers lit grills to celebrate the independence of their adopted country. By sundown, some seventy-five partygoers clustered around the flatbed of a truck that was spread with ribs, marinated chicken, corn, plantains, and beer. The revelers danced around a boom box situated next to the buffet. The dealers sampled morsels as they did business, shouting in their phones above the festive music.

"*Coño. ¿Dónde estás? Tengo el Starbucks.*" ("Where are you? I have the Starbucks.") Penknife snarled into his walkie-talkie, holding it a few inches from his ear in an attempt to hear above the music.

The show began at 9:30 P.M. sharp. The muchachos set off rockets in the middle of the street, hitting the undercarriages of unsuspecting cars that barreled down the hill. Orange, green, and purple sparks swirled in the air. Drawn by the displays, a police car drove by just as red streaks swooped by a fifth-story window across the street and narrowly missed the billowing curtains. A helicopter provided further cover overhead. Then three fire trucks screamed up Broadway and the law enforcers followed them, leaving the illegal show to continue.

Several days later we missed our dawn subway train from Queens. As luck would have it, the one day we arrived late everyone else was on time. The workmen restively circled outside the gate. They couldn't get into the house because the mason was painting the front steps.

"That costs thirty-three dollars a gallon," Mr. Kamal the mason said huffily as his many nemeses demanded passage up the stairs. "You'll mess up my work."

Alex looked at his watch as though it would dry the paint. "Better hurry up. I've got an emergency in Westchester."

"You people always have emergencies," Mr. Kamal retorted.

"Yeah, what type of emergency, *coño*?" the plumber mocked. "Lunch emergency?"

Boris moaned, with a melodramatic hand on his forehead. "These Spanish men, always complaining. It gives me a headache."

I was furious, too. The color was not the neutral gray that I had chosen. Instead, it was a startling turquoise better suited to a public swimming pool. All we needed were pink flamingos and we could pretend we were in Miami. As I complained, Mr. Kamal testily explained that he had some paint left over from another job. I should be glad that he was saving me money.

"Paint is paint," he snipped, turning his back to apply another coat.

"I don't like this particular paint."

"It's cheap."

"That's not the point."

John put his hand on my arm and forcefully whispered that this was not the time to argue, while seven men with sharp tools were demanding access to the property. He fashioned a bridge from a plank of wood that had been destined for a windowsill and the men bustled across. They jostled one another with hot coffee and ladders.

I thought I saw a familiar figure flash past into our putative home.

Sure enough, when I followed them in, I saw none other than Salami limping along purposefully with huge metal coils wrapped on each shoulder. The weight accentuated his lopsided gait. Alex waved him on with a cinnamon doughnut, careful not to spill his coffee. How dare the workmen allow Salami in? The nerve! They knew how much we wanted to keep him out.

"Can you believe the muscles on this guy?" Alex said admiringly.

Salami guffawed manically. "Jack of all trades."

"Get the fuck out of my house," I said.

"Whoa," Alex said gruffly, holding the doughnut up like a stop sign. "Let him finish the job. Put it there, *mano*. Nice and gentle."

The cables deposited in the living floor, I pushed ten dollars into

Salami's hand. "Buy yourself lunch, breakfast, whatever. Just get out of here."

Salami beamed. "Thanks, Mama. They paid me already." He limped over to the muchachos next door, waving his treasure. "I'm a rich man!"

As I stood on the stoop steaming, Mr. Anderson appeared like an imp in front of the gate. He waved his hand vigorously. It was gloved despite the seventy-five-degree weather.

"Come, darling. I want to show you something. My accolades." Mr. Anderson hooked his arm in mine and led me to the basement entrance of his house. I was intrigued. What could he possibly mean by "accolades"? We entered what appeared to be a private conservatory: two mahogany grand pianos, a small upright, and an antique organ. Mr. Anderson motioned for me to sit on a soft teal sofa. I moved aside a purple toddler-size teddy bear to make space.

My eyes took in the room. An inspirational rhyme hung on the wall amid framed pictures of concerts. It went:

Life's battles don't always go to the strongest or fastest man.
But sooner or later,
the man who wins is the one who thinks he can.

Mr. Anderson sat at the organ and played "Silent Night" in the July heat, his gold signet ring glistening above the ivory keys. He tried a fugue next.

"I love Bach. This modern music they have today with all that screaming and hollering—oh, how can they stand it? And they're making millions of dollars! I was brought up in a strictly classical style, in the churches. I never liked jazz."

Strains of merengue rose from the street. Did he dislike Latin music, too?

"Oh, it's nice to hear one number, but then . . ." He thumped his foot on the pedal. "I was just telling a cousin of mine," he said above the music, "it doesn't make sense for me to get angry. I made up my mind when I was fourteen years old not to get angry anymore. When I was fourteen, my mother was mad because I threw my brother's cap into the yard. She said, 'You devil.' She whipped me; in those days parents were allowed to whip their children. That made an indelible impression on me. I decided then never to get angry."

I pondered his words as I sat next to the large teddy bear. Yes, what was the point of getting angry? It wasn't going to make Salami, or the house, go away. My energy was better spent trying to get along with everyone. I sank back into the cushions and closed my eyes to the soothing Bach.

Chapter 12

NICE BONES, ROTTEN ORGANS

Nature, like music, had always soothed me, so I hired a gardener to clean out the backyard. The outdoor space would provide a needed refuge from the construction chaos, I figured. As it stood now, we couldn't really use the yard due to the crowded spruces, ivy, and weeds that choked the pathway. The gardener suggested clearing out the rectangular center so that we could sit under the dogwood tree without contracting poison ivy. He scattered white pebbles to reflect the sun and to bring out the hues of the lilac in back.

We quickly discovered that despite the cosmetic changes, our garden wasn't much fun. It smelled bad from the crab shells—Salami and Charm liked seafood—and the bags of excrement in the adjacent yard. To add to the mess, residents of the corner apartment building hurled rubbish from their roof into our garden. Each time I wanted to enjoy my outdoor terrace, I'd have to pluck out glass shards and dirty Q-tips before sitting down on the bench fashioned from a slab of slate and cinder blocks.

There was one corner that I avoided completely. It attracted swarms of flies and gave off such a putrid stink that I couldn't face going there. One day we finally gathered our courage and pulled the weeds aside with thick construction gloves to see what was there.

I instantly regretted our curiosity. Two rusted syringes stuck out of the earth. The vials were filled with brown blood.

"Hmm," John said in his typically understated way.

I stared without relish, contemplating what infections might fester on the needles. "How long do you think they've been there?"

"Hard to say."

"I don't want to think of what's on them. HIV, hepatitis . . ."

"Don't touch them."

"Salami?" I asked. "Maybe it's a warning. Like a voodoo doll."

John considered this. "It's possible the doctor, the former owner, put them there. To scare off intruders."

Whoever was responsible, we had to get rid of the things. I tentatively lifted the syringes, making sure not to touch the tips. Then I wrapped them in old towels, threw them in the trash out front, and went across the street to warn Clarence to take care when handling the bag.

The incident put me off gardening for a while.

One day while eating lunch in the kitchen, I noticed a pamphlet that the building inspector had left during his visit. It was written by the Ubells, a father-and-son pair of engineers who offered advice in magazines and on WNYC radio. They had acquired near-celebrity status among rehabbers for their folksy on-air delivery, and rumor had it that they inspected eight hundred buildings a year. These men were the pundits of structural cracks.

"Is Your House Healthy?" the title asked in bold letters, with a drawing of a stately Victorian. A handy checklist was provided. "Your house is probably the biggest invested [sic] you've ever made," it began. The booklet then listed fifty things that could go wrong.

All were chillingly familiar. I read that clogged gutters and poor insulation could destroy our health. We were warned of rotten wooden siding, damaged heating equipment, and bad stairs that caused more than two million injuries a year. *Extremely hazardous* chimney flues emitted toxic fumes that could cause asphyxiation or explosions. The pamphlet assigned point values to each of the following ills:

- water leaking through cracked walls
- mortar erosion, causing chimneys to shift
- broken windows
- misaligned doors
- excessively squeaky floors
- broken treads on the stairwells
- corroded water pipes and valves
- insufficient electrical outlets
- stained and cracked toilet bowls
- missing and loose tiles
- a lack of ground-fault circuit interrupters
- malfunctioning vents
- water accumulation around the furnace
- inaccessible plumbing shut-off valves
- banging pipes
- exposed wiring
- extension cords nailed to baseboards

The final offense was what we journalists call the "kicker"—a dramatic flourish that concludes an article. "Work performed by unqualified individuals," read the finale. I added up my score: 250, the worst possible.

"Wow. Do you have troubles," the pamphlet confirmed.

It then advised me to try to do as many repairs as possible myself, and failing that to call a professional. Here, too, I realized that I had erred. I hadn't gotten recommendations from neighbors, nor had I contacted three contractors for competitive estimates. I didn't examine the workers' previous jobs. I didn't call my local Better Business Bureau to check on their Customer Satisfaction Rating. In short, I was a failure.

As if this weren't enough, the Ubells helpfully included a newspaper article about toxic mold. This menace was rapidly spreading through bathrooms in the greater metropolitan area.

I called the Ubells for an appointment. When I explained the problems, they promised to come right away. Ubell junior arrived, scrutinized, and pronounced. He revised the engineer's original assessment that the house didn't need much work. No, it needed emergency surgery: concrete-filled iron supports, new beams, the gutting of various rooms.

"The house has nice bones but the organs are rotten," he said. He lifted a loose door saddle to make a point. The wood floor and joist below crumbled under his foot. Then he escorted us on a dirgelike procession from room to stricken room. He spoke like his checklist:

"Take down that bug-infested ceiling in the basement.

"Rebuild the bathroom there.

"Repoint inside bricks and install insulation.

"Replace all windows.

"Strip and repaint external pipes.

"Build walls around the boiler to meet code.

"Install encasements over the electrical cables."

Ubell took a deep breath. "Parlor-floor kitchen: Install new flooring, moldings, ceiling, and Sheetrock."

He paused again. "Second floor: Scrape lead paint from the window bars and remove the sink. They're leaching chemicals."

"The top floor: new flooring. Re-anchor the central staircase leading from the basement to the third floor. Replace broken steps."

Manuel the carpenter consulted his clipboard, reviewing the list with neat little marks. I tried to keep up, jotting in shorthand.

"That's all you need to do. Shouldn't cost more than seventy-five thousand dollars. Got it all down?"

The notion that we would have to spend an additional $75,000 on unforeseen house repairs—and keep the bickering workmen around even longer—thrust me into despair. The sense of chaos within our alleged sanctuary was compounded by the constant presence of Salami outside. He hung around at all hours, begging for attention.

"Mama, let me have a look at the house," he pleaded. "I can make it beautiful."

No way. I wasn't going to allow that maniac into the building.

Just to remind us of his presence, Salami roared outside the front window the song *"I'll be watching you."* He did the Hustle, saluted like a soldier, anything to get our attention. When straight, Salami was clownishly annoying, but when high he ranted in a way that didn't inspire faith, to say the least. Still, I made a point of remaining on benignly conversational terms. If I was cordial, perhaps Salami would be less likely to clobber me during a mercurial mood switch.

During these edgy talks, I learned that Salami was originally from New Jersey. His real name was Oscar and he came from a "good family."

"They don't do drugs or any of that. My father used to work as a salesman for a supermarket service," Salami said proudly. "But he liked to drink and I think he has a job in a bar now. I don't really keep in touch since my mother died five years ago. I had problems with my family over drugs."

This piece of information gave me some pause. I never before thought of this menacing caricature as a real person who had lived in a house with electricity and parents. But of course Salami was someone's son. Maybe his father still loved him.

Salami said he came to this neighborhood ten years ago to get away from some problems—I thought it best not to ask what they were—but the problems "caught up" with him. Still, Salami was proud of his personal work ethic.

"I'm a Virgo, so I'm a perfectionist," Salami explained one day, as he applied wax with a round sponge to a thug's tan Mercedes parked in front of our house.

"My mother always said, 'Anything you do, be the best at it. If you're going to be a bum, be a good bum.'" Salami added hastily, "I'm not a bum. I'm a hustler."

He suddenly groaned and stretched, rubbing his bad leg. "Man, it's hurting me today. I need to take something for it."

"Is that why you smoke crack? For the pain?"

"Nah. My girl turned me on. She put the pipe in my mouth. I liked it so I continued to do it. It wasn't always good, though. Someone gave it to me mixed with heroin. That's called 'chasing the dragon.' It almost stopped my heart. I was sitting outside in my shorts, holding my stomach and heaving."

"Did you ever want to stop?"

Salami smirked and jerked his head at his house, where Nose and other dealers were sitting on the steps. "I can't as long as those guys are here. Temptation."

Charm sidled up and Salami squeezed her shoulder with rare tenderness. She was so grateful for the affection that she plastered her body against his, practically strangling him.

Salami coughed as he freed his windpipe. "Mama, my little hangout partner is a home decorator," he said proudly, his voice still weak from the choking. "She's furnished our place with beautiful stuff from the street. It looks just like Paris. You should hire her."

I got a chance to look at Charm's design handiwork a few days later, after Bob the broker briefly threw Salami and crew out of the house next door, with the help of the 30th Precinct. Every day for a week, Bob installed a huge padlock on the front door, which someone— we suspected Salami—would then cleave off at night. The dealers made clear that they still considered the steps their turf and would not budge as Bob plodded up and down with containers to remove the junk piled inside. I had mentioned that Manuel had a friend who was interested in buying the house, and the broker invited me inside for a peek.

He met me at the front door wearing a face mask. Flashlight in hand, he led the way into the darkness. The lack of electricity and the boards tacked on the windows created complete blackness. *Gee*, I thought. *Charm really has strange taste.* As we progressed slowly to the back of the first floor, I gagged as I recognized a distinctive smell, that of a refugee camp without flush toilets. Bob said that hundreds of flies hovered above the toilets, which were filled to the seat. He had hung sticky ribbons from the ceilings and splashed disinfectant into the bowls, but the insects persevered. They slammed against the doors with loud thuds.

"Hoh cahn peepel leeve leek dis?" Bob asked.

"What?"

He inhaled through his mouth and slipped the mask down. "How can people live like this?" The mask went back up.

We moved downstairs to the basement. The steps afforded sufficient privacy to double as a bathroom, and the oozing floor was like an urban swamp. Cockroaches floated on mangroves of broken pipes. The drain was stopped up by used condoms, Q-tips, and crack vials.

Back upstairs, Bob trained his torch onto the butane burns on the turquoise damask wallpaper. I noted that Charm took a liberal approach to what Martha Stewart might call "junk shop chic." Every piece of wounded furniture was missing an arm or a foot. (*She really ought to get that fixed; it could be worth something,* I thought about a seatless cane chair.) An amputated dresser (circa 1930s?) stood next to tall pocket doors, which looked suspiciously like they might belong to my house. Salami's electronic cache was scattered in random piles: carcasses of amplifiers, doorless microwaves, vacuum cleaners missing hoses.

Bob led me out to the garden. The light hurt our eyes upon impact, and we took deep breaths. He leaned against a wall as he adjusted the mask strap. "Don't suppose you'd want to buy this house, too, would you?" he asked.

I had no interest. But others did.

As word spread that a honky had moved to the block, several white house-hunting couples dropped by each week to see how we liked living here. To them, Mr. Anderson and Mrs. LaDuke didn't exist. After all, the old-timers were black and had lived here for forty years. As the (generally African-American) real estate agent would stand back discreetly, the putative buyers would lean over and ask in a slightly hushed tone, "What is it like?" meaning, "What is it like for whites?"

Often the visitors felt compelled to offer decorating tips, as though we were doing up the house for *them.*

"You painted white! A historic color would have been more appropriate," scolded one prospective buyer. "You didn't do your research. It should have been lavender or ocher, certainly not white." He spat the word *white* as though it caught in his throat. This was not what Boris the painter wanted to hear, twisting like a pretzel to reach an elusive corner in the vestibule, thirty-six feet high. He exhaled a string of Russian ex-pletives: *"Mozgoyob, govorit kak v luzhu pyordnut. Muravyov tebe v shtany!"* ("Brain fucker, he talks as if he farts in a pool. May you have ants in your pants!")

One couple from the Upper West Side was so abrasive that they even tested the patience of my normally tolerant husband. John nick-named them Mr. and Mrs. Bleach for their obsession with cleanliness. For reasons known only to them, the pair wanted to buy Salami's homestead instead of one in the suburbs. But they were scared of West Harlem and barged into our home regularly to seek reassurance. We couldn't figure out why they were looking here. But as our acquaintance grew, we intuited the reason: Mr. Bleach was keen and his wife wasn't.

They kept returning, vacillating on the property as they mounted the crumbling stairs. For once, I welcomed Salami's appearance. The wife would recoil as the odorous squatter told them that he owned the house.

"Can't you make him go away?" she once whined.

"No one can," I said solemnly. "Not even the police. He's like a boomerang."

The couple's timing was such that they often chose calamitous moments to seek our advice. One day Mr. Bleach charged into the basement just after the plumber had hacked open a pipe. The house-hunter's eyes blazed with rage as water sprayed his T-shirt.

"You fucked me up!" he hissed. I thought he was blaming me for the soaking. But no, I had committed a far worse transgression.

"Termites. You told my wife this street had termites. Now she's to-tally spooked."

Mr. Bleach stomped out, muttering, "Fucking shit." John turned to me with a gleaming smile. "I think we're rid of him," he said, and sug-gested a triumphant dinner.

After six weeks more of mayhem, the electricity and plumbing were just about done. It was hard to believe that the worst of the reno-vation was over. The lights switched on and water flowed fine from the bathroom taps if we used a wrench to turn them on. Manuel would stay on, to work his way through Ubell's checklist. Boris would follow be-hind for touch-ups.

John went to the bodega to fetch celebratory beers and we invited a German acquaintance to see our proud handiwork. Gudrun was an architect recommended by our nurse friend, Marla, who had suggested Harlem to us in the first place. The architect had bought a similar wreck several blocks uptown that she was fixing up, and she had repeatedly, strongly, advised us to hire a professional general contractor.

"You shouldn't mess around with a house," Gudrun had said, handing us her business card.

Like most Dutchmen, John didn't like taking orders from a German. Although my husband was not yet born even by the end of World War II, Hitler's invasion of the Netherlands remained fresh in his family's collective memory. Of particular offense was the fact that the Germans had stolen the beloved Dutch bicycles to make their retreat. John had, needless to say, resisted the architect's many suggestions. Now we couldn't wait to show her our great job. I handed Gudrun a Czech Pilsner to ready her for the grand tour. I fantasized that the architect would lavish praise over how well we novices had done.

She fixed her eyes on an exposed plastic pipe in the basement, frowning sternly.

"That is PVC. Do you know what that means?" Gudrun didn't wait for a reply. Of course I didn't know. "Polyvinyl chloride. It's illegal. If the house catches fire, it'll melt and you'll suffocate from the noxious fumes."

She leveled us with such a disapproving gaze that I felt it might stop my breathing all on its own. I meekly agreed to get new pipes.

The secretary of the plumbing company was defensive when I called to complain, and she explained that the man they had sent was a trainee. "He's got great potential. Be patient with him," the secretary insisted. When I expressed concern by threatening a lawsuit, she agreed to deploy a more senior man to redo the job. In the process of putting in new pipes, he broke others. We called another company to clean up the mess, but these new plumbers ruptured even more parts of what we thought was our wonderful new and improved water and heating system.

John did the remaining work himself. Of course, we kept this information from the German architect.

Chapter 13

A PARKING SPACE FOR MOM

John's presence and the intensity of the construction project made me feel more anchored than I had when rattling around the house with only Raul as company. Now that I was reassured that my husband wouldn't start a fight with Salami or leave me because of my impetuous house purchase, I could relax a bit about our new life. The panicked midnight calls to my sister subsided. Since John was so fully convinced about the project, I could finally admit my doubts to him. He remained steadfastly optimistic that all would end well.

However blasé John might be, though, I couldn't fully calm down about the drug crew outside. In the two months since we had taken over the building, the worst-case scenario—being physically threatened—had not transpired, but it was a tense coexistence at best. Things superficially seemed fine—Miguel had more or less held to his promise to keep his boys off the property, although periodically I'd find them leaning on the gate. He was pleasant, even gentlemanly. Our relationship, if you could call it that, was precarious, though. It was forged out of pragmatism, after all. How could I trust Miguel, a criminal? I had heard stories about drug gangs attacking informers. We got along only because we needed to, not because he really liked me. Our very presence threatened his interests.

As for Salami, I never rested easy around him. Crack made people volatile and violent. If I knew one thing about addicts, it was that they would burglarize, and even kill, for a fix. Salami's clownish antics might be amusing, but he was a scary clown from my worst childhood dreams. Even when he was behaving like a puppy that wanted attention, I didn't forget Salami's unpredictability.

Inside the house, the top floor was all set for us to move in. However, while the house was ready for us, we weren't quite ready for it. Our belongings still had not arrived from Russia; in fact, they still hadn't left Moscow. The moving company told us that sneaky customs officials were holding them hostage on the dubious grounds of missing stamps. The amount demanded for the ransom was worth more than the goods themselves, but the movers thought that eventually the customs people would accept a reasonable bribe. "You just have to be patient," the company told us.

Leticia had offered to sell us spare furnishings when she sold her house, but this was becoming an abstract prospect, as no one seemed interested in buying on our street. As usual, Mom had a solution. Although fit of mind and body, minus the normal age-appropriate high blood pressure and sciatica, Mom had been muttering lately about the "hot breath of mortality." She was nagging us to clean out her garage and what was once my bedroom so that she could die in a tidy house. I didn't like the morbid tone of this talk but was happy to oblige, as we didn't relish sleeping on the former owner's stained mattress.

The bounty consisted of furniture that had belonged to my two grandmothers: a mahogany armoire, a lovely tiger maple desk and bureau, and the "guest" bed from the basement. My father was the grandson of a carpenter and had made the bookshelves and cabinets in our Queens house. To continue the tradition, Mom bequeathed his saws and hammers to John so that he could build whatever was missing.

In return for Mom's largesse, we offered to clean her garage of un-worthy items. She walked behind us, supervising, as we tossed junk into a big black garbage bag: chipped terra-cotta pots, a rusted rake that could have caused tetanus, a leaky hose.

We worked speedily, and got to a wall shelf that held several metal containers of desiccated paint. I climbed up on a step stool ("You can take that, too") and my mother watched in rare quiet as I tossed the old paint into the trash bag. The shelf was now bare, except for a dented Maxwell House coffee can. Just as I grasped it, Mom yelped.

"Put her down!"

"What?" I recoiled, the tin in my hand.

"Your grandmother!"

"What?"

"Grandma's ashes are in the can. Don't throw her away."

I looked at the can, then at my mother, and back at the can. My grandmother had died thirty years ago. What had her remains been doing in the garage all that time? Sure, like any daughter, Mom had had "issues" with her mother. But I knew my mother loved her and had made great sacrifices to care for Grandma when she was dying from Alzheimer's. She had come to live with us when other old people would have been dumped in a nursing home.

"You have some explaining to do," I said archly.

Mom replied testily—a little too testily, I thought. "We never got around to distributing her ashes. Grandma loved to travel. Remember how she traveled all over the world? So I wanted to scatter her at Kennedy Airport. But you can't just walk onto the tarmac and empty a pot of . . ."

I cut her off. "We can't leave Grandma here."

"I'll move her eventually."

"This is no resting place."

"Look, there's nothing we can do about it right now. We'll sort this out later. Let's focus now on getting this stuff out of here."

I mulled this one over. What would happen to Grandma? Would my mother eventually relinquish the ashes to me for a more serene resting place? And what would I do then? It was a solemn responsibility, to dispose of these remains properly. It wouldn't do to simply exchange the shelf in Queens for one in Harlem.

The next weekend we drove out to Queens in a hired van to pick up our meager possessions. Raul came along to help. He and John loaded the suitcases, the furniture, and the boxes of books that I had stored at my mother's since college. I momentarily thought about snatching Grandma's ashes, but it occurred to me that the workmen might accidentally throw the can away if we brought it to the house.

The plan was to drive in convoy into Manhattan. The men would take the van, and Khaya and I would join Mom in her maroon Subaru. However, John, having witnessed my mother's treacherous habit of cutting off bigger vehicles driven by large, swearing men in muscle shirts, apparently decided it was safer to go solo, and he hit the gas. We lost sight of him even before we hit the Fifty-ninth Street Bridge into Manhattan.

After years of driving on some of Africa's more dubious roads, where you can go as fast as the speedometer allows, provided you can swerve around the roadblocks and bathtub-size potholes, I was not mightily concerned with the possibility that we might crash. I did feel a little alarmed, however, when an enormous pedestrian, enraged by my mother's road manners, smacked her car door with a stick at a traffic light and shouted, "I'll kill you, bitch." Fortunately, the light changed and Mom sped off.

I was more apprehensive about what Mom would think of our house. My mother had shown remarkable restraint in not visiting until now. She'd taken at face value my vehement, repetitive insistence that this was a sound financial investment. Since I'd kept her uninformed so far as to the narcotic nature of the block, to say that I was uneasy about exposing her to Salami and company was a gross understatement. This was a big deal to me. I wanted her approval.

As we hurtled toward Harlem, I conjured up a nightmarish scene: Salami grabbing my mother from behind while Charm bit her knees and the dealers brayed in laughter. Naturally, I betrayed none of these fears to Mom, who kept her eyes on the road as she muttered at pedestrians racing out of her path.

In order to prevent disaster, I had planned our move for early on a Sunday morning, before trading opened. However, we had gotten off to a late start. To my dismay, the whole crew of reprobates was out on the steps of the abandoned building as we pulled up to the house with a screech. Adding to my worry was that there was no sign of John. I really wanted him there for support when my mother crossed the threshold for the first time.

Mom created quite a stir. She had spotted an opening among the double-parked cars and narrowly missed hitting an old woman crossing the street as she zoomed into the tight space. As my mother struggled with her automatic lock—the windows went up and down and back up again—Salami sidled over and opened her car door. To my horror, he gallantly offered his arm as Mom got out. As much as I wanted to intervene, I didn't dare reveal my anxiety to Mom.

"What a nice young man." She smiled brightly at Salami.

"Yeah, well . . ." I replied unenthusiastically.

Salami leered at me. "Mama, I know how to park in tight spots." He swiveled his hips Elvis-style behind Mom's back.

"Stay away!" I growled, as I opened the back door. Inside the car, I took Khaya firmly by the metal choke collar to intimidate Salami. "He bites."

The arrival of a wolflike beast and a white woman in her seventies who was connected to me had a sobering effect on Miguel, who watched our arrival with undisguised dismay.

"*Mi madre,*" I said, with a wide sweep of my hand, holding Khaya's collar firmly with the other. "Mom, these are the neighbors."

"*Encantado,*" Miguel answered stiffly. His eyes darted to the street, where a mattress van was honking to get through. "I see you found parking," Miguel added, with little relish.

Sensing an opening, my ever-resourceful mother set to bargaining without the aid of my Spanish translation skills.

"Would you mind keeping an eye on the car while I'm in"—she peered at the numbers on the houses, and then pointed—"there?"

"Yes, *Mami,*" murmured a suddenly docile Miguel. "Anything else?"

"Nothing for the moment. But thanks for the offer."

"*Sí, señora.*"

Mom beamed and we climbed the steps of the building. As we

reached the top, John drove by in the van and shouted that he was looking for a parking place and would continue circling until he found one. Miguel ignored him.

Mom's denial mechanism was in full gear as she strode through the house and up the staircase that was coming off the wall. She clucked appreciatively over the square footage and airy ceilings. My mother didn't say anything about the asthma-inducing mold, or the death-defying steps. She didn't utter a word about the folly of sinking every last penny into a drug lair. If she had any thoughts about her daughter's bad judgment, she appeared to put them out of her mind.

I noticed a gleam in my mother's eyes as I introduced her to Boris and Manuel, who lined up as though for military inspection. As a social worker who specialized in family court and troubled youths, Mom was expert at establishing trust with all sorts of people. Within minutes she was chatting away with the workers as though she had known them for years. Before one could say "skim coat," they were exchanging numbers to do work at her house in Queens. Wait a minute! Mom was poaching. What if, succumbing to her forceful charms, the workmen abandoned our jobs for hers? Boris must have sensed that this was a woman who knew how to bargain, and he cited quotes that were a fraction of what he charged me, even though he would have to drive an extra half hour out to Queens. He looked at me somewhat sheepishly and explained, "She's a widow. She lives alone."

Mom not only outdid me with the contractors; she had also done her homework on the neighborhood, and informed me that we lived a mere nine blocks from Fairway, a food market that was a temple to gourmets in the metropolitan area. It was right by the West Side Highway, and people would drive from as far as New Jersey and the northern Westchester suburbs just to buy the fresh kumquats or whatever obscure Basque cheese had come in. Having lived so many years abroad, I had never heard of Fairway, and was amazed that our neighborhood had a desirable amenity besides narcotics to draw rich suburbanites in SUVs. Perhaps they shopped there after purchasing a kilo of coke on my block. In any case, Mom had heard that the emporium carried a particular low-fat buffalo mozzarella that she liked, and as John had still not arrived, she decided to pass the time shopping. As I escorted her back to the car, Salami was in the throes of yelling at Charm. He was upset about something being missing and leaned her up against a Mercedes as he screamed, "Where'd ya put it, bitch?"

"I'm not telling you."

"You better."

With a sideways glance at Charm's emaciated figure, Mom noted this interchange briefly. Then, without obvious concern, she returned to searching for her car keys in her pocketbook. Behind her, Salami berated Charm for being lazy. The poor woman was cringing under the assault, making a whining, strangled noise.

"You're useless," Salami spat at Charm. "Why can't you be like other women? Look at Judith. She's building a house. I bet she cleans, too."

This caught Mom's attention and she whipped around. "She doesn't do windows."

My mother measured five feet three inches and was seventy-one, but she was no frail old lady. Indeed, Mom knew how to get what she wanted from people. Being a good professional, she had studied her psychology books and could bend anyone, even a hardened criminal, to her ferocious will.

She returned from Fairway with several plastic bags of organic delicacies and what could only be described as a beatific smile. She had found that elusive grail that makes New Yorkers ecstatic: the perfect parking space.

This spot wasn't only directly in front of the house, my mother told me. None other than Miguel had provided it.

"There I was, driving in, and he told someone else to move and to give me the space. And that nice young man who was there before, the one with the limp . . ."

"Salami. He's not that nice."

"Yes, well, he stood in the street and held up the traffic so I could maneuver into the space. So when I got out I asked the other one . . ."

"Miguel."

". . . if he would do this again, and lo and behold, he said, 'Yes.' You see, nothing ventured, nothing gained."

I could just see it: the local cocaine boss nodding indulgently as my petite mother stated her list of demands. What would she do next?

She told me. "Then we got to talking and I mentioned I had just been to Fairway. He said he would save the spot for me if I wanted to scoot out again."

John and Raul arrived shortly thereafter. For a good two hours they had been trying to find a parking space for the van, and were irritable as they brought our belongings into the house. "They don't mark streets properly in this country," John grumbled. "You only see signs after the turnoffs."

We owned so few possessions that the act of moving in was even more unsettling than bivouacking in an empty house. Driving over from Queens took more time than unpacking our meager goods. We had to put such disquieting thoughts aside, though. The dog was agitated and needed to calm down, lest something terrible happen.

Khaya ran from room to room, sniffing with relish at the remains of the workmen's Oreo cookies. The dead woman's mattress particularly excited him, and he buried his nose in it and inhaled deeply, his tail furiously wagging. He knocked over a can of super-white eggshell paint (thirty-three dollars a gallon), swept through the puddle, and became a giant walking brush that smeared the oak doors. It was time to get him out of there before he ran up more damages than the plumber.

"Come on, boy, let's check out the 'hood," John said. He pronounced *hood* to rhyme with *dude.* John attached a chain to the dog's choke collar and we set out.

"It's a gorgeous evening. I want to see the mansions on Sugar Hill," John said.

Just then we heard a ruckus in front of the corner deli on Broadway. It was the familiar sound of a mob shouting, *"Hijo de una puta"* ("son of a whore"). We approached and saw nothing unusual: just two hundred people yelling at a cop. However, the object of their ridicule was unusual: a sneezing Rottweiler. Police had sealed off the corner with yellow tape, and inside the cordon the police dog circled a brown bag from which a kilo of white powder spilled out. The hound brayed fiercely, brandishing yellow fangs. His handler, a fleshy policewoman, tried to calm him.

"That's the dog's mother," someone roared, to hoots from the crowd. "Son of a bitch."

The cop wore an "I wish I wasn't here" expression as she tried to subdue the meaty Rottweiler, but he continued to rise on his hind legs, madly sniffing the air.

"Don't you love this neighborhood?" I said to John. "It's a circus."

Just then the Rottweiler turned toward us. His giant nostrils quivered in Khaya's direction, and the sniffer dog snarled as he rose on his powerful legs once again. The Rottweiler looked like a fiendish dancing bear that I once saw in Moscow. Khaya crouched like a wrestler, ready to fight. Uh-oh. This was not good. Although our dog was mild-mannered with humans, he could be extremely provocative with his own species.

I feared Khaya's eighty pounds were no match for this crazed behemoth, who was seething with adrenaline and coke. This was like pitting a sixth grader against Mike Tyson on one of his ear-chewing days.

Suddenly the leash jolted. It was my husband—180 pounds of solid muscle—taking over the reins. "Time to go, boy," he said, hauling Khaya toward the house. Our pet whipped around for a last howl at the police dog, but John managed to yank him away.

Heading back home, we passed Mr. Anderson on his evening stroll. He was humming a fugue. "Lovely night," he crooned, oblivious to the mayhem around him.

We were almost home. Just a few paces and we'd be safe. As we walked by the vacant house, Salami called from the darkness, "Nighty-night, folks. Don't let the bedbugs bite."

I shuddered at the thought of sleeping next door to the source of this disembodied voice.

Tranquillity continued to elude us back at our alleged sanctuary that night. I felt vulnerable with only a chain-link fence separating our garden from Salami's, and I checked the locks of the kitchen door several times to make sure he couldn't easily break them. That wasn't the only disturbance from the rear of the house. The yellow security lights in Mrs. LaDuke's yard glared like prison searchlights right at our pillows.

The sound of the crowd outside was like a drone, or more like a

roar, that was punctuated periodically by a shrill female shriek or
"¡Coño!" Musical anarchy, meanwhile, flared up. We had thought that
the bedroom would be quiet, as it faced away from the street. We hadn't
considered that the apartment dwellers in the back might enjoy blasting music, too. The adjoining gardens served as a canyon that ampli-
fied noise. The hyper merengue of the virtuoso Johnny Ventura came
in from the north. Mexican *ranchero* music floated from the west.
Salami's falsetto rose above all else like a deranged solo. Then, just
when we thought it couldn't get worse, an African-American man from
Clarence's building parked speakers in his window and called, "This is
war!" as he turned on Public Enemy. The music discharged at 110 deci-
bels:

*"Our freedom of speech is freedom or death / We got to fight the
powers . . ."*

The muchachos didn't appreciate this particular musical contribution, and with shouts of *"Coño,* nigger," they cranked up the Ventura. I
didn't think more clamor was possible until a helicopter clattered
overhead.

Finally, after what seemed like an eternity but was probably only an
hour, the hullabaloo died down. I checked my watch: It was 3 A.M. I fell
asleep to the sounds of Salami and Charm shouting abuse at each other.
"You bitch" and "Get off me, shit" wove into my edgy dream along with
the whirl of the copter.

At 5 A.M. I awoke to another party from the back of the house—the
clamor of birds feasting in the mulberry branches that hung from
Salami's yard. I peered outside to see a winged party of woodpeckers,
thrushes, finches, robins, sparrows, and starlings. They were pecking
the newly sprouted berries, and one another, flapping, singing, war-
bling, warning, mating, and doing the Macarena, for all I knew about
backyard ornithology. I lay awake listening grouchily.

John snored. The dog's legs moved as though he were trotting in
his sleep. I folded the pillow over my head, closed my eyes, and thought
of BB guns and what I'd do if I could get my hands on one. Somehow
that lulled me to sleep.

Chapter 14

QUIS CUSTODIET IPSOS CUSTODES?

A couple of evenings later, I actually heard a gun, although of a louder, more lethal variety than a BB. Fifty or so people ran up Broadway, bristling with chatter and adrenaline while pointing to a grocery store down the avenue. A rumor rippled through the crowd that an armed man had taken hostages and a helicopter was on its way to rescue them. As the crowd hopped up and down, four police cars screeched up to the curb and cops with guns drawn poured out.

A mild-looking man in reading glasses slid up beside me, with an amber beer bottle in his hand and a bemused expression on his face. Then he addressed me in Latin.

"Fortis cadere, cedere non potest."

"Huh?"

"Fortis cadere, cedere non potest." He sounded like my seventh grade teacher, who had insisted that the language of Caesar was not dead.

"My Latin's rusty. Subtitles, please."

" 'The brave may fall, but never surrender.' That was my high school motto, at Kingston College in Jamaica." He offered a hand with neatly cut but grimy nails. "Mackenzie."

I had seen this man around for a few weeks now. His handsome, intelligent face and dignified bearing reminded me of the actor Morgan Freeman, minus a few teeth. Mackenzie squatted in the basement of Clarence's building, and in return for free lodging helped the super put out the garbage on pickup nights. On nice days, Mackenzie set up a plastic crate in the shade and studied a *Daily News* rescued from the trash, his bifocals halfway down his nose as he fished into a packet of Newport regulars. Mackenzie spoke no Spanish but was on high-five terms with the Dominican dealers and apartment dwellers. He was teasingly playful with the kids, and the women trusted him to keep an eye on the young ones while they did errands around the block. Mackenzie walked with a hesitant manner, as though he wasn't used to large spaces. I suspected that he had just come out of jail, a not uncommon story here in West Harlem.

"You're new here?" I asked.

"Not really. I've lived on these streets for twenty years. Used to live around the block."

"Lemme guess. You're back from upstate."

"No, Jessup, in Maryland."

"Drugs, right?"

He laughed sardonically, a bitter spurt. "What else?"

I eyed him expectantly.

"I took a package to Baltimore on the bus. I got busted at the depot when I arrived. It was coke from one of the Dominican gangs. I did two and a half years."

"Not your first time?"

"Third. Tax evasion was the first." Mackenzie scrutinized me closely. "I got a favor to ask. I need stuff to read. Can you lend me books?"

"Sure. What type?" Mackenzie didn't have a chance to answer. The police were dispersing the crowd and coming toward us. Mackenzie did a smooth dance step and slipped down the basement stairs, calling over his shoulder, "Here's another one: *Quis custodiet ipsos custodes?* 'Who shall guard the guardian?' "

I was amazed, to say the least, at how forthcoming Mackenzie was. But he was so clearly out of place, despite the not unusual homelessness and drug use, that maybe he yearned for a kindred soul. It wasn't as if a lot of people spoke Latin on this block. Mackenzie had no doubt observed me, as I had him. There wasn't much else to do on the street if you weren't dealing drugs, and he had rightly pegged me as the bookish type. I wanted to encourage this acquaintanceship, if not for intellectual company then to make an ally. My arrangement with Miguel could fall apart at any moment and I needed protection.

I was thinking about developing other guardians as well. On evening walks, John and I made the acquaintance of a soigné West Indian woman named Icilda; our dog liked to hump her terriers. As Khaya vented his lust on her pets, Icilda told us about herself. She was a community activist with a network of thousands of people who fought for the many social causes in West Harlem. Many of these folks had been politically active since the civil rights movement and were now fed up with the filth of the noisy dealers who came to these streets solely to make money and couldn't care less about people who actually lived here.

"We're sick of it!" Icilda explained.

She told us about the activists' formidable organizing techniques, this being one of the more politically vocal communities in Harlem. These energetic residents could mobilize a petition campaign or rally within hours. In order not to miss meetings, the activists brought their kids along with coloring books and instructions to sit still. There was a fair amount of horse-trading on issues: "I'll come to your picket if you'll sign this letter."

All throughout, I heard, activists gave careful thought to racial calibration. This reminded me of my father's work to bridge white and black communities. The West Harlem organizers tried to strike the right mix of black old-timers who lent wisdom and credibility, rich whites to whom white politicians would respond, and young professionals of any color who represented Harlem's future. Professional experience was used to best advantage. Architects prepared cases to preserve buildings. Actors from the area were particularly good at giving stirring testimonies. Bankers met with the Harlem Empowerment Zone officials to seek loans. Lawyers provided pro-bono advice; writers edited communiqués.

"You should think about getting involved," Icilda said.

I saw her point. Of course I wanted be a good citizen. I was annoyed by the dealers and was within my rights as a taxpayer to complain about criminals. Nevertheless, I felt uneasy about going behind the back of my new "friend" Miguel. What would happen if I called the police and he found out? Rafael had warned me of the dangers of informing on dealers. There was also the issue of hypocrisy—something I didn't like to admit to. Like many people of our generation, John and I had dabbled in drugs when we were younger. Like many foreign correspondents, we could be described as enthusiastic drinkers. So who was I to complain about the narcotics business? And whose stoop would the muchachos sell in front of if not ours? Would I simply be pushing the problem onto someone else?

I was also ambivalent about losing my alleged journalistic objectivity. Going to meetings would be in keeping with my politically active family—heck, my sister and father had spent endless hours at these types of things. But reporters are expected to cultivate an elusive state of impartiality. This is relatively easy to achieve when abroad—as a foreigner, I was already an outsider and couldn't vote in local elections. In contrast, now I had joined a community in which I had invested all my money, sweat equity, and emotional capital. I wasn't working as a reporter at the moment, but I planned to again. At that point, I didn't want someone to accusingly say, "Aha! She took sides!"

I told Icilda I would think about getting involved, and I was doing just that during an afternoon stroll with Khaya, when a buxom Hispanic girl fell into step with us. She was walking a white husky pup named Kilo that belonged to her uncle, who was "out of state." The girl, Esmeralda, explained that she was thirteen, lived in the corner apartment building, and needed cover.

"The dealers hit on me," Esmeralda said. "They won't leave me alone. They talk all sexual and comment on my butt." She exhaled loudly, as though it would erase the men from the street. "No one will hassle me with that big wolf. Can we walk with you?"

If I had a daughter, I wouldn't want her treated like that, I thought. We set off together.

The dogs did their bit and we walked slowly back to Esmeralda's building. I escorted her to the door and we made plans to meet up for future walks.

I went back home and thought some more. Then I called Icilda.

Having decided to join the forces of organized citizenry, I could finally enjoy a *Law & Order* moment. Since I had gone straight abroad when I began my journalism career, I had never covered the police beat, unlike so many of my colleagues. My only exposure to New York cops and prosecutors was TV.

My first meeting was that of the 30th Precinct Community Council, a forum set up to improve relations between the police and residents. Drugs were among various matters that were discussed—the others were vandalism, run-of-the-mill violent crime, and teenage gangs. I was advised to take a roundabout route to the precinct so as not to arouse the dealers' suspicion. The muchachos never seemed to show interest in my whereabouts once I left the block, but I nevertheless complied with instructions, looking over my shoulder. No one followed me.

At the precinct, I was ushered into a big room decorated with mug shots tacked up on the wall. A map with stars marked the sites of burglaries, rapes, and homicides. Few on my street, I noticed with satisfaction. Maybe Greg was right that the muchachos protected us.

The meeting had the air of a church lunch for seniors. The vast majority of the thirty people sitting on the uncomfortable metal chairs were retired black women. I was the only white person except for the three cops seated at the dais. A thin divider separated us from the front desk, where two mangy characters were being booked.

An elderly woman in a newsboy cap led me to a visitors' book, where I was supposed to write my name, address, and telephone number—just within peeking view of the two handcuffed crack addicts at the front desk. They eyed me with curiosity while I signed and the woman outlined the drill.

"The only thing we don't talk about openly," she said loudly, "is narcotics. The detective will introduce himself. If you want to talk, do it in private in the halls."

The perps eyed me intently.

I took a seat next to two grandmotherly women who were discussing a street near mine.

"It's terrible. It's only going from bad to worse."

"I just don't let them get away with that in my face. I don't pay them mind."

"They do it right in front of the school. My grandchildren see them sell."

"My Lord. Did you hear? She said she had to move away. She said, 'I just can't take it anymore.' "

The meeting was called to order. An old man wearing an oversize blazer asked the company to stand as he led them in prayer: "We walk by faith, not by sight."

One of the cops stood up and reminded everyone that drug-related information would be kept confidential. He added, "Our goal is to enhance the quality of life in our community by continuing enforcement efforts against drug trafficking and to address problems like drinking in public, excessive noise, illegal gambling, et cetera."

The audience looked at him dully.

The officer then recited a roll call of statistics. Nearly 550 buildings in the area had been enrolled in the trespass affidavit program over the past decade. The narcotics eviction program had secured over fourteen hundred vacates of drug traffickers and other illegal businesses.

He then went on to discuss other issues, such as a clean-up of graffiti and a warning to lock doors and windows carefully.

Aware that no one could talk about what really mattered, the cop reminded the audience, "If you want to talk about narcotics, we'll take a walk in the back." At this pronouncement, a handful of people rose. They filed past the perps to meet the commander in the hall.

The ladies next to me remained seated.

"Won't you join them?" I asked.

"There's really no point, dear," said the plumper of the two. She patted my arm companionably. "We've told him before."

Her friend agreed heartily, with bobbing head. "He knows what we think."

"So what *can* one do?"

"Pray," said the first woman. She put on her coat and picked up her cane.

Discouraged by the mild nature of the meeting, I next went to a clandestine one with members of the D.A.'s office and the police. This gathering was attended by residents of some nearby streets, whom Icilda had called "the hard core." This group, I was assured, was articulate and vociferous.

As a leftover from the time when muggers prowled the streets, people preferred to travel together to the meeting. I was told to wait at a designated corner at dusk for a van driven by one of the residents. Right on time, a solid woman with bad teeth drove up and honked at me.

"You must be the new one. Hop in."

The van was littered with candy wrappers and small plastic toys. The driver, Ethel, explained that she was raising her two grandchildren. "Push that stuff over."

More people piled in, hands were shaken, and the van lurched downtown.

The group had mastered cop slang, and the talk was of "wires," "take-downs," and "collars." There was a new commander, Thomas Cody, whom one woman described as a "teddy bear."

Everyone in the van except for me was black. I asked whether there was outreach to the law-abiding Latinos on the block. There was silence.

"You mean those Spanish people?" someone said in a scornful tone that I, as a white person, couldn't use without charges of racism. "We don't trust them."

We pulled up to the building where the meeting was to take place. We were cleared to go upstairs after the guards checked our names on a list and sent us through an X-ray machine like those in airports. Awaiting us in a sterile warren of cubicles with fluorescent lighting were undercovers with big scars, men in dark suits who processed the cases, and a lumbering Irish captain in uniform, who, just as the woman had said, resembled a Gund bear.

Other residents were already in the room where the meeting was to take place, including a well-dressed lawyer named William. Because he and I were both white, it was assumed that we were acquainted. There were quite a few elderly black women. A movie-star-handsome black man, Bailey, introduced himself as a professor from one of the nearby colleges. One woman had an infant with her and apologized for the crying. No one, I noted, was Dominican—although Dominicans made up nearly half the population of West Harlem.

The commander briskly called the meeting to order. People volunteered painstaking notes about apartment numbers and overheard conversations. The residents described perpetrators and their street aliases and recited the license plate numbers of out-of-state cars. One detective asked if anyone had an empty apartment that undercovers could use for stakeouts. There was a short debate about the merits of videotaping transactions.

The main achievement recently had been the indictment of twenty dealers at two apartment buildings on the northern corner of our block. These had nothing to do with Miguel's crew, nor Clarence's building, nor the other drug-stash buildings on the southern corner of the block, nor the crack houses on my street. We listened with rapt interest. A yearlong telephone wiretap investigation had busted the gang, which had supplied major traffickers in New Jersey, Pennsylvania, and Massachusetts. Coke worth $390,000 had been seized. This was a fraction of the dealers' proceeds, but the band was deemed broken up.

"As you can see, we're making progress," Commander Cody said.

Bailey was annoyed. "Why aren't there more take-downs?"

The white lawyer joined in. "I used to live in Midtown. This drug activity would never be tolerated there. Why won't the police deploy more officers here? It's racism."

Cody sucked in his breath and caught the eye of a detective with a scar snaking around his chin.

"We can't just arrest people because they're standing on the street."

Bailey leaned toward him. "We call, we call, we call. A police car comes fifteen minutes later. By then the guys are halfway across the bridge to New Jersey. *You* aren't doing your job."

The detective with the scar got defensive. "Hey, look . . ."

Ethel interrupted him. "I can't call. They'll know it's me. No one else would call in the building. I got beaten up a few years ago. My grandchildren live with me." She sounded weary, as though she had said this two thousand times before.

The commander responded just as tiredly. "We're the second smallest precinct in the city but we make the most narcotics arrests. We just don't have enough resources. We collar drug dealers, but then they get replaced by fresh ones from the D.R. If anyone can get immigration into the ball game I'll take you out to dinner."

The room processed this in silent resignation. Someone changed the topic to a homeless "hotel" down the hill on a desolate stretch near the river. The triangular brick building was a freight house from 1928 that would have been converted into expensive lofts if located in Tribeca. Instead, it housed more than a dozen squatting vagrants, who skulked around trash cans looking for food. The building had no working plumbing and let off a rancid stink. The sheer size of the colony, and the remoteness of the spot, made people scared to walk by.

"It's a blight," said an artist who lived up the street.

Cody lamented that there was little he could do. It was private property. "We've called the owner. It's up to him to block it up."

This provoked more derision. "That's ridiculous."

"It's the law," retorted the commander.

One of the undercovers weighed in. "Look, you didn't hear this from me. But you can seal up the building yourself with plywood and cinder blocks. Go early on a Saturday before the neighbors wake up, so no one sees you." He paused. "Make sure you don't seal anyone inside."

What a simple, elegant solution, I thought. We would become urban guerrillas as the cops turned a blind eye. But there was a hitch. How were we to check inside without risking life and limb at the hands of a dozen or so Salamis?

People looked at their watches and the meeting was adjourned. As I stood up, the undercover with the big scar sidled over.

"I've seen you talking to those dealers on your street. You should keep your distance. They're dangerous."

"You mean Miguel?"

He blanched. "You know his name?"

I puffed up my chest and in my best foreign-correspondent swagger explained about my past. No "I was stuck in crossfire" was left out. I informed the detective about the time I had walked on a smoking mine dump in Luanda that had been blown up by rebels. I described how my plane in Zaire was stormed by half-naked looting troops. I told him about the close call with the Rwandan machete man. I was really on a roll here—the ambushes, the snipers, the howitzers, the dictators. I was one cool customer.

"I know what I'm doing," I said.

The undercover listened quietly. *Now he gets who I am,* I thought.

After a long silence, and a strange look, the cop spoke. "You know what? You're a lunatic. Why would you put yourself in such danger? You should be locked up."

I thought about the cop's words as I rode down in the elevator. He had a point. I had come back to the United States ostensibly seeking stability and safety, and then had plunged right into mayhem again.

I wasn't the only one sending contradictory messages. Cell-phone numbers of various law-enforcement officials were handed out at the meeting, with express instructions not to distribute them widely. We were also assured that our identities would be kept secret and that there was no way that the dealers would find out that we were discussing them behind their backs. However, this cloak-and-dagger discretion melted once I was back on my block. Officers did not think twice about yelling "Hello!" from their marked cars as they drove by. Others waved ostentatiously if we passed on the street.

After raids, there was a lot of stagnant time when the detainees sat handcuffed in the vans while the officers did searches and placed calls to the precinct. During these lulls, plainclothes cops came up to the gate if they saw us sitting on the stoop, and made chitchat until it was time to leave for the station. I hoped for their sake that they didn't return to the same spot twice. Or maybe they just didn't see any harm in striking up a conversation with a white homeowner.

"My favorite part is booming," confided one unshaven undercover with an oversize silver hoop in his left ear. He draped himself on the gate. "You know, breaking down doors. I'm always the first in. I'm very fast and I have no qualms about pulling the trigger." He tapped the holster on his waist enthusiastically.

Mr. Boom lowered his voice confidentially. "You want to know the real reason I go first? I'm vertically challenged. I have less chance of being hit because I'm a small target. My boss took me out for a drink and told me that!"

He took a good look at my small frame. "You'd be good at this— you're very short. You know, the drug dealers will trust a female more than a guy."

I told him I'd keep that in mind.

"I'll tell you a trick. You develop a character. I stay in character but get out of cop mode. So I'm the white guy from Queens or Jersey who's scoring. I'm also good at bar duty, because I'm such a good drinker." Mr. Boom eyed my beer bottle. Then he resumed his sales pitch.

"I love this job! I have a front-row seat to the best show on earth. I walk into a Starbucks anywhere and I own the place. If the shit hits the fan, I'm in charge. It's a power trip. It feels good!"

I made a mental note to remember this the next time I went to a Starbucks.

The cop's colleagues across the street shouted at him to get in the van. With a peppy "Have a good day!" the officer jogged to the vehicle and drove off.

The world of activism quickly accepted us, and while the solidarity was warming, the fear that Miguel might find me out was not. However, the upside was that just one meeting with the cops opened up a whole new social life that I hadn't even dreamed existed. Feeling under siege creates an instant sense of community, and suddenly we gained a firm place in the neighborhood, regardless of our race or profession— a rare phenomenon in status-conscious New York. No hazing was necessary to join this club, other than living the experience. Our new acquaintances accepted us simply out of shared anger at failed law enforcement. Out of the blue, we had a social niche and went from being complete outsiders to regulars at barbecues, parties, brunches, and teas. And at more meetings, of course.

What with all the issues, I could easily have gone to one or more gatherings a night. There were groups for tenants, seniors, parents, and homeowners. I heard about a surplus of drug treatment centers, bad schools, homeless shelters, and halfway houses. Asthma was widespread, what with a sewage treatment plant, marine transfer station, and diesel-bus depot nearby. People were trying to clean up the parks. They were pushing for architectural landmarking.

As much as I cared about these matters, I was so busy with the house rehab that I didn't have time for anything but police meetings. Being a more principled journalist and determined to remain apolitical, John rarely went to any gatherings, politely coming up with excuses about cabinets that had to be sanded. As time went on, I realized that these gatherings provided an opportunity to bond as well as to vent. The jiggling van that ferried organizers served as a social club where people compared notes on schools and arthritis remedies. It was also a venue to get tips on workmen and swap tales about the drug activity.

One time, I mentioned the syringes in our garden.

The group fell silent, considering this.

"Jeez," someone gasped. "That's radical."

"Apropos of that, listen to what my neighbor found in *his* garden," said one woman.

"What, a body?"

"Close. An automatic weapon and a block of cocaine. *Pure* cocaine."

"Lordy."

There was a pause. "How'd he know it was pure?"

"He brought it to the precinct."

"He should have kept it to pay for the house rehab," suggested one crusty old fellow.

Chapter 15

PIONEER LIVING

I never would have imagined myself doing this. Driving over a land mine, perhaps. But not climbing into a garbage Dumpster to extract oak shutters. Yet here I was, scavenging for the decorative remains of a nearby house, which was being gutted by a developer with little appreciation for Victorian pocket doors. Next to me, deep inside the skip, a dude with four earrings on each side tugged at a pedestal sink.

"How's your street?" he asked between grunts. He was making little progress.

"Terrible." The shutters were trapped under a rusted bathroom cabinet. I might need his help. "Ow! And yours?"

Grunt. "Terrible."

The cabinet moved. Got them! Just then, another dude,

this one in a bandanna and leather pants, climbed into the Dumpster. "You should check out 144th Street. Someone threw out an awesome clawfoot tub!" he called out from the bowels.

"Yo, how long you been in the 'hood?" Earrings asked. I supposed it was the rehabber equivalent of "Do you come here often?"

"Three months."

"One year here. Still doing up the house."

I caught sight of a red bandanna. Leather Pants emerged with a bounty of door handles.

"Look at these brass beauties. They must be from 1887," he said. He regarded my shutters as though they, too, might be worth something. "Hey, I got some great walnut spindles. Got anything to trade?" Leather Pants took a notepad and pen from his tool belt and scribbled. "Here's my number. Come by tonight if you wanna take a look. We're having a party."

The police meetings gave me a sense of being part of something larger than our house and block, and helped me understand better why my father and sister liked activist work, despite the long hours and little or no financial reward. Community gatherings fostered a sense of mission and camaraderie—something that I sorely missed from my foreign-correspondent days. The meetings also introduced us to a new, strange world: rehabbers doing up wrecks. It was an eclectic clan who spanned all races, with a high proportion of teachers, musicians, and clothing designers. There was even an immunologist and a court translator. Despite our varied backgrounds, we all shared something important: Everyone else thought we were crazy.

Misery likes company, and for the first time in months I felt normal. Not only that, I felt cool! These people made the ordeal seem so hip.

The outsider brotherhood reminded me of being a foreign correspondent. Then, no matter how well I spoke the language or romanced the locals, I was always out of place. Even if I made friends with genuine inhabitants, it was tempting to hang out with other expats who also had to carry their passports when they left the house. The shared status exerted a strong pull. You understood one another's loneliness, you spoke the same language, and besides, while you griped over a bottle of wine, weren't some of those local customs infuriating? No doubt about it, we newcomers to West Harlem didn't fit in here, either. We huddled together at the sole funky café, Largo, which was a way station for City College students and aspiring poets who gave slam readings on Tuesday nights. Largo was the only establishment that would have fit in the East Village, what with the stripped brick walls that were decorated with artistic black-and-white photographs. This was the only place in West Harlem that called spaghetti "pasta" and served goat cheese on salads—with lettuce other than iceberg. The owner, Marc, was a Dominican former cop who grew up in the neighborhood and had visions of a hipster West Harlem where sushi and baguettes became a regular part of the local diet.

The undercover Gino pronounced Largo "a decade too early for this neighborhood," and we scruffy rehabbers also felt ahead of our time—or maybe behind. We didn't pay sufficient attention to *buena presencia*, or smart presentation, like most of our neighbors. Our ilk could be spotted from afar in grubby construction boots and dented station wagons. (Not that John and I owned a car. We couldn't afford the insurance.) I had what many Dominicans called "bad hair" and didn't straighten the frizz like the neighborhood women did.

Indeed, I didn't like to admit it, but living in West Harlem as white upper-middle-class interlopers was akin to being an expatriate. And as much as we welcomed meeting likeminded souls, we didn't want to fall into the foreigners' trap of complaining about the locals. If John caught me so much as mocking any neighborhood habit, such as playing loud music at 3 A.M., he would adopt his most sanctimonious Dutch tone. "We made a point of immersing ourselves abroad. You should do it here," he lectured. "We shouldn't lose touch with the 'real' West Harlem. Let's not forget why we moved here."

While I in turn spat at him for being a politically correct European, of course he was right. How dumb of me not to think of this myself, in fact. Damn that humanist husband of mine. That was one reason I loved him. Luckily, I had John around to remind me of my own skewed moral compass.

Real estate agents had less appreciation than we did for the original inhabitants of the block. They generally referred to us arrivistes—

white or black—as "pioneers," a quaint yet galling term that implied no one had lived here before us. Mrs. LaDuke apparently did not count, although she had moved to West Harlem in the 1970s. In fact, most "pioneers," like us, were less intrepid than simply financially stretched. The pioneer spirit, such as it was, took hold in part because we were priced out of the areas that we would have preferred.

Although claiming to be color-blind, the agents described West Harlem as "emerging," the code for "poor area of color." This shorthand also implied that the area had a low hipster quotient. "Pioneer" was a lower category than "gentrifier"—the latter implied that sushi had arrived. It is rather like animal migrations in Tanzania—first the wildebeest come, then the predators follow the meal ticket. In the equally mercenary world of New York real estate, usually a critical mass of pioneers settle in distressed neighborhoods before more mainstream gentrifiers feel reassured that enough cute cafés serve roquette. As the agents reminded us, gentrifiers wouldn't go for the fried pork rinds at El Floridita as long as the menus were written in Spanish.

West Harlem was unlikely to morph into an oasis of upscale eateries partly due to the plethora of churches, which were located on nearly every other block. As one aspiring restaurateur ironically noted, he couldn't get a liquor license for a property in proximity to a house of worship, yet meanwhile the crack trade was buoyantly lively in front of churches. Even if the liquor license could be obtained, the $15,000 rents for storefronts that were inflated by drug-laundering clients were prohibitively expensive for small-business owners.

The scarcity of struggling artists was another count against gentrification, although a few bohemian refugees had been spotted trickling in from artsy Williamsburg, where there was a lot of warehouse space that had been converted into artists' studios. Most painters couldn't afford an entire brownstone, and the layout of four narrow floors didn't lend itself to open, airy workspaces. Instead, our district tended to attract black lawyers with an appreciation of Harlem's past, or teachers with extended families in need of rental income. The one sizable contingent of creative types consisted of architects, especially from Europe, such as Gudrun, who had provided us with plumbing advice. As foreigners, they were intrigued by Harlem's legendary name and were hungry to put their imprints on empty shells—nor were they above hunting through Dumpsters themselves.

Despite the inconveniences of raids and dealers, it was a form of pride to live on a truly awful street. This reminded me of war correspondents who would compete at the bar with tales about being in the line of fire. Just as being shot in the chest—and surviving—won a journalist great kudos in Africa, so rehabbers acquired vaunted status if they camped in a total shell without a functional stove. Our situation was downright cozy compared to some others'. We were humbled by one daring artist couple who feared that their preschooler would fall through the holes in their floors, or that they'd be murdered by the menacing tenants who lived above them. The landlords erected a barrier to ensure that they didn't encounter the lodgers while eviction proceedings were under way. Now *that* was pioneer living. But we won prestige by living next door to Salami. Everyone knew Salami, and mention of his name would send eyes rolling.

"He's so in your face," shuddered the white lawyer, William. "Aren't you scared?"

Although I often was, the irony was not lost on me that Salami was the true pioneer. He had camped in trains, parks, and empty, abandoned buildings. He had been taking bucket baths for years. No doubt he could teach us a couple of tricks about living in stark conditions, if we dared ask.

So could Mackenzie. I felt surprisingly comfortable with this Latin-quoting squatter, except on Saturday nights. (That was the only time, or so he said, that he indulged in crack, with an attractive streetwalker named Star. It was Mackenzie's version of date night, which so many of our married Upper West Side friends were advised by women's magazines to schedule.) Aside from his dating choice, I appreciated his caustic wit and the way he managed to keep his dignity intact. Mackenzie never begged for food or money, but never lacked for either due to his ability to charm a wide array of people. The kiosk man gave him free newspapers. The Dominican restaurant on the corner fed him gratis.

The lawn-chair ladies invited him for home-cooked meals. And we gave him the *Times* crossword puzzle and books.

Mackenzie made me reflect that any of us college grads could have fallen likewise, and only by the grace of God had not. His undoing, in fact, began with rich white lawyers much like the ones I went to school with at Harvard. Mackenzie was a promising sociology student in Los Angeles in the late 1970s, when he was offered freelance work as a paralegal. It paid so well—$6,000 a month—that he dropped out of college and overstayed his student visa. The attorneys tipped him in cocaine mixed with water and sniffed from a spray bottle. Mackenzie quickly got hooked.

Ironically, greed, and not drugs, sent him to jail. A random audit by the IRS revealed he had pocketed $30,000 due in income tax. After eighteen months in federal prison, Mackenzie discovered that no one wanted to hire an ex-con. His family rejected him, too. Mackenzie drifted for eight years and then took a Greyhound bus to New York. There he began "that hobo life," bivouacking in Central Park, on rooftops, on the A train. "I slept on the A train for months," he said. "You get the best sleep. The A train is the longest line—that's two and a half hours from the Bronx to Far Rockaway. By the time it makes three trips, it's daylight."

Unlike the song popularized by Duke Ellington, the A train was not what had brought Mackenzie to Harlem. It was the shelter on Ward's Island, which arranged a job for him to survey the homeless in West Harlem. That's when Mackenzie first smoked crack. He liked it so much that he moved here in 1989. Thus began a decade of bouncing between various crack houses and prison. These days, he supported himself with maintenance work for Clarence and the aforementioned handouts. And of course he lived rent-free—every Manhattanite's dream.

As our acquaintance deepened, I grew to admire Mackenzie's Zen-like acceptance of his circumstances. His tiny room in the cellar was as spare as a cinder-block jail cell, but Mackenzie said he didn't mind. "It's something over my head. No one bothers me. If I'm reading, my mind is more than in that room."

His only furnishings were a fan, a bookshelf fashioned from discarded planks, and a mattress covered by an orange sleeping bag. He kept a bar fridge in the adjoining corridor so that it wouldn't create heat in the airless room. He neatly hung his parka and shirts from a water pipe and stored other clothes in a duffel bag. He didn't have a bathroom, so he borrowed the super's hose to fill up a bucket to bathe and used the toilets in the park. Mackenzie made do with a garbage bag if he urgently needed to go at night.

The room was his refuge. "I dabble a bit in crack and weed. You won't see me on the street then. I'll be in my room reading, resting."

A common pastime among the pioneers involved commiserating about unprincipled workmen who had reneged on deals. Even our most annoying contractors were mere bumblers compared to some miscreants who had fled the state in a blaze of debt and pseudonyms. Our job was a relatively quick one, too, apparently. Three weeks swelling into a few months was nothing compared to four years of broken promises and still no roof. One man was trying to hunt down a sleazebag who had disappeared with $100,000 worth of advance payment. Other neighbors had angry scenes in court. Gudrun's renovated house burned down when construction was 90 percent finished, after a workman started an accidental trash fire. The contractor of another house installed a staircase twenty feet off the stipulated design. The homeowner, who paid him nearly $500,000 for the renovation job, complained of plumbing that was so poorly done that pipes leaked on his new and very expensive maple floors.

Entertaining resembled camping trips—with a lot more booze than was portable in a backpack. We went to a few barbecues that were held in gardens, not for the joys of al fresco dining but because a hibachi was substituting for a stove due to the delayed installation of a kitchen. A memorable fete was staged in a gutted house where candelabras were attached to the stripped brick walls. Electrical cables hadn't yet been laid.

Our contribution to the pioneer social life was to invite folks over for police-raid parties. Our street was notorious for these operations, and we made the best of the events with a merry "If you can't beat 'em, watch 'em." Since we didn't own a television set, the undercovers sprinting by became our main source of entertainment.

"Hey, there's a good one on," we'd tell friends, and they'd come over. We'd sit on the stoop, open a few bottles of Presidente, and watch the show as the carrot-colored sun set over the Hudson.

As much as we liked Mackenzie, we often daydreamed about ejecting the other denizens of the pavement, or the "visitors," as John called the muchachos hanging out front. We resorted to a juvenile code talk—even speaking Russian, a language neither of us was overly fluent in but which we safely assumed the dealers did not understand.

Among our crowd, there were more creative problem solvers. Two actors with a flair for the dramatic developed a particularly effective method of crowd dispersal. When the sidewalk radio-playing got too loud, the husband, Sheldon, climbed the six flights to his roof with a bucket of steaming water laced with Pine-Sol disinfectant. Then, like a medieval knight hurling boiling oil from the castle ramparts, Sheldon dumped his hot mixture onto the heads of the men below.

That served two purposes, he pointed out. "I cleaned the sidewalk of their urine and scared them off, too."

It wasn't a permanent solution. "Of course they come back. But we have a respite while they change their clothes."

His no-nonsense wife, Donna, preferred a more direct approach. Walking up to the dealers and, standing right in their faces, she'd tell them that she was a witch and would put a spell on them if they continued to hang around outside her house.

"A lot of them are surprisingly superstitious," Donna recalled. "They run away when they see me approach."

John and I spent more hours dreaming up outlandish tactics than actually taking action. Although we wouldn't admit it out loud to the other pioneers, we didn't actually wish any harm to the local peddlers. We simply wanted the guys to sit somewhere else.

Clarence recommended that we spread lime on the steps, but that solution was short-lived. The enterprising dealers simply placed cut cardboard on the steps before they sat down.

Our mentor's next suggestion was more radical. "Try tar," he said. "It's hard to wipe off." We didn't want to mess up our own stairs but had no qualms about the abandoned house next door. John took the bucket down from the roof and was about to spread it with a brush until he had a thought: It would make it impossible for the owner to sell her house.

We consulted a neighboring pharmacist about concocting a chemical that would explode upon contact with urine. My husband's reasoning was that the boys wouldn't want to risk damage to their *cojones*. The pharmacist pondered the matter, but his reply was not encouraging: "Phosphoros?"

We thought back to South Africa, where extreme measures were common to protect the hearth. People routinely kept guns by their beds, or put razor coils and electric wires on top of the fences. Being a more lawful kind of place, Harlem called for a milder scheme. We decided to unleash the "weapon" that had worked so well before—Khaya and his feral looks. Who could forget the time we parked him in our Johannesburg patio? The dog scared off a burglar, though he also scared off the security guard who came in pursuit, summoned by the tripped alarm. The poor guard clung to the top of the wall, mouthing, "It's a jackal," while Khaya gazed on, puzzled.

Pulling off such a ruse here would be tricky, though. Anyone with normal observational powers would eventually realize that Khaya was as vicious as cottage cheese, especially around people. Lest the secret get out, we developed a "Stand back—he's vicious" stance to prevent him from licking hands, as he was so wont to do. This took some work, as the dog was getting on in years and not so receptive to new tricks.

From the day Khaya bounded into our house, we kept on his choke collar and shouted, "Down boy!" at every given opportunity. "Be careful—he bites," I told the dealers. I also dragged the creature as quickly as possible around the corner on walks, so that he wouldn't move his bowels in front of the muchachos. I didn't want them to see me stooping in an undignified way behind the animal's butt—it somehow undercut our fierceness.

In order to further enhance our street cred, I presented Khaya as *"mitad lobo,"* or "half wolf." So what if the wolf lineage could be found only on a family tree thousands of years ago?

Not realizing that Khaya was docile, the dealers hurriedly crossed the street when we approached. To John's great satisfaction, dapper Miguel tensely leaned against the wall. However, Salami saw through the ruse and mockingly howled, "Werewolf!" when we passed. "Nice doggie!" he'd shout in his falsetto.

We couldn't fool Clarence, either. "That animal is a marshmallow," he said. Much to my annoyance, Clarence stroked him softly under the chin in front of the dealers. Khaya rolled over and submissively offered his belly for scratching. Thanks to Clarence, everyone on the street eventually saw Khaya for what he was—half pillow, not *mitad lobo.* Our cover was blown.

Chapter 16

WAYS TO KILL A CAT

Khaya may have been gentle, but no dog in West Harlem howled louder in the thick August heat before a thunderstorm. The summertime scene out front of our house hinted of the Caribbean, what with the chicken braziers and ice vendors calling, *"Coquitos!"* Families poured out of their apartments for the barely fresher air, joining the usual cluster of domino-playing dealers on the sidewalk. The tree in front of our house offered the best shade on the block, and the crowd underneath included seniors and a man who had been shot who used a breath-operated wheelchair. The patriarchs pulled their T-shirts up to their armpits in order to ventilate their ample bellies.

The chug of air conditioners created such a load on the

corner building that the electricity went out on a nightly basis. Then the fights commenced. People were so irritated by the temperature and humidity that any minor provocation served as a pretext for violence: a smile at someone's boyfriend, tossing a baseball at a car. Events took a predictable turn. A crowd would gather around the sparring pair, either holding them back or egging them on, depending on the whims of the onlookers. (On a hot night, they tended to savor a good brawl.) Things never got too rough, though. At most a woman would pull the ponytail of another. Penknife, true to his name, pulled out his weapon a couple of times, but he never actually slashed anyone.

During the worst of the daytime heat, the dealers created their own version of water sports by prying open the block's two fire hydrants. Because we were at the bottom of a hill, the water ran down from the top like a stream, pooling in the potholes. The old folks sitting in beach chairs stuck their swollen feet into the rivulets as though at the edge of the sea.

The hydrant on Broadway at the bottom of the block was for the pros. The muchachos created geysers that gushed a thousand gallons per minute—enough force to knock over a small child. There was quite a lot of skill involved in controlling the flow; it took more than one pair of hands to cup the spigot. The muchachos had an annoying trick of diverting the fountain toward passersby, especially pretty girls, who got so soaked that their thong underwear and nipples showed. Occasionally in their zeal to drench young women, the boys hit the odd mother with a small child, or a pregnant lady. Then the elders got up and yelled at them.

Salami took advantage of the spray to shower. He had no reservation about stripping down to his shorts and lathering soap onto his naked chest with the same rag he normally used for car polishing. When he had a sizable audience, Salami hammed up the bath, slapping the cloth locker-room style against the hydrant and pounding his fists on his well-formed pecs like a gorilla. *"I'm singing in the rain!"* he howled.

The jets of water were so strong that drivers rounding the corner went into reverse as soon as they caught a glimpse of what looked like a car wash on speed. Those who couldn't back up rolled up the windows and powered through the water as quickly as possible. This created a menace for the informal day-care center that was the street, where kids dashed back and forth under the spray without heeding the traffic. Mackenzie made it his job to police the children, dragging them firmly back to the curb. "Every year someone gets hit playing in the water," he grumbled. "There's a public pool five blocks away. Can't their parents bother to take them?"

So much water had exploded from the hydrants this summer that it soaked the telephone cables. The lines that I had waited so patiently to install went to static. The fire department issued periodic warnings about the risks of lowered water pressure, but the cops just ambled by and let the water flow. "Aw, let 'em blow off steam. It's fucking hot," one lieutenant said.

Miguel was less sanguine. His clients refused to drive through the deluge. After receiving one too many complaints, Miguel sneaked up on the boys once as they were drenching a comely redhead.

"*¡Coño! ¿Qué estás estuviendo? ¿Amarando el chivo?*" ("What are you doing, goofing off?") Miguel yelled. It was the only time I'd ever seen him lose his cool, and his pawns were suitably shaken. They quickly went back to the abandoned house, with regretful looks at the pretty girl's plastered shorts.

Despite the fact that we finally had a functional kitchen at our disposal upstairs, we often felt too sapped to cook. The heavy air of summer drained our desire to create more heat on the stove, and the sight of flies buzzing around the gray chicken thighs at the butcher on Broadway wasn't enticing. We continued to subsist on takeout from El Floridita, even as we were growing tired of the *cubano* sandwiches.

Such culinary monotony could induce madness, as I knew from visiting offshore oil rigs in the North Sea. The men on board overcame their cabin fever in the middle of that watery nowhere with deluxe meals. Chefs offered amazing spreads of succulent variety over the fortnight the men were secluded. They weren't allowed to drink on the rigs, they weren't a book-reading bunch, and they didn't have a wide selection of movies. Delicious repasts provided the only way to unwind.

I was feeling a bit like an oil worker in need of distracting meals.

The all-consuming construction project dragged on. Manuel was still working his way through Ubell the engineer's checklist, with the painters repairing the ensuing holes. However, dining diversity wasn't a strength in this neighborhood. Even the nearest Chinese takeout, the Sing Luck Garden, specialized in fried chicken and fries alongside the mediocre Cantonese menu. Customary fare in the Dominican diners on Broadway was *la bandera*—which was stewed meat, red beans, and rice. Another standard was tripe, never one of my favorites. The nearest Jamaican goat curry was seven blocks away. We had to take the subway to eat Italian.

An idea for a change came from the street. I noticed that the boys ordered their lunch from *comedores,* or family-run caterers that operated out of nearby apartments. These enterprising chefs posted menus of Dominican specialties on lampposts, public telephone booths, mailboxes, and storefronts on the busiest drug-trading corners. Every day at 1 P.M., the dealers placed orders via cell phones and used car hoods as dining tables when their meals arrived in aluminum containers. The hand-scrawled and photocopied menus came from three distinct outfits that all offered the same six-dollar deal: a selection of *la bandera* and salad.

Each eatery served a specific gang turf. La Chory was active on Amsterdam Avenue. Sazón Gladys staked out Broadway, and Sazón Niño advertised on side streets. As competition ratcheted up, the caterers vied to outdo one another. La Flaca (the Skinny One) embellished its menu with an Art Deco font. Sazón Gladys added a slogan: *"El Mejor Sabor Latino"* ("The Best Latin Flavor"). La Chory experimented with creations such as codfish potatoes and roasted pork with eggplant.

Despite the aggressive advertising, the proprietors were not so entrepreneurial when it came to cultivating new clientele. As a stranger with a gringa accent, I had a hard time finding anyone who would take my order.

The first call was to Dulce Cena (Sweet Dinner), whose motto was *"Si la pruebas, te quedas."* ("If you try it, you'll stay.") The gruff man who answered the phone wouldn't give me a chance.

"Who's that?" he demanded.

I told him where I lived.

"Who sent you?"

"No one. I saw your sign."

"What sign?"

"There are signs all over Broadway."

"I don't know what you're talking about." *Click.*

The next place that I called operated out of one of the more notorious drug buildings on 144th Street. After I convinced the man that I was not a member of the police force, he said he didn't take orders for fewer than ten people. When I assured him I could easily place such a big one, he presented another obstacle. I lived too far away—three blocks. No amount of cajoling could get his delivery people out to make the trek.

"Sorry, *mi amor,* that's awfully far," he said apologetically.

I had different problems with another place. It seemed that, this being 3 P.M., I had missed the lunchtime rush, and all that remained was some fish stew that even the cook did not recommend. "I can't guarantee it's fresh," she said.

I was out of luck at the next three places. Defeated, I gave up and walked to El Floridita with a complaining stomach.

Meals aside, we savored the semblance of ordinary life that the now-serviceable top floor provided. We kept chilled water in the fridge and showered in a bathroom free of workmen's footprints. We had a haven to escape to, and while strong, the smell of paint grew fainter by the day. Before, I had felt very much like we were playing house, or that at best we were squatters. These were the first steps of taking ownership.

At about this time, Cleo arrived from Moscow.

Cleo was a dear friend from our days in Russia, and we were so close that I thought of her as a surrogate little sister. Like me, Cleo had grown weary of the harshness of Third World life and now had moved back to the soft familiarity of New York. Cleo's medium-term future looked bright: She had landed a job at a prestigious publication and had enough cash saved to buy a two-bedroom apartment in a desirable section of Brooklyn. But while she waited to finalize the sale, she had to find temporary lodging, and her two high-strung dogs made this near impossible. Both animals had been strays in Russia, and before their rescue had been viciously attacked by marauding packs and starved of decent meals. The trauma of foraging on cruel streets had left deep emotional scars, and no amount of pampering—sleeping on her bed, trips to the dog shrink—could erase their painful past. When left alone during thunderstorms, of which there were many this season, the hyper beagle tended to chew up wood doors and shit on Cleo's prized Turkmeni carpets. The vet prescribed Prozac and tranquilizers. Cleo's giant German shepherd was not on medication but perhaps should have been, as he spent his days nervously gnawing his foot into a pulp.

Cleo's inability to find a sublet that would accept the dogs was causing her anguish, and she visited us one day seeking consolation. We led her to the garden to calm her frazzled nerves, and served El Floridita coffee, arguably not the best sedative. As the starlings squawked and Khaya thumped his tail at our feet, Cleo burst into tears.

"I can't put them into a kennel after all they've been through." She wept. Cleo knocked over her coffee. Smelling the milk, Khaya came over and put his head on her knee.

I felt immensely privileged, compared to our poor friend. I had a whole house, even if most of it was uninhabitable. My dog had a roof over his head. I had a partner to share life's pain.

Then I thought again. Actually, things were pretty dire. We were going bankrupt, and there was no sign that this draining construction would ever end. When it finally did, we might not find employment for a long time. As I contemplated a life of penury and debt, an idea came to me, a wonderful solution to everyone's problems.

"Move in with us!" I exclaimed. I ecstatically rose and embraced the startled Cleo, trampling her pedicured toes. She winced.

I explained: If Cleo rented our now-finished top floor, we could earn much-needed money while helping a friend in need. We could share the kitchen; that ought not to be a problem as we all got along well. So did our dogs; we used to walk them together in Moscow and they were the best of friends. What's more, Cleo spoke several languages, so she could help us with translation with various workmen.

"It would be win-win for all!" I said.

Cleo didn't need much convincing. "Yes! Yes!" She blew her nose, signaling that the crying was over.

John was quiet throughout all this. He shot me a cautious look. "Where would we sleep?"

"The second-floor bedroom, where we were planning to sleep."

"We weren't planning to sleep there *now*. It's not finished."

A trifling matter. Men. "It will be soon. Cleo, when do you want to move in?"

Cleo arrived radiant and early the next day. Her spiky mules clicked on the parquet floors as she entered with her two dogs, four suitcases, and five pounds of Eukanuba weight-control dog food. It is worth commenting that Cleo is a sultry woman with charcoal eyes and glowing skin who has often been compared to the actress Halle Berry. She dressed to emphasize her ample bosom and hips, features that were not lost on the workmen, who tried to peer into her turquoise halter top as she knelt to pick up her bags. The men jostled to carry her dog pellets up to the comfortable top floor. While they gazed at Cleo's well-waxed legs, I was left to my own devices to drag our belongings down to the uncomfortable second floor.

Aside from overlooking the perils of doing business with friends, I had disregarded the health effects of sleeping in the middle of a construction project. The painters were still doing touch-ups in what was our new bedroom. Plaster dust rose in puffs from the bedsheets. The mattress took on the odor of perspiring men, who sat there during their breaks. Within days John and I had developed rasping coughs.

But this was the least of our problems. Salami had become infatuated, achingly and poignantly, with our new housemate. Charm seemed to have disappeared—I hadn't seen her for a week—and Cleo was clearly the new object of his affection. Salami mooned around outside the front gate at strange hours, hoping to glimpse his new beloved. The lyrics from "Obsesión" took on greater meaning as he passionately belted out *"No es amor, no es amor."* (He dropped the falsetto to appear more masculine.) The exercise machine reappeared outside the church, as Salami ripped off his shirt in the hopes that his naked torso would excite our good-looking tenant.

Salami's performance had the effect of frightening her instead. I couldn't blame Cleo; we had grown accustomed to his clowning, but his fangs and rants were understandably unsettling to a newcomer. Despite our assurances that Salami was *probably* more bark than bite, on her way to work, Cleo cantered past him as fast as she could on her high heels, her alarmed eyes purposefully fixed straight ahead behind dark sunglasses. As she passed, Salami delivered a running commentary on her wardrobe and speculated over what delights lay underneath.

"What a shirt! Look at that, everyone! Mama, you're my lady!" he called out one day as a harried Cleo hugged a shawl over her bare shoulders.

"Look at those pegs! Mama, you make the sunshine dim," Salami pronounced another time. "Don't forget to smile! It won't mess up your hair."

The only time Salami fell silent was when Cleo appeared at the landing with her dogs, which she increasingly made a point of doing. Salami gazed appreciatively, but cautiously, as the huge shepherd stalked past.

The more Cleo ignored Salami, the more he tried to attract her attention. One morning, after he had unsuccessfully tried to provoke a nod with the greeting "Yoo-hoo, Mama! Take me with you!" he desperately intercepted me as I headed toward El Floridita to fetch the usual rounds of coffee. His hands shook, and his eyes had a disturbing gleam that made me suspect he was high.

"Mama, I gotta talk to you."

"Later, Salami."

He quickened his pace to mine and leaned in, insistent. "This is important. Your friend is gorgeous."

"Yes."

"Do I have a chance with her?"

I considered sugar-coating it for a moment, but what was the point of lying?

"You're not her type."

"She doesn't like black men?"

"No, it's not that."

His brow furrowed with thought. "I'm too short?"

"No, Salami. It's, uh, you know, the crack."

His face took on a relieved expression, and the bare gums flashed in a smile. "You tell her I'm gonna make good. Tell her I'm cleaning up my act. Please. Pretty please."

I tried changing the subject. I asked Salami about Charm. She hadn't been on the street lately. Was she in jail?

"What's it to you?" He turned from cajoling to threatening. "You keep out of my life."

Shortly after Cleo moved in, John and I came upon a weedy empty lot while walking our dog. There, a dozen feral cats in assorted degrees of mange munched on rats and discarded fish heads. These survivors were normally shifty, so I was surprised when a longhaired tabby rubbed against our calves. Judging from her trusting nature and glossy coat, this animal hadn't been on the street for long, and we figured she was probably someone's pet that had lost its way. The cat seemed to think that it had found it again when we took off, following us the seven blocks home. It shadowed us up the stairs, meowing insistently as I took out my keys.

"Why not?" I said to John.

"Why not? We have a dog. Cleo has two. Our house is a mess."

As I opened the door, the cat resolved the issue by slithering past. John tried to catch her, but the wily creature got away. She jumped onto a box in the living room and began licking her paw. That was that.

We named the cat Siber, at the prompting of a Russian friend, Gees, who insisted that she was a Siberian breed rarely seen west of the Ural Mountains. Clarence the super dubbed her "Trouble." True enough, she spread fleas and kept us up all night by sprawling on our pillows. Instead of ridding the house of vermin, Siber dragged live mice and cockroaches into the building, only to let them go after growing bored with batting them around. Siber got stuck on our terrace and stranded in trees. She fell into the cesspool cellar of the corner apartment building, to the great amusement of Penknife. We grew accustomed to knocks on the door by Clarence to alert us of new mishaps. Meanwhile, Khaya suffered from an intense attack of jealousy, and this perfectly house-trained dog now marked his territory everywhere throughout our new house. I wouldn't hear of letting Siber go, however. The cat fulfilled some deep emotional need, though at first I couldn't pinpoint what it was. I fretted excessively over every matted hair. Then it struck me one day as I cradled the mewing animal after her latest terrified escapade on the roof. She was my substitute baby.

Cleo's dogs didn't share my appreciation for Siber. Their months on Moscow's hungry streets had refined all instincts to hunt. At the slightest whiff of cat, they'd bound down the stairs, dragging Cleo as though on a sled.

One morning I awoke to what sounded like a murder under way. *"¡Van a matarle!"* ("They're going to kill him!") a man's voice shrieked. I threw on a robe and bounded downstairs to the corridor, where Raul pressed against the wall, hand over his opened mouth.

He looked on in shock as Cleo's two dogs leaped onto John's chest, baying for the blood soaking his hair. John's hands were above his head as he kicked at the dogs and shouted at Cleo to control the curs.

Cleo was frozen like a statue, her hands extended as though she were still holding the dropped leashes. Her lips didn't move.

"¡Ayúdanos, señora!" ("Help us, lady!") Raul screamed. "They are going to kill us all!"

I threw myself upon the dogs and tried to pull the little one off John by grabbing her waist. It was like wrestling a hairy anaconda, but I managed to pin her down by stepping on her tail, while she screeched in protest. The shepherd then promptly sat and began chewing his foot.

Raul gaped at me, horrified. I looked down and realized that my bathrobe had opened. The sight of my naked body jolted Cleo back to action, and she took hold of the leads from the floor. "Damned cat," she snarled, dragging the dogs upstairs.

"Speaking of which, where is the damned cat?" I asked.

"On my head, dummy," John said.

I looked up. "On" was not quite the operative word. "In" would have been more appropriate; Siber's sharp talons were embedded in John's scalp and he was having difficulty extracting her without ripping more flesh.

"I got her out of the dogs' reach, but she extended her claws to fight them off," John said with gritted teeth as he succeeded in lowering the animal to the ground. He stuck a hand onto his crimson crown and winced.

Back on terra firma, Siber straightened her back and yawned, without an appreciative look at her savior. She calmly licked a bloodied

paw and smoothed down some errant hairs by her ear. Then she ambled off to the garden, bushy tail whisking back and forth, and plunked
down to sun herself by the rhododendron bush.

I heard a ferocious bark in the distance. Was that Khaya? Where
was he? He had been absent during the fracas. I found the *mitad lobo*
lying on his back in the kitchen with his legs in the air like a yogi, oblivious to the pandemonium. His gorgeous eyes were closed in beatific
meditation.

John refused to go to the hospital, even after I steered him to the
bathroom mirror to study the Red Sea on his head. "It's just a scratch,"
he said, dabbing the three-inch gash with a towel. John relented only
when Boris the painter complained about the crimson droplets that
speckled a newly minted wall. John came back from the hospital six
hours later, cleanly sewn up with five stitches but complaining about
the American health care system. ("A six-hour wait just for a few
stitches. What inefficiency. And you have to pay!")

Thereafter we established a strict routine, whereby Cleo would
telephone or yell before descending with her pets. We then dashed
around the house to find Siber and held the squirming cat until the
barking procession returned from relieving their bladders. For the
time being, Siber was safe.

Chapter 17

THE MEN FROM MONTENEGRO

We didn't feel our house was safe, though, as water dripped through the rotten sills of our nineteen windows. Aside from the leaks, there was also the noise from outside. Salami stationed himself in front of the window, shouting, "Anyone home?" whenever he knew we were there. He repeated this hilarious "joke" every few minutes just to torment us. What with his jarring chorus and the unremitting merengue and shouts of drug traders, we were going mad.

As we contemplated the repair of the windows, John suggested that we retain as much as possible of the original glass-and-wooden frames. "These are the real McCoy," he said, running his hand over the antique rope pulleys and metal weights. Indeed, they were lovely, in a frayed sort of way. How-

ever, a cursory inspection revealed that most of the cracked glass would
have to be replaced. Besides, double-paned windows would keep out
the din better. As for the wooden frames, Manuel offered to strip the
six layers of paint to see what could be salvaged. But after his heat gun
seared off a large chunk of wood, we sadly accepted that these, too,
would have to go.

Now we knew enough to solicit several bids. A couple of phone calls
to distributors revealed that the cost of ordering windows from an established company like Andersen was prohibitive, as none of our windows measured standard sizes. To make matters worse, no two were
alike, jacking up the cost even more.

This meant that we had to go with ugly aluminum-and-plastic
frames that slide and click to open. After a random scan of the Yellow
Pages, we interviewed a weedy fellow who fished from his briefcase a
small model window a foot high. He acrobatically flipped and flapped
panes to show their insulating capacity, until his pinkie got trapped in
his display model. The salesman moaned as he tried to pry the digit
out. This only made it stick more. Blood dripped between the tiny
panes.

John read the directions that came with the kit. With a nifty twist of
pliers, he freed the finger and guided its owner out the door.

He turned to me. "Let's seek references next time."

The next candidates were a refreshingly masculine team from the
former Yugoslavia that a friend of my mother's had recommended.
John dubbed the trio the "Men from Montenegro." With grim "I've
seen things no man should talk about" eyes that reminded us of Russian mobsters, the men arrived uniquely dressed for workmen. They
were kitted out in Eastern European chic—black turtlenecks, leather
jackets, and slicked-back hair. We spotted no visible dust on their tas-
seled loafers, or signs of perspiration, despite their heavy apparel in
the summer heat. John harbored doubts about their work-worthiness,
but I was reassured by the references from a major hotel chain. I also
liked their offer to complete the job in two weeks, and to throw in the
last two windows for free.

The dapper trio briskly marched from room to room, speaking in
clipped Serbo-Croatian as the foreman took measurements with a
stainless-steel tape. After a mere half an hour, he came down to the

kitchen and barked the price in a voice that brought to mind Slobodan Milosevic.

John and looked I at each other. The quote was suspiciously reasonable.

"We can't go wrong," I insisted.

John disagreed. He felt uneasy about the workmen's proposal for the kitchen, which currently had two slim frosted windows that blocked the leafy scene outside. We wanted to gaze out at our estate while eating, so the Men from Montenegro suggested cutting out half of the back wall to install a single picture window. This would involve demolishing the two columns in the middle, in order to carve a rectangle measuring five by eight feet.

Aesthetically we loved the idea. John, however, possessed doubts about its structural viability. He pointed to the water-soaked ceiling and pulled out a splintered piece of windowsill as evidence. "It's just fragile wood adhered to fragile bricks. The wall might collapse."

"No problem, no problem," the natty foreman insisted. "The wall and aluminum frame will support it."

"The wall will probably collapse," my husband insisted pleasantly.

The foreman surveyed John with pitying condescension. "My dear mister. I do this all the time. The frame is as strong as iron. No problem."

John waved me into the dining room and we conferred.

"I don't think this guy knows what he's doing."

I, however, with customary impatience, wanted to move forward immediately.

"These guys handle the Sheraton Hotel, John. They're not jokers."

"Judith, I feel uneasy about this."

"Relax. They're pros."

My steamroller persuasion prevailed. Or perhaps my husband had grown weary of fighting me. Two weeks later, the Montenegro triad returned with a van full of new windows, carrying them in gingerly without sullying their herringbone jackets. Salami appeared on the scene to offer assistance, but the foreman silenced him with a hardened glance. The trio deftly knocked out the existing windows without shattering them, and then created the frames on the spot. This was done with an elongated bar with a handle, with which they bent the aluminum plates into rectangular frames. After the new frames were inserted, the men squeezed rubbery caulk around the edges with a rocket-shaped gun.

"Jeez, look at this," I gasped, after they finished the top two floors. I had never before imagined how light our house could be. The shimmering glass reflected the sun, where there used to be grime and slime. The walls looked whiter and even the floors shone.

The Men from Montenegro stacked the old wooden beauties outside the house, leaning them against garbage containers. I felt a pang knowing that these pieces of 1888 architectural history would be thrown away with bug-infested mattresses and dirty diapers. Salami was standing watch in the hopes of nabbing some work, and he leaned over to contemplate the resale value. He shook his head angrily.

"You crazy, Mama? This is vintage heritage. You're lucky you're not landmarked. They'd fine you a fortune for throwing these away." He loaded a couple panes on his baby carriage and wheeled them to his lair, muttering, "Rape, they're raping Harlem."

The Men from Montenegro returned inside to work on the piéce de résistance: the kitchen picture window. This was a more complicated job, as it entailed more than simply knocking windows out of the sill. I remained on the stoop, to make sure Salami didn't tamper with the workmen's van.

After an hour, I heard a loud rumble: the unmistakable sound of crashing masonry.

I ran into the kitchen, gaping at where the back wall once stood. It looked as though someone had lobbed a mortar into the back of the house. Layers of brick and cement had crumbled into a two-foot pile of fragments. Dust smoked from the pile. The collapse exposed a gigantic ant nest that would have made an instructive display for a science museum. Hundreds of liberated insects streamed from their tunnels toward an open Oreo bag on the floor.

The Men from Montenegro silently stared at the ants crawling from the wreckage. The foreman glanced at his watch and said something in Serbo-Croatian to the crew. They began packing their gear and brushing powder from their trousers.

"Where are you going?" I boomed in a schoolmistress voice.

"Madam, I must depart. It is two forty-five. We do not work past three P.M. on Fridays," the foreman intoned.

John's eyes bulged. "This is unacceptable. You haven't finished the job."

The foreman disdainfully stamped on an ant with his Italian loafer. "I regret there is nothing we can do. This is our custom. I do not abuse my workmen." Said men shook their heads sadly. They gathered up their jackets, peering inside the sleeves to ensure nothing had crawled inside.

"We will resume respectfully on Monday at ten A.M.," the Milosevic voice said. "I will call first to confirm that you have a new windowsill. I cannot install a window in these conditions. You will have to rebuild the sill."

"You can't just leave like this." John drew himself up to his full six feet, one inch, for greater authority. I feared my husband would become confrontational.

The foreman sighed. "I must go, my friends. I must go." He grew less apologetic as he neared the front door, commanding briskly, "Call a carpenter. I don't want to waste my time on Monday."

The telephone rang just as John slammed the front door behind the Men from Montenegro. Mrs. LaDuke was on the line.

"What happened? Your back wall fell down."

I explained our predicament.

"Take care of those ruffians next door," she warned.

Oh, no. Salami. We had taken down the iron security bars to install the new windows, and there was nothing but air separating any crazy crack addict from the hole that was once our back wall. Salami and his cronies could creep in and invade our house again.

I sprinted out the front door into the dazzling sunlight to check on Salami. Our neighbor was deep in siesta on the stairs of the abandoned house next door, sprawled out like a starfish. His malodorous head rested on the sharp edge of a step, an unlikely pillow for anyone but the profoundly unconscious. I couldn't see his chest move under his sleeveless basketball shirt. Was he alive?

Of course I didn't want Salami to die. However, I was relieved that he was in no state to come charging into the house. Whew—we were safe for now. But perhaps not for long. I ran through various scenarios. It would be perfect if someone would remove Salami from the premises and store him in a safe place until we got a new back wall. What if he woke up too soon?

John and I were not the only agitated souls. Miguel was nervously watching the top of the street. Shifty glances in my direction indicated that he didn't want me around. He made a typically Dominican gesture that I'd seen on the street before—he held his left hand still and waved his pointer finger back and forth. The sign looks vaguely obscene and means: "Stay away. I'm serious." Miguel shook the finger again for special emphasis, and then he tried to steer me from Salami, hooking his arm in mine.

"Salami is tired. He had a long night," Miguel said with an insistent tug. "He'll be fine after he sleeps it off." Miguel saw something, let go of me, and moved away.

I followed his gaze to a police car pulling up. It braked with a lurch, and out walked a cop. I asked him to check on Salami. The officer bent over and felt Salami's pulse.

"He might have had an overdose," I said. "Shouldn't we call an ambulance?" I held my breath.

Salami expelled some foul air and said, "Doughnuts." This reassured the officer. "Nah, he's okay. But call if he doesn't wake up tomorrow."

The notion that Salami might awaken prematurely made me so anxious that I kept running to the front of the house to check on him, much to the irritation of Miguel, who was still awaiting a connection by the curb. While I scurried about and John called Manuel, John sprayed glass cleaner on the ants, which by now were venturing into the living room. John made good progress drowning the wriggling black lines before they reached a hole in the floor that led to the basement, but a few broke through his chemical barricade.

The drama flooding through the telephone line energized Manuel, who agreed to drop the job he was working on in Brooklyn and come to our aid. "It's a matter of life and death. These people could be murdered in their sleep!" I heard him tell the unfortunate woman whose bathroom he was tiling. "I must go to Harlem!"

At this moment there was an insistent knock on the door. Perhaps it was the Men from Montenegro, now repentant? A medic coming to carry Salami away? Or maybe it was, please no, Salami.

The steady smile of Mackenzie, the Latin-quoting homeless man, met me at the door. His reading glasses were missing a lens. He held out a thick hardcover book.

"Catullus. I heartily recommend this translation. It's more elegant than most."

I looked at the volume of Roman verse. The book was still in its crisp jacket.

"Uh, thanks," I said, noticing from the corner of my eye a new marching battalion of ants. "Er, this is not a good time."

"Say, do you have any Dashiell Hammett? I like those old-fashioned detective books. I imagine him with the hat."

"Oh, yeah," I said absently, moving toward the ants and squishing a formation with my boot. "Try the hallway. Boxes are there."

Mackenzie peered into the kitchen and came out. "Hey, man. Sorry about your wall. Looks like a mess. What's in the boxes?"

I described the Marxist trove that the previous owner had left behind. Mackenzie smiled mockingly.

"Ah, the classics. I read all that when I studied sociology at UCLA. It was the sixties and we were all into social revolt. That stuff gives me a headache now."

He chattered on, oblivious to my mounting distress. "Mind you, I'll read anything. When I was in state prison in Jessup, oh man, I tore up the books. Books saved me from going crazy. I read more books than anyone who had ever stayed there. Three to four a week. There are horrible jails, and then there are jails where the time passes fast because there's no stress. My first jail had a great library. When I went upstate to Cape Vincent—that was my third jail—they gave me an intelligence test. I scored so high that the lieutenant said, 'What the hell are you doing here?' I told him, 'There's a first time for everything.' "

Mackenzie sighed as he rummaged through the complete works of Karl Marx. While he reacquainted himself with dialectical materialism, a clunk that sounded like a grown man falling resounded from the kitchen.

I not so gently ended our salon. "Mackenzie, I'm sort of busy right now. Take the books. We'll talk later."

He looked disdainfully at me. "You white folks, always looking at your watches. People in Harlem take things slow."

This was not the moment for a discussion on Harlem's inner Zen. I led Mackenzie to the door, resisting the urge to glance at my watch. He barely looked up as he made his way out. "I'll be back for that Hammett."

An hour later Manuel appeared and promptly began taking measurements to clean up the mess. As he pushed wedges of rotten windowsill into the garden, John pointed out a minor problem: We still lacked security bars. He went to the hardware shop and brought back a huge tarp of blue plastic sheeting, the type the United Nations uses to provide emergency shelter for refugees. John's plan was to hang it over the hole in the wall to deter would-be invaders and keep out the rain.

"Just like Burundi. It will make you feel at home," John joked.

I'd seen hundreds of these tarps and knew just how flimsy they were. "This isn't going to keep Salami out."

"What else can I do? If it makes you happier, I'll sleep downstairs with Khaya and a metal bar."

I eyed him dully. "That won't protect us."

"It did in South Africa, crime capital of the world. Remember how Khaya scared those burglars? They wouldn't come over the wall."

"Salami knows Khaya's a wimp."

As we debated the dog's merits as a security guard, Manuel went to buy supplies and promised to come back early the next morning. I crept up to bed, and then out of it four times to check on Salami, opening the front door a crack. He continued to slumber peacefully on his front steps, unaware of his chance to reclaim our house. I went upstairs and lay down on my bed, fully clothed and with a Swiss Army knife by my side. Eventually, I feel asleep.

I would have stayed awake if I had known that John was in no shape to provide resistance, even with an iron bar and dog. Before retiring, John had made a foray to Mercedes's bodega for provisions and then fell deeply asleep on the dead woman's mattress in the living room. His slumber was aided by lots of Budweiser, lethal stuff after not eating all day. John was snoring so loudly that he wouldn't have noticed if a platoon of crazed addicts tromped in.

I jolted awoke at 8 A.M. with a dream that our illustrious neighbor had made himself at home in the kitchen and was frying an English breakfast.

"Hey, Mama, want some scrambled eggs?" The nightmare Salami leered from our Chambers stove, wearing a white chef's jacket.

Fully conscious, I crept downstairs with pounding heart, half expecting to find a machete embedded in John's skull. Instead, he was cementing bricks while Manuel sawed a plank of treated wood for the windowsill. By lunchtime, a new wall had risen from the ashes, with a perfect rectangle for the picture window.

We had a wall, but still a big hole, and I wanted to be fully confident that Salami wouldn't creep in. I peeked out the front door, and with great satisfaction saw that the next-door steps were empty. But then I heard a shriek, akin to the delighted fear of a child on a Ferris wheel. Salami barreled down the hill on his blue baby stroller, knees raised up to his shoulders, hanging on to the back frame with his hands. I spotted the white flash of his remaining teeth as he raced past.

We admired the handiwork as we ate lunch that Saturday. Manuel seemed satisfied and I was over the moon. Still, something troubled John. He peered at a section of Sheetrock on the wall adjoining the window. "I'm just going to take this away," John said, peeling back a section with a knife. He frowned, and cut some more.

After an agitated night, I needed a break. I ventured out to scout for tiles to replace the ones that the plumbers had smashed. Manuel had recommended a supplier downtown that specialized in 1940s ceramics. When I returned four hours later, the kitchen as I had known it was gone. The floor, the ceiling, and the Sheetrock walls had all vanished.

Manuel stood on the precipice of the room, surveying the gigantic hole. Meanwhile, John crouched against the bare wall that adjoined Salami's house, spraying window cleaner on a huge tunnel of writhing, slimy insects.

"Termites," he said glumly.

I wasn't sure which was making me feel more nauseated, the recoiling vermin or the splintered piece of my house that Manuel held up as a sad offering.

"We had to do it," Manuel said, in the sympathetic but firm tone of a doctor explaining an emergency amputation. I was so merged with the house that I felt the surgery keenly.

Manuel explained that the men pursued John's suspicion that the kitchen was rotten from water damage. They ripped out the basement ceiling to find that the insects had chewed up the joists and beams to the consistency of sawdust.

While they worked, the men exiled Khaya to the garden so that he didn't fall through the abyss that was once the floor. The dog howled in protest, primordial, pained cries evoking a lonely wolf on the frozen steppes.

The phone rang. It was Mrs. LaDuke. "What on earth happened to the animal? He's braying like a banshee."

I filled her in, and joined Manuel at the edge of the chasm. He avoided my watering eyes. "New floor," he mumbled. "I'll give you a good price."

A kitchen floor is priceless. I waved "Whatever," and Manuel hopped into his van and screeched off to Home Depot for supplies. By Sunday night, the kitchen once again had a floor and walls.

The Men from Montenegro called on Monday before coming up. They had left precise instructions: They needed an opening this wide, that high. I gathered that they were skeptical that we could meet their exacting standards.

"Madam, I hope you're not wasting my time," the foreman said with a chilly Balkans inflection. The crew entered slowly, cradling the plates of glass between them. I held my breath as they slotted the pane in. It fit perfectly. They screwed a couple screws, caulked the cracks, and wished us a good morning—all before finishing their coffees.

Now that we had a restored kitchen, it was time to end the urban camping trip. Our Russian furniture had finally arrived in New York and we called the movers to deliver it to our house. This was great! We could get settled at last and begin thinking about proper jobs. We paced throughout the house, debating where to put our three thousand books. We couldn't wait!

This excitement about unpacking was a novelty for me. In my past unchained existence abroad, I actually liked it when the movers placed my belongings in cardboard boxes and took them away. Life felt purer with only a couple of changes of clothing. Who needed all those paintings and pots? I felt lighter, although admittedly somewhat inconvenienced, living out of a single suitcase. In my previous incarnation abroad, I would feel a sense of regret as the moving truck pulled up with all my belongings, and the accompanying heavy responsibilities of bills and real life and laundry.

Now in New York, though, I felt differently. I wanted our belongings so badly that it hurt. Who knew that I could crave a chair this way? The longing was almost physical. Our house felt too empty and I was desperate to unfurl the Dagestani rugs on the floors, marking them as our own.

Someone else was excited about our move. As the moving truck pulled up, Salami stood at the curb and made circling gestures to help the driver park. He then planted himself at the gate and offered to help the men carry our 156 cardboard boxes from the vehicle to the front steps. He meticulously counted every carton aloud, telling the movers, "I'm real strong. I won't drop anything." Salami wouldn't budge when I asked him to.

"What, are you scared I'm gonna rob you?" he challenged.

In fact, I was, although I wasn't going to admit it to him. It occurred to me that maybe Salami hadn't burgled us before because he knew we didn't have anything to steal. Now we had 156 boxes' worth of stuff. Would our security situation change now that we had a microwave? Salami wasn't reassuring me, as he counted the boxes and uttered, "One hundred and fifty-six," with a greedy expression. As my chest tightened with alarm, I tried to remember the breathing exercises Manuel the meditation master had taught me.

Distraction came in the form of Clarence, who ambled over to join us after watching bemusedly from across the street. As ever, he was eager to share his views. "Why you people need so much stuff? What's all that, clothes or something?" He tossed a cigarette butt close to a cardboard box marked BOOKS.

When the moving men dumped the last carton in the living room, I managed to shut the door on Salami. John and I pounced on the pile with a box cutter and sliced yards of tape open. After a mere twelve boxes, I wanted to close them up again.

This confirmed it. We were living in a sitcom, albeit a crummy one. It looked as if we had just thrown all our belongings at each other. Nearly everything that could be broken was. Shards of poster glass and Hungarian plates jutted angrily from the supposedly protective paper balls. Statuettes from the Ivory Coast had lost noses. A mask was impaled on the remains of a bowl. Only stems remained of hand-blown Mexican goblets.

Worst of all was the damage to the long yellow table, our precious talisman that we had dragged around the world. Its legs were splayed like a fallen racehorse, the middle section fractured.

I felt like stabbing someone with the box cutter. How could they do this to us, and why of all moves, this one? I had moved countries eight times before, and not even a mug handle had chipped. Leave it to the corrupt Muscovites. Our bribe must have been too small. The table had carried a lot of weight before. How could anyone break it without jumping up and down on it? John's first theory was that the Russian movers who packed our belongings in Moscow were drunk, entirely plausible considering the smell of vodka that had accompanied them. Then he recalled that the men were on leave from a paramilitary unit in Chechnya notorious for abusing civilians. That must be it: They had turned their aggression against our furniture.

Despite the lack of a serviceable table to dine on, the next week we decided to hold a housewarming party with the surviving crockery, filling in the shortfall with plastic cups. The party would double as a farewell for Cleo, who had finally bought her own Brooklyn apartment. In good pioneer style, we planned to sit on cartons in lieu of chairs. As we still lacked a kitchen sink downstairs, we washed lettuce with the garden hose. We hung glass lanterns with candles, less for romantic atmosphere than because we didn't trust Alex's electrical work.

Ever since we had returned to New York we had tried to persuade particular friends to visit. Yet even people who had lived through the siege of Sarajevo were frightened; their image of Harlem hadn't advanced since the 1977 looting. The anxiety was color-blind; two seasoned black reporters who had seen terrible things in Africa refused to take the subway here. To accommodate our party guests, we scheduled the start of the roof-raising party well before sundown. However, this did not stop most of them from taking taxis rather than the subway, and arriving with excuses that they'd have to leave early.

Here at the house, John reconstructed the smashed table by hammering in metal supports. I was ready to shout, *"Poyekhali!"* again.

As the guests arrived in their cocktail dresses and fragrant coifs I realized that I had forgotten what perfume smelled like. In fact, I had forgotten how to dress in civilized company. I felt quite chic these days just by taking showers and had lost the art of dressing up. As it was, we still hadn't unpacked our party clothes; I wouldn't even know where to find that little black number that would have been more appropriate for this event, rather than my customary work jeans. At least I had cleaned under my fingernails.

The evening was the first in days that it wasn't raining, and a welder put the window bars back on while the party was under way. He and John created fireworks at they powered the soldering machine. The sparks shone among the fireflies. As we sat in the garden, kicking aside CDs and broken bottles thrown from the corner apartment building, we listened to the whine of the machine and hosed down the salad. People busied themselves, imagining where we could plant other buds. It was a lovely evening with a soft breeze, marred only by a carrion smell emanating from Salami's hovel. The visitors made admiring sounds as they paced the square footage of the yard.

"This is bigger than my apartment!" I overheard a friend say.

For this most festive occasion, I decided to cook one of our favorite dishes, prawns drowned in beer. The dish was tasty but, most important, required only two minutes' cooking time—one simply plopped the shrimp in the liquid with some spices and boiled it up. I also put up pots of flavored rice and corn and black beans. A typical Caribbean meal, fitting for our new neighborhood.

As the men put back the window bars, I uncorked more bottles of South African pinotage. Pouring it into plastic cups, I toasted our friends for their patience with us, and John for his equilibrium. They in turn blessed our new home, in Spanish and Serbo-Croatian.

Before we finished, the phone rang. We tried to ignore it, but the ringing continued, urgent peals, seven, eight, nine, and then ten.

I picked up the receiver, and Mrs. LaDuke's contralto flooded through the receiver. Something was wrong. She was sobbing, terribly.

"I'm sorry," she keened. "Our, our new friendship is ruined."

She was weeping so hard that I couldn't make out what she was saying. I looked out across to her garden and saw her pointing frantically at the ground. It occurred to me that she had a prime view of our party. Damn. I should have invited her. How insensitive of me. The poor woman must feel left out. What a stupid way to alienate such a fine woman. It was bad enough we had crackheads next door and dealers in front. Now we had pissed off a neighbor of whom we were extremely fond. What bad manners.

Something else was troubling Mrs. LaDuke, however.

"She's dead. In my garden."

Oh, no, I thought. I imagined Mrs. LaDuke's petite Filipino tenant pruning the pear tree in their collective garden as some drug-addled fiend jumped her. Please, don't let it be true.

Mrs. LaDuke continued. "Tore her throat with his teeth. I recognized the white collar."

White collar? "What are you talking about?"

"My dog killed your cat. She's lying in the garden, poor thing. The welding machine drowned out the noise. The cat tried to jump over the wall but didn't make it. I feel terrible. Please forgive me. Thunder's killed five other cats, but never a friend's."

In the background, someone clinked a knife on a glass lantern to make another speech: "We thought they were crazy, but look what a lovely home they've made."

I steered John into the kitchen, where I whispered the bad news. We agreed it was better not to spoil the party by mentioning it, and stoically sat through the toasts to our allegedly tranquil oasis.

I was surprised by how bereft I felt the following two weeks. I'd feel a stab every time I found little reminders of Siber: a flea on a pillow, a tuft of tawny hair that floated over the wall from Mrs. LaDuke's killing fields. "It was just a cat," I told myself. But her death had revived thoughts of the baby we had lost, the very incident that had inspired us to move here in the first place.

Morbid thoughts descended upon me. I thought about Grandma's undignified purgatory in the garage. I obsessed about the victims of shelling in Angola whom I couldn't get to the hospital in time. When I went to Mom's house, I averted my eyes from my father's pictures. Images of decay intensified when the exterminator found termite nests in the garden. I began listening more attentively when our workmen claimed that the ghost had returned. Raul insisted that the phantom had slapped him in the face.

"A woman. Tall and thin," he said. "She had long fingers like serpents."

With my morose mood came nausea. All food now made me feel sick, except dry pretzels.

"It's probably stress." John stood outside the bathroom one morning as I retched from the smell of coffee.

I wasn't convinced. I rummaged through packing carton number twelve and fished out a small box. I went into the bathroom, pulled out a stick, and peed on it and then watched the line deepen from pink to magenta. I took out another stick, and yet another, to be absolutely sure. The same thing happened. According to the instructions on the box, I didn't need any more proof. I was pregnant.

Chapter 18

CHARMING APARTMENT, WITH DOORMAN

I never knew before that a person could shake from joy. I dashed into the living room, where John was discussing a poorly erected beam with Manuel, and, forgetting all customary decorum, waved the urine-soaked stick at the men.

John did not realize the importance of the moment and glanced over vaguely. "The rubbish is over there," he said and pointed, annoyed. While the trusty carpenter—who had sired quite a few children in his time—shot me a knowingly happy look, I pulled the mystified John toward me and pointed exaggeratedly at my midsection. "Pregnant. Me. Baby."

John came close to shrieking, Dutch style. "That is wonderful!" he said, beaming. Then he bent down and kissed my still-flat belly.

. . .

In the coming days, we shifted emotional roles. John became the effusive one, who, contrary to all caution, informed everyone we knew of the news. I, on the other hand, grew uncharacteristically circumspect. I had an irrational fear that talking about the pregnancy would jinx it. I couldn't believe that I had gotten pregnant so easily, and even less believed that this one would be successful.

Nonetheless, I had enough latent optimism to consult the doctor about proper steps to ensure a safe gestation. This time, I was going to do it right. I'd stay in bed all day, forfeit all sweets, stop swearing, even watch baseball games, if that's what it took.

It was good that I was so preoccupied with the goings-on inside my body. This self-involvement no doubt softened my reaction to some unwelcome changes on the block.

August in West Harlem resembled Paris, in that everyone who could afford to left town, although in this case to visit relatives back in the Dominican Republic. The crowds on Broadway thinned and parking spots miraculously appeared. Mercedes left her bodega in charge of a relative, and it was harder to flag down gypsy cabs, as the Dominican drivers went back to the island. Even the corner ice vendor left during this prime business time.

The exodus, unfortunately, included Miguel.

I stepped outside one morning to collect the newspaper to confront six unsmiling youths leaning on the gate. I had never seen these guys before and they displayed little interest in making my acquaintance. The tallest, whose halolike Afro topped a non-angelic face, was in the process of buttoning up his fly, having deposited his bodily liquids on my *New York Times.* His buddy in the oversize jeans dropped a half-eaten Egg McMuffin atop the soggy, smelly mound.

I was suffering from morning sickness, which in my case also lasted throughout the afternoon and evening as well. The stink of the piss and egg made me retch. So did the full sight of the mess, which I hadn't taken in before. The steps were strewn with chewed orange peels and crack paraphernalia covered the steps—glassine bags, bottle tops, vials with colored tops. I stifled the urge to vomit.

"Who the fuck are you?" I demanded, once I had sucked in my

breath. I was a mother (well, sort of—I was three weeks pregnant). I had to defend my territory. No child of mine was going to grow up with such disrespect on the front steps.

The urinator glanced at me with irritation and put earphones in his diamond-studded ears. The other five guys eyed me dully.

Miguel wouldn't put up with this. Even Penknife wouldn't act like this.

"Where's Miguel?" I demanded.

No answer.

"When is he coming back?"

The tall one shrugged. *"No sé."* ("I don't know.")

"Haw, haw, haw," the urinator guffawed. "She thinks he's coming back."

Wasn't he? Were we back at square one? Please, no. I didn't have the energy to start over again. A wave of nausea hit and I sat down and breathed deeply.

Clarence came over with a broom and a scowl. The youths wouldn't budge, and Clarence cleared his throat loudly as he swept around them. He intentionally moved the broom within an inch of their toes. The urinating one swore, *"¡Vete al carajo!"* ("Go to hell!"), but moved back.

"The summer shift is the worst," Clarence muttered. "The punks go home and send substitutes. Buckle your seat belt. These guys don't care about nothing."

Clarence was right. As the days went on, the disarray on the stoop reached the fetid proportions of when we'd first moved in. Ribs, used condoms, chewed gum, and beer bottles—they were all tossed on the steps. Clarence lugged a giant container of Pine-Sol when he came to clean, in order to wash away the smell of piss. Each time I left the house, I felt nervous. What might these guys do? I was pregnant now. Would they harm us? I wanted Miguel back, amazingly enough.

I probably would have been even more upset, except for the fact that Salami was suddenly gone next door. Out of the blue, without warning, I woke up one morning to find his house sealed up, with plywood on the windows and a formidable metal lock on the door. A big sign proclaimed that the property was for sale, again.

This was unexpected. Actually, it was extraordinary. I'd always imagined that Salami would depart only under extreme duress. I had a vision of armed cops pulling him bellowing down the stairs. But, no. Salami went so quietly that I didn't hear even a "fuck you."

Any sane person would want to get rid of the stinking hulk next door. Not this owner. She mysteriously fired her broker when a prospective buyer met her asking price. Then she went through eight more brokers, raising the price to an exorbitant $450,000. What was she doing? The house *had* to sell. Salami would come bolting back if he got wind of this.

When Willie Kathryn Suggs entered the picture, Clarence said, "That's it. The block's gonna turn."

Suggs was widely known as the doyenne of the Harlem real estate market. Unlike most of the white brokers who recently had discovered Harlem, she had lived in the neighborhood for many years. A woman of considerable savvy, Suggs managed to get quoted in *The New York Times* as the main voice of uptown real estate, and was spectacularly successful in breaking price barriers. Early on in my own house hunt, I gave up looking at her listings because they were so expensive. La Suggs had a reputation for toughness, and few competitors would dare muscle into her turf. Now, seeing her white board with the red cursive script hanging in the window next door, I felt safer than if twenty cops were stationed along the sidewalk with Uzis. If anyone could sell that wreck and keep out Salami, it was Willie Kathryn Suggs.

To make her job easier, we offered Suggs a yellow electrical cord that could extend from our garden into hers. That way, she wouldn't have to rely on flashlights to show the property. As a further sweetener, I offered her prospective buyers use of our bathroom. "We can serve them iced tea, too," I added, anxious to please.

Suggs nodded indulgently, no doubt used to such accommodating treatment. "That," she stated curtly, "would be in your interest."

Sunday after Sunday the property was advertised in *The New York Times* real estate section. People came, sighed, and made offers. They begged. They used our toilet and drank our Earl Grey. But the owner proved too much, even for the formidable Suggs. After a few weeks, her sign came down. The seller had turned down the latest bidder, and like many an agent before her, Willie Kathryn Suggs bowed out.

The house, I feared, would never get sold.

• • •

We had unpacked all of our books, and Mackenzie regularly came around to borrow reading matter. Poor Mackenzie. He was upset that he couldn't get a library card, being a homeless person whose visa had expired.

"It's not right," he complained. "I need books."

Being a well-brought-up man—he was the son of a physician from a "proper family" in Jamaica—Mackenzie felt compelled to give me books in return. Many of his offerings were Roman classics or works of sociology. He particularly enthused about one treatise about race relations, *Color-Blind* by Ellis Cose. ("*Kirkus Reviews* called it 'a positive contribution of the highest order,'" Mackenzie said in his endorsement.) This was more lofty fare than I could handle at the moment, but I invited him in for coffee while he perused our bookshelves.

Before I knew it, we'd established a routine whereby Mackenzie would drop by just as we were having breakfast. We'd offer Mackenzie coffee ("black, two sugars, please"), along with *The New York Times* crossword puzzle. He'd help himself to fruit. Mackenzie was losing teeth—only the front two remained, giving him the appearance of a benign hare—so he asked that we save him the ripest bananas that were easy to chew.

I looked forward to these "kaffeeklatsches," as Mackenzie called them. Like us, he was a news junkie. Unlike us, he had a television, so he could inform us of the latest turn of events. He had managed to pirate cable into his cellar so that he could view the BBC ("I prefer the European take on current affairs"), and he'd furiously ring our bell to alert us about major world developments.

Mom sometimes joined us, with books for Mackenzie. "She's cool," Mackenzie remarked, recalling their first meeting at our front door. "Here I was a raggedy black man coming up behind her as she was struggling with the key. She didn't flinch or anything."

Mackenzie approved of Mom's reading taste as well. One Sunday over brunch they discovered a shared love of the Victorian writer Anthony Trollope. With an ecstatic gleam, Mackenzie put down his untoasted bread and ran out to his cellar. He returned minutes later with a well-preserved edition of *The Small House at Allington*. It was one hundred years old.

Mom's face glowed as she gently handled the volume. "You don't want it?"

"Nah," Mackenzie said nonchalantly. "I'm cleaning out my library. Too much clutter."

He then offered three paperbacks by the British humorist Tom Sharpe. Mom smiled affectionately. "My husband loved these. They're very funny. You sure you don't want them?"

"No," Mackenzie sniffed. "His stuff gets tired after a while. If you read his works in succession you see that they're formulaic."

Mom considered this. "You're right. I'll pass."

As their literary friendship deepened, Mom offered to use her social-worker contacts to help get Mackenzie out of the cellar. "He's such an erudite man. There are agencies that provide housing and jobs," she mused.

After wavering, Mackenzie accepted her offer. However, Mom's research yielded only sad news. Mackenzie's lapsed visa and jail record precluded a placement. Mackenzie took the news stoically, though with misting eyes.

My anxiety about losing the baby deepened with time, despite all signs that it was developing fine. I was almost too scared to hope for a successful outcome, yet had to be pragmatic. Since I was obsessed with creating the perfect conditions for a safe pregnancy, our top priority became wrapping up the messy construction job and removing the last vestiges of toxic lead and chemicals from the window bars and pipes downstairs.

John felt he could finish these final tasks himself. Nonetheless, I was having trouble letting go of Manuel, Raul, and Boris the painter, who by now seemed like family. After months of complaining about the renovation chaos, now I didn't want it to end. The construction had co-cooned us from responsibilities like jobs—and each other. What would it be like to be alone with John in this big house? Until now we had gotten along well, but we were both argumentative by nature, and the presence of others encouraged us to keep up a united public front. Would we suddenly turn on each other, or grow apart? What would we talk about, aside from the pregnancy? I didn't voice my fear to John but sensed that he felt similarly. He tended to avoid being in the same room with me, and stayed up late reading in the kitchen after I had gone to bed. Each morning, he would come up with more chores for Manuel.

The dillydallying came to an abrupt end when I reviewed our checkbook to settle up payments. We had already paid the plumber and the electrician a collective $33,000—quadruple what had been budgeted. Now we learned that the painting job would cost us $18,000. (When I blanched, Boris pointed out that he had used sixty buckets of plaster compound. "That was more than any job I've done," he insisted.)

The maxim among rehabbers is that you end up paying three times the initial estimate, but we did far worse with Manuel. His original quote had been $3,000. We owed him $35,082.94.

That left just $7,000 in our account.

We hastily convened a good-bye party before we ran up more bills, making a final run to El Floridita for coffees and *cubanos.* Talk turned to what came next. We had helped the painters and Manuel find work with other rehabbers in the neighborhood. Raul was harder to place. My sister had a lead about a karate program in Queens, but the employer lost interest when Raul mentioned his jail record.

"What are you going to do?" I asked, anxious for our friend. He was such a great guy, and his kids were so sweet. How was he going to support them? Would he, heaven forbid, turn to selling drugs in desperation? Raul poured himself another Tropicana orange juice and contemplatively inspected the label. He held up his glass, as though to make a toast. "Juice! The muchachos need fluids. I will sell them fresh juice!" Raul went on to explain that he wanted to try to manufacture organic beverages in his tiny kitchen and hawk them on drug-trading corners. He had already scoped out which were the busiest.

I was skeptical, to say the least. Yes, the dealers developed a thirst standing in the sun all day. But surely fruit drinks were an odd sales pitch for men who sold narcotics? I couldn't quite see the dealers going for Raul's exotic concoctions of melon-cucumber, or honey-radish. This was a Fanta and beer crowd, after all.

Raul was a smarter businessman than I gave him credit for, however. In the days to follow, word got out through *Radio Bemba* that vitamins enhanced virility. The muchachos were abuzz the moment Raul pushed his grocery cart onto Amsterdam Avenue with five-gallon jugs. In a scene reminiscent of Moscow food shortages, the dealers were lined up the length of the block. They generated so much demand that even Raul's formidable strength was tested as he blended gallons of citrus in his tiny kitchen and hauled it downstairs to the street.

"Business sure looks good," I commented one day, taking my place on the queue. On the recommendation of the cocaine dealer in front of me, I ordered a mango-and-carrot medley.

Raul grunted as he lifted another container. "Good? I can make a hundred dollars an hour. That's more than in construction. Hey, gimme a hand with that cup, please. That's it, don't drop it."

While Raul watered the dealers, John finished installing the kitchens in our apartment and the basement.

It was time to look for tenants. We approached this venture with foreboding. Who could forget the story of the house next door? Its decline began, legend went, with villainous lodgers. The pioneer grapevine shook with cautionary tales of tenants who wouldn't pay rent and then won squatting rights.

"You can always replace a beam. Not a bad tenant," warned Mrs. LaDuke.

After one week of advertising with a real estate broker, we began to understand why our neighbors had settled for unsavory tenants. West Harlem still had a rough reputation and was a such a hard sell, that real estate agents tended to list it as the Upper West Side, which was a good fifty blocks south. Our agent sneakily called the area "H. Heights," in the hopes that callers would think it was the more affluent and whiter Hudson Heights.

"That's unethical," I protested, when I saw the ad.

"We're not lying." She snatched the newspaper from me as though that would remove my objections. "You have to lure them in. Otherwise, no one will come."

Her ruse didn't work. Nor did our assumption that our low rents would attract students from the two nearby colleges. City College, two blocks away, wasn't an option, as most students commuted from lower-rent areas elsewhere. As for Columbia University, the broker said it had deemed our neighborhood too dangerous to recommend.

Not to be deterred, she advised us to set an even more ridiculously low rent, and advertise an open house. Her reasoning was that the pack mentality would encourage a competitive frenzy that would drive at least one person to impulsively sign a lease, much as I had when I bid on our house.

It seemed like a good idea. Even if it wasn't, we didn't have others. We swept the street from the top of the hill down to Broadway, filling three contractor bags full of rubbish, to give the illusion that this was a "clean" block. We vacuumed the tenants' quarters, all the while dreaming of signed checks. I had a mental image of sliding my ATM card and hundred-dollar bills zipping out. We set up pots of orange marigolds on the back terrace, wiped down the exposed pipes in the basement, and placed an antique beveled mirror on the fireplace mantel. It actually looked homey.

Then we sat on the stoop and waited for the house-hunting hordes to arrive. Weather was on our side, a sunny sparkle with a soft breeze. We timed the open house for 10 A.M., before drug dealing began. The real estate agent was puzzled. "Why so early?" We just said that we had things to do. We didn't want to scare her off, too.

Precisely at 9:55 A.M., Salami appeared next door, out of nowhere, with furniture piled on a dolly. We hadn't seen him since he had been evicted. Why did he choose this, of all times, to return? Salami tested the lock of his old home, realized he couldn't pick this one, and then busily installed a "living room" on the front yard, complete with an Oriental-style carpet and couch. For an added touch he set up a standing lamp and swivel chair. I groaned.

As soon as Salami spotted attractive white women clasping real estate ads heading toward us, he jumped out of his chair and leaned on the gate. He had put on a Greek fisherman's cap, which he fancied made him look more like a doorman. "Come in, ladies, come in," he said, ogling them.

Our erstwhile neighbor played doorman as twenty-four prospective tenants filed through our gate. He introduced himself with a bow. "Salami, local crackologist."

We couldn't persuade him to leave. Not even with promises of money.

"What, are you racist?" Salami challenged.

How could this be happening? Was I stuck in a horror movie that continually rewound? We couldn't allow Salami to sabotage our tenant search. I called the police and reported a trespasser. "He looks crazy," I noted.

When the officers came by to check, they simply laughed through the open car window at the sight of Salami. He was stretched out on his lounge as a tremulous blonde sprinted past. "That guy is too much!" chuckled one enforcer of the peace.

After that debacle, we lowered the offered rent yet again. It didn't help. People telephoned, visited, and then didn't call back. Finally, finally, we thought we were in luck with a white couple who seemed promising—middle-aged, good credit, jobs. The real estate agent was convinced that we had a shoo-in. "They know the house and *love* it," she bubbled over the phone.

When the middle-aged white couple came to the door, the man looked oddly familiar and I welcomed him with my most radiant smile. The goodwill didn't seem to be mutual, though, and for some reason the couple remained rooted on the threshold. The broker was oblivious to their bristling, and while the husband kept his hand on the door handle she mouthed behind his back, "They love it."

Apparently, they loved it too much.

"This was *our* house," the male hissed hoarsely, spraying saliva. "*We* wanted to buy this house, and she, that woman"—he pointed at me, jabbing the air with a chewed fingernail—"outbid us."

His wife glared at me. Even the real estate agent looked affronted.

"These people stole our house," the male continued, pulling his wife's arm. "Let's go, honey."

The agent turned to me, looking defeated and ever so suspicious. "I don't know what else to do. I don't have any more clients."

We went the route of the desperate, listing the apartment in a dubious free-ad publication. After two weeks we finally got a call. One call. It was from a pair of aspiring teenage actors. Aidan and his brunet boyfriend were hauntingly pretty boys. But despite their physical charms, they were not the sort of people one would want to depend on for income: nineteen-year-olds away from home for the first time, dismal credit rating, no discernible income, and a fragile romance. "We've been together two weeks," blond Aidan said, nuzzling the other's neck. The whiff of untrustworthiness was as strong as their patchouli oil.

Of course, we took them.

The house felt safer now that we had tenants. All the comings and goings—and there were quite a lot; these boys had an active social life—would discourage even the most tenacious burglar. In any case, Miguel returned from his vacation looking rested, and his normal crew of muchachos was back, too. The steps were clean again. What a relief! As for Salami, amazingly, our downstairs actors didn't seem to mind him at all. They even amiably chatted with him by the gate from time to time.

On one of those occasions, Salami broke from his conversation to grab my arm.

"Mama, it's my birthday. You got anything for me?"

My face must have betrayed my skepticism.

"Seriously, Mama. It's today, September sixth. I'm thirty-nine."

"No way. You can't be that old."

"I am," Salami insisted gravely. "Cross my heart and hope to die." He made a cross sign in front of his face.

He seemed so earnest. Why not? I pulled ten dollars from my jeans pocket. Salami grabbed the bills and kissed them. "Thank you, thank you!" This provoked hoots of derision from the steps next door, where the muchachos had been watching avidly. "Did you see that?" Penknife howled. "*La carpintera* gave him money!"

I fixed my eyes on Salami. "You look great. What's the secret?"

Salami puffed up his chest and flexed those formidable biceps. "Drugs keep me young, Mama. I'm well preserved."

He danced some steps, wiggling his lopsided hips, and then swung around to face me with a belligerent face. "Mama, thanks for the present. But I got an issue with you. I heard you been telling people that I soup. I want to make clear: Salami doesn't soup."

What was he talking about? "Okay, you don't soup. Got it."

I crossed the street before Salami's mood could turn even uglier. Clarence was at his sentry post.

"Clarence, what's souping?"

"Darned if I know. Why you ask, girl?"

"Salami said something about it."

Clarence practically spat. "Salami? What you doing, making friends with Salami? I saw you give him money. Don't you have a brain? Now you never gonna get rid of him. He's gonna tell you it's his birthday every day."

Sure enough, Salami was standing outside the gate when I opened the door the next day. I took in his stale smell as I tried to wiggle past. "Mama, I want you to know I appreciate what you did. I was starving. I used to think you were evil. You're okay."

"Thanks."

"Mama, I won't forget you."

"That's okay, Salami."

"Really, Mama. I'll make it up to you."

"Really, it's nothing." I moved away.

He climbed on the gate and swung on it, calling out: "Mama, I'll make good. Just you wait."

Chapter 19

STATE OF EMERGENCY

S alami's words "Just you wait" had an ominous ring that set off a burning release of acid in my stomach. What exactly did he mean by "make good"? Could this positively phrased remark be even worse than a threat? I hoped it didn't imply that Salami would forever hang on the gate like a nasty limpet.

The tempo of my worries sped up with the omnipresent merengue. This type of music is akin to salsa injected with speed and it has a manic effect on most people, especially high-strung neurotics like myself. The music never stopped in October, which was one big party: It looked like the New York Yankees would meet their city rivals, the Mets, in the World Series. I might explain that baseball is the national sport of

Dominicans, and West Harlem was Yankees turf. The team had a profusion of Dominican talent and the stadium was within walking distance of my block. Signs hung on cars proclaiming, METS FANS NOT WELCOMED. I once saw Penknife smack a guy for suggesting that the rival team might win. I didn't care either way, but having grown up in Queens, I would have supported the Mets by default. This was not to be broadcast, however.

We got into the local spirit and bought a television to watch the Series. Each victory by the Yankees brought a night of frenetic street celebration, and sleep was utterly impossible after the team ultimately won the World Series. Everyone who could be was out rejoicing, even the paraplegics in wheelchairs and small children who would normally have been long asleep. They could be forgiven for *haciendo la bulla*, cranking up the Luis Vargas, and honking car horns.

As I lay awake that night worrying about money, the music punctuated my calculations of how long our savings would last. We were down to our last $3,000, and I subtracted what we still owed people in time to the thumping 2/4 beat. As the percussion hit the downbeat, I'd remind myself that we didn't have jobs. For all we knew, I thought, as the clamor rose, we might have difficulties getting work.

John had built desks for us so that we could polish our résumés. The red oak had an arresting grain, and John perfectly fashioned the furniture for our individual heights. I had never before worked at a desk that fit me so precisely, and I felt all set to go. Except for one small problem. Despite the nice linen paper on which we printed the mailed-out CVs, we failed to find gainful employment. Our grand plan for New York had been based on the dot-com boom, in which newspapers and startups hungered for seasoned writers. "We'll get jobs just like that," I had reassured John before we left Moscow, holding up the pages of editing/publishing/content positions advertised in *The New York Times*.

Things had changed enormously since then, however. Nasdaq had collapsed, bringing down with it advertising and jobs. Now companies were firing instead of hiring.

We had an added problem. What I thought would be a routine visit to the obstetrician revealed that my innards had been so scarred by assorted Russian and African medical procedures that I risked losing our baby if I stood upright. Starting in a few months' time, I would have to remain in bed, lying flat except to go to the bathroom or to checkups.

This discovery punctured the other facet of our Grand Plan: that John would leisurely figure out what he wanted to do with the rest of his life while I put on my suit—the one with the expanding waistband to accommodate a growing baby—and charged out into the world to replenish our bank account. Our assumption had been that I would find work more easily since I was American and English was my native language. Now I was soon to be flat on my back and John had to find something immediately.

In between sanding desk legs, we made the rounds with the few colleagues whom we knew here. Neither of us had ever worked in the United States before, so we didn't have a wealth of American contacts to draw on. The handful of people we called delivered the same dark news: sackings, buyouts, early retirement, pink slips.

After one particularly depressing lunch with a colleague at *The Wall Street Journal,* where we heard about yet more hiring freezes, I suggested that we cheer ourselves by visiting the top of the World Trade Center. The sterility of the endless lobby made us feel insignificant, and I figured that going thirteen hundred feet in the sky might give us a sense of power. Ah, a respite from life's worries! Ears popped as the elevator climbed 107 floors, and we rode the escalators and walked onto the swaying platform with a dizzying sense of disorientation. Out on the observation deck we gazed at a tiny metropolis a quarter of a mile below and felt detached from earth and its complications. (The sense of an out-of-body experience was helped, no doubt, by my single glass of red wine, prescribed by the doctor for cramps, at lunch.) I had been going to the Twin Towers ever since they had been built in the early 1970s, but this was the most perfect view I'd had yet, a clear vista over the harbor and silver water beyond. We located the rectangular green of Central Park and then traced the air to the general location of our house.

"These are some formidable buildings." John leaned on the railing to contemplate the distance to ground level. In my pregnant state I wasn't taking any chances and steered my husband forcefully to the elevator, and then down to the safer level of a concourse café. Under the soothing influence of lager (for him), I suggested a backup plan. Being journalists, we didn't have many skills besides persuading people to talk and then writing down what they said. But we, meaning John, of course, could always drive a cab while awaiting an opening in his chosen field. As a last resort, he could take the various workmen up on their offers to go into business with him. (They all wanted a "white face" to get contacts and so more business.) Meanwhile, I was fairly certain I could get the odd editing assignment that could be done lying down.

None of these prospects was terribly appealing, but the flush of alcohol convinced us that life wasn't really all that bad, and we jovially gossiped on the subway home. Once there, a long series of calls flashed on the answering machine, most having to do with money owed to various people. Near the end, however, was a message from a colleague from when I had covered OPEC in the 1980s. A senior editing position had opened up at her publishing group, which specialized in covering the oil market. The company was looking for someone to report on Iraq and the United Nations. Would John be interested?

He started a few days later.

The good news was inside the house: John was employed, which would resolve our money worries for now. The bad lay outside, in the backyards.

At six-thirty one morning, as Mrs. LaDuke fed the pigeons, a man sneaked up behind her and smashed a brick onto her well-coiffed head. Tyrus was a lanky, quiet fellow who did odd maintenance jobs for the church next door, such as cutting the overgrown weeds in its back garden when neighbors called the Health Department to complain. Out of pity, we once hired the fellow to lug away bags of shattered Sheetrock.

On the morning of the attack, Tyrus had smoked too much crack, and jumped across the connecting back gardens behind the brownstones. Maybe he thought he was flying. Measuring more than six feet, Tyrus had no trouble swinging his long legs over the four-foot-high chain-link fences. Mrs. LaDuke was startled yet also highly affronted, and wrestled him to the ground while hollering for help. Thunder the cat killer did not spring to her defense—he was inside the house and didn't respond to her calls. To Mrs. LaDuke's rescue came her tiny Filipina tenant, who threw her ninety-six pounds at Tyrus. The two women managed to pin him down on the patio under the pear tree, and called the cops from a cordless telephone.

Mrs. LaDuke was sitting on the brute's chest when the police arrived. "I got him," she told them, shaken but triumphant.

I was sleeping more soundly than usual owing to my pregnancy and didn't hear the commotion. I only learned about the incident the next day from Mr. Anderson, who heard about it from Mrs. Campbell, who heard about it from someone who heard about it from yet someone else. "I'm frightened," a subdued Mrs. Campbell said. The incident unnerved me, too. Had I been deluding myself all these months that the neighborhood was safe? Here I had been worrying about Salami. What other dangers were hidden among us? And what could be done to protect our vulnerable elderly neighbors?

With a racing pulse, I called Mrs. LaDuke to check on her. She sounded rattled and her contralto voice had lost its normal vigor. But she was justifiably proud of her composure under attack. "The nerve!" she said indignantly. "And I had just had my hair done!"

In a role reversal, I began looking out the back window regularly to ensure that Mrs. LaDuke was okay. To my astonishment, she was out in the garden the next day, and the next, bravely pruning her rosebushes for winter. Never fear! I saw the cordless phone within reach, on the patio table.

As we moved into November, the weather grew colder, and the sharp wind sent plastic bags and rogue Mylar balloons snagging on the tall metal gates. With the change of seasons, the sounds of the Mister Softee ice cream truck gave way to the calls of Mexican vendors selling *churros*, the fried dough pastry that goes so well with hot chocolate.

"It's gonna be a bitter winter," Clarence warned. "You're gonna go blind with the cold," he said ominously, pulling his cap down farther over his eyes. The ever-inappropriate Russian coat no longer closed over my swelling midriff. I took inspiration from the street, figuring that the dealers must be on to something as they stood all day in harsh elements without shivering. Yes: I bought a black North Face jacket. This prompted sarcasm from Clarence—"Whaddya trying to do, blend in?"—but I didn't care. The parka kept out the cold, even if the police might think that I had gone over to the dark side.

Physical comfort was first and foremost on my mind, considering the risky nature of this pregnancy. No more the devil-may-care journalist, I was forty-two and had miscarried twice. My previous angst about the house now seemed petty compared to the prospect of losing the baby. The doctor detailed any number of reasons I could miscarry: run-of-the-mill chromosomal defects, Ashkenazic genetic flaws, premature labor, age, overexertion. Even the medical tests to ascertain if the baby was normal were accompanied by a small risk of miscarriage.

Against all odds, by month five our baby was deemed healthy, despite the fact that the image on the ultrasound screen resembled a chicken wing caught in a snowstorm. However, the doctor feared the forces of gravity would prove too much, and ordered me to commence the bed rest. Much to my surprise, and that of everyone else who knew me well, I welcomed the inmobility. During the process of rebuilding the house I had discovered that I was perfectly happy to neglect my brain. Just in case my intellect reawakened, John made regular runs to the video rental shop and left me with a continually refreshed stack of films. The maternal instinct had not yet kicked in, and to offset the boredom of confinement, I found that the more violent and action-packed the movies were, the better.

Surely one reason I didn't mind the imprisonment was that my doctor embraced the European approach to pregnancy—a daily glass of red wine to relax the cramps. This had the effect of relaxing the rest of me as well, and my few sips felt like one long cocktail hour. On a more productive note, I found I could balance my laptop on my growing belly, and took on some freelance editing work that I could do in bed. Before he went to work, John left me a plate of food—healthy stuff like salmon, berries, and romaine leaves—that Khaya would eat while I snuck downstairs to feast on ice cream, making sure to close the window shutters and duck down so that Mrs. LaDuke wouldn't see me. (She had recovered sufficiently from her assault to resume her guardian duties, and phoned every time she peered through her back window and saw me on my feet in the kitchen. "Get back to bed, young lady!" she'd admonish. "I'll tell that husband of yours that you're misbehaving.")

Mrs. LaDuke's concern about the baby's welfare spread to other neighbors, who checked in while John was at the office, bringing fattening food and conversation. I grew expert at waddling to the front window and dropping a key down to visitors waiting below on the street. Then I held court, stretched out on our couch, while my guests regaled me about life on the outside.

Sadly, my strict regimen of bed rest did not deter real estate agents hoping to show us off to nervous potential buyers. Clients had to be reassured that this white couple was truly planning to raise a child in this scary area. ("Really, it will just take a minute," one broker said, pushing past my bulging abdomen as I opened the front door. "Don't trouble yourself—I can make my way inside.") Up the block, Leticia had finally sold her house, to a white couple, no less. The arrival of these additional Caucasians had the effect of attracting even more pale-faced house hunters.

The dealers were far more solicitous to me in my delicate state. Because I was skinny, the pregnancy began to show early on, and I wasn't shy about confirming news of the impending birth, knowing the venerated position mothers generally hold in Latino society. Sure enough, I gained a new level of status among the muchachos, who now graciously helped carry my bags up the stairs and held the gate open on the rare occasions that I left the house. The sight of a belly sticking out like a torpedo was cause for public comment in West Harlem, I found. Strangers exclaimed from across the road: "God bless!" Much to my surprise, the local Don Juans apparently deemed my bloated state attractive now that I had gained nearly half my body weight. They purred, *"Que preciosa,"* as I lumbered by.

Eventually, the chicken wing in the sonograms took on a more human appearance, including, on one visit, an unmistakable set of male genitalia. As I rode home from the doctor, I called Mom, John, and my sister, but no one was there. Wanting to share the news with a human rather than an answering machine, I announced our unborn's gender to Miguel as he held the taxi door open for me. *"¡Un hijo!"* ("A son!") Miguel called excitedly to the street.

Oops, a narcotics dealer was the first to know. This was truly a strange start.

• • •

As the pregnancy advanced I rarely went to community meetings, but the activists kept me apprised of what was going on. They were particularly keyed up over Bernard Kerik, a bulldoggish man who had been named police commissioner in August. On paper Kerik seemed a good ally, and he was more willing to meet with the activists than his predecessor was, though he had a particularly alienating tendency to bark, "I've met with you people more than any other community!" Kerik was a veteran of narcotics undercover work in Upper Manhattan and had pursued cocaine traffickers in Latin America, which seemed to augur well for his getting tough on drug merchants in West Harlem. But this brusque son of a hooker lost friends among the activists by demanding that cops fill out a two-page questionnaire explaining why any person was searched. The policy was supposed to make policemen more accountable, but, not surprisingly, the result was that many did fewer searches to save themselves the extra paperwork.

Nonetheless, the year 2000 would end with some impressive figures for West Harlem: 5,891 drug-related arrests—a 22 percent increase over the previous year. The D.A.'s office crowed about having ten major investigations under way.

"So why are the dealers back on the street after being arrested?" demanded Icilda. She and other frustrated advocates decided that they needed to make a louder stink, and they declared a "state of emergency" to attract public attention.

One of the main firebrands was a young marketing executive with the suitably inflammatory name of Daryl G. Bloodsaw. He pronounced it deliberately, "Blood Saw," for dramatic effect. A Georgia native who had changed his surname from Barnes, Bloodsaw was a tall, smooth man with perfectly draped suits and a special chemistry with older women. Enamored of Harlem's legendary history, he had bought a brownstone on hallowed Sugar Hill. Bloodsaw had some aspirations for political office and wanted to clean up the streets.

Bloodsaw went house to house to mobilize a presence for a February 10 meeting, where organizers would make their proclamation. The campaign had a catchy ring, and even people not normally given to meetings were curious to attend. As it was an "emergency," I left my gestating bed for the evening.

The gathering was held at one of Harlem's less attractive buildings, the drab Public School 153 on 146th Street. Hundreds of women, mostly over forty and Hispanic or black, filled the institutional auditorium that normally was used for school assemblies. Sitting at the dais was our uncomfortable-looking precinct commander, Captain Cody, and various representatives of local government and the D.A.'s office. Bloodsaw opened proceedings with a declaration that West Harlem was under siege.

To the cries of "Right on!" he made his demands:

"Money collected in police stings must be reinvested in the community." ("Yes, sir!")

"Reimpose the loitering law!" (The middle-aged women in the audience jumped up and waved their arms in response.)

"Greater INS and IRS involvement!" ("You tell them!")

"Double the number of police officers!" ("You bet!")

He ended his oratory by evoking the words of James Baldwin: "The fire next time!"

Some of the old ladies unfamiliar with this seminal book on race relations looked discomfited by the mention of flames, but most rose to their feet and cheered. A mike was passed around to lodge complaints. Each time a politician stood to defend his record, the crowd roared back, "That's not enough!" The elected officials slithered out the door as soon as proceedings closed.

Councilman Stan Michels, who was white, was the only politician who followed up. He didn't normally pay a lot of attention to West Harlem, which accounted for a virtual sliver of his large turf. We speculated that Michels was advocating for us in the hopes that we would support his proposal to extend term limits so that he could remain in office longer. Whatever his motivations—sincere shock at the plight of his constituents might have been one of them—Michels fired off a blizzard of letters to City Hall and law-enforcement figures. Among other measures, he called for the attorney general's office to assume more responsibility in prosecuting drug dealers, greater coordination with the IRS and INS, and the seizure of property of landlords who tolerated drug activity. He also adopted one of the activists' pet suggestions: confiscating the cars of questionable out-of-towners.

I was a bit skeptical this would lead to anything. However, Bloodsaw reported that Mayor Rudy Giuliani had called a Town Hall meeting on this subject, the first in this political hinterland in his nearly eight years of office.

I wasn't going to miss this one, either, despite heavy snow. Plodding up to the institutional gloom of P.S. 153, I found dozens of very cold elderly people ankle-high in snow. The doors were shut. The crowd circled a white mayoral aide, who curtly declared, "We'll have to cancel. There's a blizzard warning."

Bloodsaw's elegant form emerged from the cluster, and he put a suede-gloved hand on the aide's arm. "We've come all the way out here in the snow and so can the mayor," Daryl said in his smooth purr. "Surely he's not going to dis these women." The old ladies shivered for extra effect.

Then someone shouted the magic word: "Racist!" and women began hissing, "He's racist, Giuliani's racist."

The aide murmured something into his phone, and then announced to the assembled company that there had been a misunderstanding, not to worry, of course the mayor was on his way. The doors of the school swung open and ushers materialized to briskly escort the old folks to seats. There was so much spillover that people stood in the aisles and in the entranceway. They craned to see the mayor's bald pate as he rushed to the podium surrounded by security men.

A shrewd opportunist, the man who introduced the mayor was Congressman Rangel, whose heartland was central black Harlem and who had snubbed the last meeting. Clearly this one was more politically useful. Flanked by Kerik and other city commissioners, Giuliani sat hunched over, displaying the bored air of a man who felt he was wasting his time.

The meeting reminded me of a Baptist church session without the spiritual goodwill. Giuliani would make a statement, something like, "We're making more arrests," and the chorus would shout back, "Oh, yeah?" Booing erupted when the mayor suggested that residents walk their streets to see the improvement.

"*You* take a walk," the crowd bellowed.

Giuliani shook his head. "Now, now. Let's be polite."

A woman asked if police officers downtown were paid more than in Harlem. "We don't have any quality of life in Harlem, none whatsoever.

Drug dealers are allowed to stand out in front of our houses every day, to practically invade us. Nothing's being done about it."

The mayor looked at her indulgently, like a parent dismissing a child's nightmare as imaginary. I expected him to tell her to drink some milk and go back to bed.

Kerik defended himself. "I have had more of my executive staff meet with this community than any other community since I've been in office. We have more cops up here than we've had in the last three years."

"We need more," someone yelled.

Noting that the 30th Precinct had reported nearly six thousand arrests the previous year, a woman demanded to know why there were still so many dealers on the street. "There seems to be no coordination between police arrests and what happens in court. They are so blatant and bold, it's as if they know the system better than we do."

"You don't want us to just walk up and arrest them?" Kerik asked, as if he were suggesting something outrageous.

"Yes we do!" a man shouted.

Suddenly without warning, the aides briskly collected the microphones. "Time's up," they said, and bodyguards whisked Giuliani out into the snow. Bloodsaw mouthed, "But, but . . ." as the other politicians fled.

There was virtually no media coverage of the meeting, but three days later a small announcement in the newspaper intrigued us. The city's narcotics chief, Charles Kammerdener, was transferred to the NYPD's Housing Bureau. It could only be a demotion, we thought. City Hall insisted that there was no link with the angry Harlem meeting. Nonetheless, General Bloodsaw claimed a minor victory.

Eager to keep up the momentum, the activists decided to court the various candidates who were vying to replace Giuliani in the upcoming November elections. Only one, Comptroller Alan Hevesi, showed any great interest in West Harlem. The activists chose as a venue the minimalist mansion of William, the lawyer I'd met at an earlier meeting, to impress upon the white Hevesi that prosperous white people lived in West Harlem, too. This meticulous example of uptown Soho style exuded money, and other homeowners got a bit distracted from the mission at hand as they inspected the stainless-steel kitchen. Some of the humbler members of the community fidgeted uncomfortably as they followed instructions to take off their shoes by the door. They were even more awed by the chilled Bordeaux and decorative hors d'oeuvres arranged in a flowerlike spread. Mrs. LaDuke, however, was her usual forthcoming self, and planted herself firmly by the cheese board. "Oh, boy, try this," she said, chomping on a creamy Gorgonzola.

Hevesi barely sipped his drink before starting off on the wrong note. He took one look at the expectant black faces, thought, "Amadou Diallo," and launched into an "I came from immigrant roots, too" spiel. Tolerance for immigrants was not something this mainly African-American audience wanted to hear; after all, this was a "check their documents and send 'em home" sort of crowd.

Borrowing a line from Giuliani, someone shouted, "Tour the streets. The drug dealers have overrun us." Hevesi tried to wrap up his speech about immigrant rights, but the chorus "We want the National Guard" drowned him out.

"I had no idea, no idea," Hevesi repeated, looking like he wanted nothing more than to get off those maple floors and see some drug dealers. He left quickly, without finishing his cheese cracker.

The white lawyer got a call the next day. Hevesi had in fact taken a ride around the neighborhood after the meeting and was so dismayed by what he saw that he called Kerik to urge action. "He said he'd do something," Hevesi said. "Really, he did."

Thereafter, Kerik made a point of dropping by the precinct, which seemed to raise morale there. He rode along on narcotics raids. Meanwhile, Robert Morgenthau, the district attorney, assured Councilman Michels that he was seeking increased sentences for recidivist narcotics offenders so that they would be prosecuted to the "fullest extent."

Maybe Bloodsaw was right. Things might be changing.

Then again, I wasn't sure. One day, coming back from a doctor's appointment, I found a muttering woman with shaved head and frenetic eyes sitting on our stoop. She wouldn't budge as I tried to waddle pass. Mindful of Mrs. LaDuke's assault, I clutched my cell phone as I asked the visitor to leave. She didn't like this.

"Who the fuck are you, bitch? I can sit anywhere I want. I'll take a knife and slit your bitch belly open and kill that baby inside." She reached into her pocket. I rushed into the house.

As soon as I began to breathe again, I pondered my options. I didn't think it was worth calling the cops. After all, the woman was obviously high and probably wouldn't even remember what she had said. She wouldn't come back. But when she reappeared the next day with a boyfriend who had the pugnacious glare of a boxer, I lumbered into the house and called 911. Three minutes later, seven police cars screeched onto the street, in pursuit of the pair, who had by now vanished.

Salami watched, guffawing loudly. "She went thataway," he told the cops, pointing in the wrong direction.

The dealers were less amused. They fled to the traffic meridian, peering from a safe distance at the scene. When the bewildered police admitted defeat and left, Miguel approached me anxiously.

"*Mami*, what happened?"

I recounted the details. Miguel frowned. "I know who you're talking about. *Mami*, next time, don't call the cops. Come to Miguel. Miguel will sort it out. Okay, *Mami*?" He gave the thumbs-up sign and looked deeply into my eyes. "Don't you worry, *Mami*. I'll take care of her."

A couple of days later, Miguel pleasantly asked if everything was okay.

"Yup, everything's fine."

"Good. *Mami*, you don't need to worry about that woman anymore. She won't bother you again."

Miguel's words alarmed me, and I sought Raul's opinion. What did he think happened? Could Miguel have hurt her? Despite my fear, I didn't want her harmed.

"Who knows?" said Raul. "These guys don't tolerate trash on the street."

Chapter 20

ANTON

In the final stretch of my pregnancy, I almost lost the baby to premature contractions. The crisis passed quickly, but not my fear that he wouldn't make it. I didn't feel I could stand another loss, especially at this late stage. I made up my mind that I would give up on becoming a mother if this one slipped away. While John snored loudly next to me, I lay awake many a night ordering our offspring to remain inside for the rest of the term. I channeled Mom's no-nonsense voice for further authority. "You're going to make it," I told him. "There's no choice." To assure myself of his obedient vigor, I placed bottle caps on my belly and watched as a shape that resembled the Loch Ness Monster emerged to kick them off. I tried a visualization trick that

Manuel had recommended, conjuring up the image of a robust toddler sitting in the kitchen in a high chair and hurling mashed squash on the floor. This endearing domestic scene—my next thought drifted to cleaning up the mess—served to soften the anxiety.

Though I did not believe in any higher being, the neighborhood matriarchs *were* believers, and I readily accepted their offer to pray for us at church. Perhaps divine intervention would work after all! In the coming months, sonograms revealed an energetic little being with the requisite pairs of eyes, legs, and arms. As spring approached, the *Our Lord in heaven*s grew louder for him to make it to week thirty-two, when he'd be out of danger.

In the final countdown, someone mentioned my name to a television station that was filming a program on "mature mothers." Having little to do but sit in bed and go to doctor's appointments, I agreed to be interviewed. The segment hinged on my giving birth, as the producer wanted to provide a happy ending. She quickly grew to share my trepidation about losing the baby. The crew had had great trouble finding a subject as old as I was—forty-three now—and it was apparently too late in the programming schedule to look for another. The producer called periodically, making chitchat until she not too subtly got to the point. "So . . . how's the baby? What are the chances?" When I forgot to return one voice mail, the anxious producer left seven increasingly hysterical messages.

The crew followed me to the doctor's office for my weekly sonogram, and was keen to get scenes of me preparing for what would hopefully be a happy arrival. The plan was to film me folding hand-me-down infant T-shirts that my sister had given me. They also wanted shots of my old flak jacket, to emphasize the midcareer change of lifestyle. The team chose one of Miguel's busy days, and pulled up a big camera just as the muchachos lined up for a delivery. The last thing Miguel wanted was to be caught on film making a connection, and he frantically motioned to his client in an SUV to drive on as the cameraman filmed a long shot of the street, trying different angles just to make sure the light was right.

When the crew left two hours later, Miguel berated me. How could I be so inconsiderate? He had business to conduct. Didn't I realize what I was doing?

"I would appreciate it if you gave us advance notice next time," he said curtly.

The visualization and praying must have worked. In fact, it worked much too well. After all the precautions, it was mid-May and the baby was due. I felt like an overripe watermelon. After months of limiting all motion to ensure the baby didn't fall out, I now did everything in my power to expel him. I swam a mile a day and walked another four, but at week forty the doctor still saw no sign of imminent birth. We made an appointment to induce the following week and I went home feeling annoyed about the prospect. "Can't you cooperate?" I said, tapping my belly. The moment I walked in the door of our house my water broke. It was the wrong color—green. I called the doctor, who ordered me to report immediately to the hospital.

"This could be a sign of fetal distress," she said with urgency. "The amniotic fluid is contaminated with meconium. We'll have to induce before he inhales it. Get here right away."

I phoned John at work, urging him to hurry. I needed his calm presence to erase my worry that something would go terribly wrong at this final stage. I looked at my watch every five minutes, less to time the contractions than to wonder where the hell the father of my child was. When John finally arrived at the house, I realized what had taken him so long. As a good parsimonious Dutchman, my husband had cycled home instead of flagging a cab.

"I made record time!" John said proudly. He stood in the entryway with his bike and patted the seat. Surely he didn't expect me to hop on? The contractions were making me petulant, and I couldn't believe that he was going to impose his Dutch customs on me at a moment like this. "I'm not riding that thing," I snapped. "Call a taxi."

Passing cab drivers immediately switched on their OFF DUTY signs when they saw a gigantically pregnant woman doubled over against a lamppost with an armload of towels. When we finally nabbed a car, I nearly bit my tongue trying to suppress the groans of agony each time we lurched at traffic lights. I didn't want the driver to throw me out on the street.

Checking in at the hospital, I loudly made clear to anyone wearing scrubs that I wanted an epidural. I wasn't going to have any of this natural childbirth. I had suffered enough with the ordeal in Russia and didn't need any more pain. No, sir. Drugs for me!

I repeated the epidural order as the doctor assigned me a room and set me down on the bed, giving me a shot that would speed up contractions. Hours passed before the painkillers arrived. This gave me plenty of time to dwell on memories of Moscow.

"Sorry, the anesthesiologists are all busy," the nurse said breezily, when I complained again. "It's right before Memorial Day, so many of the doctors are inducing their patients. They want to get to the Hamptons in time for the long weekend." She accidentally switched on the intercom to other rooms. I heard a woman screaming, "I'm dying! I want to die!"

After twelve hours of what felt like a horse kicking my innards, the baby crowned briefly. Then he popped back inside. The doctor tried everything to lure him out: She pressed on my abdomen, cajoled with a "Here, kitty, kitty, kitty" voice. Then she went after the fellow with an implement that resembled barbecue tongs. However, no matter how hard I pushed and the doctor pulled, he refused to exit. After a whispered exchange with John, the doctor apologetically announced that she'd have to open me up to get the kid out. "We'll make sure you get plenty of drugs this time," was the sweetener.

Shortly after the sheet was strung up to shield my eyes from the surgery, I heard an indignant first howl of life and then the words "Fuck, he peed on me!" As the attending surgeon wiped piss from her face, John proudly held up an unblemished little person with alabaster skin and a perfect scowl. "He's gorgeous," John said, with an uncharacteristically goofy look. I marveled at the sight of the baby's vivid orange hair. "*That* came out of me? Where did that red hair come from?"

Jewish Ashkenazic tradition is to name a child after a deceased family member. As my nephew had already been given Dad's name, we called our son Anton, after John's father. Aside from the sentimental import, we figured that the name would travel well in the event that we moved overseas. And for sure, it could be easily converted to Antonio in our neighborhood.

I wondered if we'd ever leave the hospital—not that I necessarily wanted to. I was assigned there for five days to recuperate, and the small sterile room felt like the coziest nest a human could make. Except for the occasional zip back home to walk the dog, John camped by my side on the uncomfortable vinyl armchair, proudly hosting the procession of family and friends who came to meet our son.

As ecstatic as I felt, my new adult status was vaguely terrifying. One *studied* to become a professional. But parenting? It was just supposed to happen, but didn't feel very natural to me. When the nurse handed me the birth certificate application, I wondered why Mom was supposed to sign the papers. Then I realized—*I* was the mother. Me! The responsibility for caring for this minuscule defenseless person terrified me—what if I accidentally dropped or starved him? I fretted about the many ways I could unwittingly sabotage this pristine baby, who had no emotional or physical scars so far.

Yet even my fears of being an incompetent parent could not destroy my wonderment. Everything about Anton seemed marvelous—his fresh smell, the alert way he gazed at the wall clock, and how he sucked on John's nose in the mistaken impression that it was a teat.

All good things come to an end, and after five days it was time for Mom to drive us home. My anxious stomach felt as though a pint of vinegar were bubbling inside as I stepped into the maroon Subaru. Now real grown-up life would truly start, away from the watchful eye of the nurses, who knew how to administer CPR. Would I fail at this new job? My unease heightened when a delegation of dealers met us at the curb as Mom pulled up. They frantically gestured at my mother to turn the wheel before she rode up on the curb and hit their domino table. Miguel nodded coolly to John. He felt compelled to pay respects during this moment of great joy, but only grudgingly, and with a barb.

"Nice red hair. Where did that color come from?"

Then, with a warm smile for the new mother, Miguel inquired if I had had an easy birth and how much Anton weighed. He asked if Anton would be drinking "mother's milk," politely avoiding the word *breast*. Otherwise, he recommended Similac formula, which he had heard was the best.

"She's breastfeeding," my mother snapped.

Salami and Clarence joined us. "That kid doesn't look a thing like you," was Clarence's comment. Salami was more gracious. "The Gerber baby! Right off the jar!" He peered into the swaddled bundle as I energetically tried to shield my precious newborn from his foul breath. Anton looked up at Salami impassively.

"Better watch out or someone will steal him for modeling." With that ominous warning, he sauntered off singing, *"I'll be watching you."*

I glanced uneasily at John. What were we doing raising a kid in this environment? What if Salami seized Anton? John gave one of his nonchalant European shrugs. "Salami is all bluff. Ignore him."

I'm not sure it actually takes a village to raise a child, but neighbors certainly help. Any tips on mothering were welcomed, as becoming parents in our forties presented a more daunting challenge than either of us had anticipated. Neither John nor I had much experience with infants; my exposure was largely limited to photographing them at African refugee camps. Nursing, I discovered, was not intuitive, and the staff at the hospital had neglected to inform me that nipples become raw and painful if a baby is left to suck too long or is positioned incorrectly. My ever-nurturing sister and her seven-year-old son paid many a visit to the house to teach me the proper way to latch on a hungry infant. My nephew, having nursed until the age of four, had some particularly insightful advice on the ideal position to aid milk flow, and which wails mean a child is famished. The elders on the street provided a further mine of information—where to rub on the belly to soothe gastric reflux, how to treat mastitis. ("Plunk raw cabbage on your breast," one granny suggested.) Miguel, too, proved to be an expert in parenting, taking great interest in the consistency of Anton's bowels. He alerted me that Love diapers were cheaper than Pampers but "just as absorbent."

Following Miguel's lead, the muchachos treated me with cordiality bordering on warmth. My new status elevated me to an object of respect. Even surly Nose politely moved aside when I walked past with Anton.

Anton suffered from colic. Miguel—who by now confided that he had sired a number of children, although he was vague on the number—suggested playing slow *bachatas*, the romantic Dominican music. "The beat soothes them," he said.

Following his advice, I rummaged through our music collection, but the only cassettes close to that rhythm were ballads from Angola sung by a gravel-voiced man named Bonga. Sure enough, the beat worked. I swayed Anton to sleep with melancholy lyrics about war and destruction.

Even with this abundance of proffered wisdom, John and I found the transition from dog owners to parents slow going. On more than one occasion we addressed Anton with Khaya's nickname: *Dikke Drol*, the Dutch for "Big Turd." This sharing of names confused the hound, who would rise slowly onto his arthritic legs thinking we were summoning him, only to be disappointed. Anton collected other monikers on the street. "Little John" was Mackenzie's choice. Clarence bestowed "Killer," and Raul called him *"El Presidente,"* a pun on the popular beer that was light like Anton's complexion.

I got lonely being with the baby all day, and I often returned to my perch on the stoop seeking social interaction, even if it had to be with narcotics pushers and a crochety super. Clarence or Mackenzie—never the two at the same time; they were bickering these days—often joined me there.

"Girl, what a dumb smile. You're in love. That kid is going to wrap you around his little finger," Clarence muttered. He stubbed out his cigarette as he dictated a health regime to help Anton's organs grow. Clarence swore by wheat germ for nursing, and omega-3.

"Give that boy fish oil and his brain will develop," he insisted.

That wasn't all. Apparently I wasn't holding my baby properly. "Neck support, girl," Clarence barked, cradling the child's head. "When you gonna learn how to hold that baby? You're gonna break his neck if you don't watch out."

I found Clarence's version of tenderness touching, and mentioned it to Mackenzie, who remained skeptical that his employer had a soft side. "He tries to impose his worldview and tells you how to eat, live, sleep. That man doesn't love children. He had no childhood of his own. He had to pick cotton in the South when he was five years old."

"What about you? You seem to like kids."

He smiled at the thought. "No doubt."

"Ever had any?"

His eyes welled. "Two. I never see them."

"What happened?"

He took a deep breath. I had a feeling that this was going to be a long story, and settled back on the step as comfortably as I could, careful to cradle Anton the way Clarence said.

"Their mother was a prelaw student. I met her at work when I was a paralegal at the law firm. She was Filipina-Japanese. Her name was Susan. We lived together, a common-law arrangement. Our twins were born in 1971, a boy, Gabriel, and a girl, Isabel. It was a secret thing in the beginning, my relationship with Susan. I had a problem with her father. He was Japanese. It really upset him that we had kids. At first he wanted nothing to do with them.

"Things came to a head when I went to jail for tax evasion. Susan didn't hold it against me; I just got caught in the system. But after I got out in 1981, when the kids were ten, her father offered me a deal: He would pay my back taxes if I would sever all ties with my kids. I owed thirty thousand dollars.

"It took me about a week to consider his offer. I wrestled with it. I thought it was best for the kids." Mackenzie choked up and looked away, his eyes shining wet. He sucked in the tears. "The kids' mother was on my side, but in Japanese society she had no say against her father. We were best of friends when we broke up."

Mackenzie paused. What a horrible story, I thought. Sacrificing your kids to pay back taxes.

"He gave me ten grand. I didn't press him for the rest of the money. The kids and their mother moved to Oakland. I let them go. I told Susan, 'Put the money in an education trust for the kids.' Susan's father died in 1985. By that time, she had sent the kids to the Philippines to stay with their grandmother."

Mackenzie focused on the street ahead. Anton made a sound like a dolphin, and Mackenzie considered him briefly. "It hasn't been easy," he said.

"Do you know where they are now?"

"I'm not sure. Their mother is a lawyer now. I think she's in Portland, Oregon. If I had the ways and means I would find them."

"You can find people through the Internet. We have a computer. We could help you look."

Mackenzie's eyes misted again. He looked away and shook his head no. We sat in silence. Anton made a rooting gesture, and I tried to distract him with a tickle. Mackenzie said, "I will find them eventually." We sat for some time more. Then Mackenzie got up, brushed off his jeans, and went across the street to his cellar.

Perhaps Mackenzie's loss was in the back of my mind as I contemplated going back to work. Right after I gave birth, I flirted with some jobs, including one that would have involved lengthy travel to unstable areas such as Sudan. As the recruiter talked about the seductive salary and benefits—the pension plan was particularly impressive—I had a vision of Anton in a babysitter's arms, reaching in vain for a breast (mine) that was in a desert ten thousand miles away. I saw myself pining for him, as I interviewed child soldiers in Sri Lanka who had lost their own mothers. No, I couldn't do this work anymore. How did I ever do it, for that matter? It seemed inconceivable that I had spent so much time among orphaned children without weeping. This soft unfamiliar person that I had become didn't want to take risks anymore. I couldn't tear myself from Anton. I had morphed into one of those New Age mothers who wore their children on their bodies all day and kept them in the parental bed at night. I couldn't imagine leaving Anton for three weeks, let alone eight hours.

To minimize the separation, I decided to work part-time, and arranged freelance writing and teaching work for the months to come. After trying to edit an article at the computer with Anton squirming on my lap, I quickly discovered even itinerant work necessitated a babysitter. We didn't have too many requirements, other than a warm, responsible person who spoke Spanish. (We wanted to raise Anton to be trilingual, learning English, Dutch, and Spanish.) After I casually mentioned that I was seeking child care, Miguel offered to introduce me to one of his cronies. Angie was the sturdy, busy woman with big hoop earrings who organized keys and meal orders in front of Clarence's building. I thought of her as the den mother of the muchachos.

For a mere instant, I was tempted by Angie's take-charge manner and the convenience of employing a babysitter who lived across the street. But of course it wouldn't do. Manuel the carpenter yet again saved the day. He suggested Miryam, a serene middle-aged Colombian woman who had babysat for his two youngest children. It was love all around: Miryam couldn't wait to pick up Anton. Anton cooed back. She was so sweet that I wanted to hug her, too.

So we hired Miryam. One thing was sure: She wouldn't get involved with the dealers. "These people are scum," she said with disgust the first time she saw the muchachos on their stoop. "Cocaine ruined my country."

Chapter 21

LATTE ARRIVES

Sometime in the spring, real estate agents came to the consensus that Harlem was hip—meaning acceptable to white professionals who could afford to renovate rapidly appreciating brownstones, as opposed to black people of lesser means. For real estate brokers, being hip had nothing to do with the jazz tradition of Harlem or the basketball stars who had trained at its city parks. Hip meant a person could shop at the expanding array of national retail on 125th Street—Disney, The Body Shop, Old Navy, and Starbucks—rather than at appealing family stores selling obscure blues records and Ghanaian kente cloth.

Fancy restaurants were opening, too. Predictably, this shift in yuppie perception didn't apply to West Harlem, still the domain of *botánicas* and discount shops. While radicchio could be nibbled farther east on Frederick Douglass Boulevard, the pioneers in Little Dominica wailed: When, oh when, will we be able to buy whole-wheat bread?

Yet, how quickly things changed, even if Sancerre vintages hadn't yet arrived at the corner liquor store with the bulletproof Plexiglas shielding the cashier. Police Commissioner Kerik further beefed up patrols to clean out the narcotics that were discouraging Gap franchises.

While the NYPD was out handcuffing Dominican youths, a developer, Emmes Asset Management, decided the time was ripe to introduce big corporations to 138th Street. Emmes reclaimed an old theater, and demolition Dumpsters parked outside to reinvent an entire block of mainly abandoned storefronts. In March, the golden arches of McDonald's arose. The HSBC bank and Starbucks soon followed.

I felt conflicted about this introduction of national chains to our little enclave of mom-and-pop stores. On the one hand, it was a relief to see the permanently scrolled-down storefronts replaced by functioning enterprises, and ones that didn't launder drug money, for that matter. Yet, like many liberals raised in the 1960s, I had a visceral suspicion of big business, and the familiar siren from Seattle had a jarring effect.

Of course, this being West Harlem, our Starbucks wasn't ordinary. The coffeehouse was financed by none other than basketball star Magic Johnson, who launched a national program to jump-start commercial retail in poor black areas. Despite Magic's good intentions, this Starbucks was a financial flop because the star had neglected to do his research. If he had, he would have realized that this was a heavily Hispanic area where coffee drinkers were loyal to their ninety-cent brew of Bustelo espresso. The notion of spending $3.12 for a giant cup of caffeinated froth was anathema. On one visit, the woman behind the till confided that she had never worked in such an empty Starbucks, "except when they're closed." Unlike the packed franchises in Midtown, where you might have to wait a good five minutes to order, the staff here outnumbered customers. During what would be the breakfast rush elsewhere, here a sole City College student or urban pioneer in dreadlocks sat self-consciously among twelve empty tables. Occasionally an undercover cop took advantage of the floor-to-ceiling windows that looked out on the drug business on Broadway. He'd pretend that there was nothing strange about an unshaven man with a walkie-talkie sticking out of his Jets shirt nursing a Frappuccino for two hours.

Things livened up, though, when the dealers learned about the clean toilets. This was an amenity in short supply for the busy salesmen, who were under pressure by the enhanced police patrols not to relieve themselves in public. Men desperate for a private pee would plunk five-dollar bills on the counter, mouth, "Venti, keep the change," and slip behind the chartreuse bathroom doors.

After witnessing a series of these exchanges, I asked the barista what she thought of her new customers. Did she care that they were narcotics traders? The young woman brightened. "They're good tippers. *Very* good tippers."

Just as key to changing perceptions of Harlem was the decision of former President Bill Clinton to open an office on 125th Street. Although his building was in the African-American heartland, a good nineteen blocks south of our abode, Clinton's vote of confidence rippled to these distant Dominican streets. From the day Clinton moved his desk into his ample suite, we began receiving telephone calls and flyers through the mail slot from real estate brokers offering free appraisals to sell our house. One zealous agent actually hand-scrawled a note, "I have a buyer who will pay cash!"

The Sugar Hill Bistro opened just in time. This was a new drinking spot, to which house hunters could repair after a long day of looking at properties. The restaurant cum art gallery cum jazz club cum oak-paneled conference room was a new concept on run-down 145th Street. Abstract paintings of saxophonists hung for sale on the wainscoted walls as actual saxophonists drowned out the conversation. In an eloquent statement on the changing times, the eclectic venue was situated in a refurbished 1880s Victorian townhouse that had previously accommodated a liquor store and a drug treatment center. We were skeptical that a critical mass of diners wanted to pay eighteen dollars for Asian pan-seared scallops, but for those who did, the softly lit garden and regular appearances by Wynton Marsalis—a friend of the owners—were nice diversions from the greasy fare of El Floridita. This commercial milestone was described by *New York* magazine as "the most exciting addition to the Harlem restaurant scene since Hillary's husband." Just the thought that a restaurant here would get reviewed by *New York* was in itself exciting to those of us who could afford the blackened salmon, if only occasionally.

There were more and more of these blackened-salmon types, testing the upper altitudes of Manhattan. That was a good thing, as we were looking for tenants for the upstairs apartment. At first I lay awake imagining Salami scaring off a new set of potential lodgers with his outdoors-parlor tactics. But it turned out that we didn't even need to advertise the space, now that *New York* had put West Harlem on the yuppie map. A friend, also named Judith, recommended two opera singers who were delighted at the thought of living up here in this newly discovered *quartier*. The female member of the pair, Vianca, performed with the Metropolitan Opera, and the male, Charles, moonlighted as a risk analyst while training to become a professional singer, too. We were puzzled as to why such glamorous and cultured people would want to live in our funky dive. But we were told that Vianca was so busy touring that she didn't have time to organize prosaic matters like housing. What's more, the two preferred brownstone living and, being Latina, the woman had an affinity for this Hispanic neighborhood.

"Really, you'll love them," our mutual friend said.

Sure enough, we were enchanted when they came over one evening for a housing blind date. They were gorgeous and urbane, and ostentatiously tanned, as if they'd just returned from St. Bart's. Vianca's beauty was such that it had to be fake, I thought. (Besides, she had the wide shoulders and exaggerated femininity of a transvestite.) The four-inch stilettos that brought her height to well over six feet completed the transgender effect. I searched closely for a five-o'clock shadow under her heavy stage makeup, but was finally convinced of her true identity by the breasts that moved so naturally inside her lacy camisole. Indeed, her goddess looks were all real! The shorter member of the couple, Charles, wore a gold Pierre Cardin belt buckle that nicely set off his lavender pressed shirt, and he had a tendency to sprinkle conversation with Parisian slang. He also had a delightful way of giggling as he flipped back the sandy hair that hung prettily over his collar.

Anton was captivated by the glitzy twosome. The mezzo admired him right back as he lay on the couch like a pasha, tickling his belly with her long crimson nails. Anton giggled and swatted at her rhinestone earrings. And then he did the unthinkable: He smiled his first smile . . . at another woman.

I was crushed. For this I had made sacrifices? I had given up my fascinating career to minister to this child. I had suffered bed rest, surgery, bleeding tits, and mastitis. And then Anton beamed his first smile at a stranger.

I was still sulking when they left the house.

As soon as we closed the door, John turned to me with an enthusiasm that I normally would have found infectious. "They're terrific!"

I didn't agree.

"Why not?"

"Because . . ."

"Why?"

"Anton smiled at her. I'm the mother. He's never smiled at me." Tears filled my eyes.

John stared at me in disbelief. "Get over it. They're delightful."

"Are they?" I took a new tack and pointed out that we had forgotten to request a credit report.

"Well, they seem rich enough." John was exasperated. He turned his back to me, a sign that dialogue had come to an end. "Look, they have respectable jobs. Our mutual friend recommended them."

I continued to huff. But I had to concede that I didn't have the energy to look for alternatives. Resigned to playing second fiddle, as it were, I called the diva that night. The next day the pair came over and signed a lease.

While I struggled with my jealousy, the muchachos grappled with how to place these stylish new additions to the neighborhood. The stunning Amazon and her dapper cohort were unlike anyone who had populated this street. No one in recent memory had carried GQ magazine or sung Tosca. But once the guys established via close ogling that her escort was no threat, they loitered outside the house to chat her up. What's more, she spoke Spanish! "She's one of us!" Penknife remarked excitedly to the others.

Salami didn't join the would-be seducers, having been chastened earlier by our former lodger Cleo. This new woman, who swanned about in limousines and floor-length gowns, was clearly even more out of his league. He moped on the outskirts as the dealers trailed her down the block, offering to do carpentry repairs or any other handiwork that might crop up in her apartment. Miguel kept a hungry distance, no doubt deeming it unseemly to flirt with our tenants.

Inside the house, testosterone was churning as well. The basement actors had ended their romance the day they moved in, and to make matters worse, the brunet had sneaked in a puppy, which I forcefully pointed out was in flagrant violation of the lease. The boy and his dog moved out shortly thereafter. Without a partner with whom to share arguments or sex, the remaining actor, Aidan, had a lot of time on his hands, and he spent many an hour lolling around shirtless as he burned cranberry-scented candles and belted out numbers from *South Pacific*. The lad was also in need of comfort, having reported various sightings of the ghost, which he claimed had a tendency to slap him when he took showers. It therefore came as no surprise that Aidan and Charles began to spend time together. As we didn't lock doors in the house, we grew accustomed to the sound of male feet scampering up and down three flights of stairs as the two *artistes* visited each other.

All was not well, however, and within weeks we became aware of more complexities besetting our upstairs tenants, which had not been evident in the initial interview. The problem was the male's musical identity. Charles's voice was on the high side, and he was training to force it down. "Baritones are taken more seriously," he explained.

His apartment mate was actively encouraging him in this pursuit. Vianca was of the belief that his two ranges reflected distinct personalities, and the tenor part of him was frivolous and prone to temper tantrums. Deeper voices were taken seriously for a reason—they were less flighty and more substantive. Vianca explained that her cohort was a tenor when he left the remains of lavish dinner parties on the table for two weeks and broke the dishwasher with an errant chicken bone. He was a tenor when he forgot to pay the rent. He was a tenor when he got drunk above our bedroom and sang, keeping time with a thumping Cristofle serving spoon. Charles was definitely a tenor when he set up a conservatory above our bedroom, without so much as a warning to his landlords—us.

I came home one afternoon to find a man in coveralls prying the front door off its hinges. Two of his cronies lifted something massive draped in a blanket from a truck.

"What is going on?" I demanded. The coverall man grunted. "Move it, lady. I'm trying to get this piano in."

Piano?

Charles trotted down in his dressing gown, talking on the cell phone. "Velvet would be divine."

"You didn't mention a piano," I hissed.

"No? Surely I did. It's very small. I wanted a grand, but they said it wouldn't fit."

He pursed his lips into the phone, and waved the men upward.

I wasn't sure this "small" thing would get inside his apartment without breaking a wall. The moving men were having difficulty maneuvering the instrument around the second-floor landing and smashed a bit of the plaster. Chips flew into the air as the men set the piano down. I heard the snap of a wooden stair coming loose from the wall.

Charles continued his design conversation, intent on resolving an issue with drapes. "Earth colors. Think the W Hotel."

I waved to catch his attention. He waved back and blew me a kiss.

The piano made its way to the third floor, and I heard it settle down—right over our bedroom. Then its owner dispatched the movers and sat down to a rousing series of scales, sung with a voice that resolutely stayed in the higher range.

That night I conferred with John about how we would negotiate reasonable practice hours. John pointed out that we couldn't easily ask that the instrument leave now that it was in the house. Nor could we reasonably ban playing during the day. I accepted this only begrudgingly. I liked quiet at all hours, as I was working at home and often napped with Anton in the afternoon because he awoke during the night. However, live music during the day was far preferable to nighttime serenades. John proposed 10 P.M. as the hour to cut him off.

Our piano-playing tenant was sprawled on the new black velvet divan, talking on the cell phone ("He had the most luscious . . .") when we came up to offer the compromise. Vianca was wearing a silk dressing gown and pouted over complaints about the piano. "I *have* to have accompaniment when I practice," she said indignantly.

Charles wasn't overly delighted about the music curfew, but acquiesced when we insisted that the piano was an unexpected arrival. "Are you sure? I thought we discussed it," he said with an enchanting pout. *"Très bien . . ."*

As a gesture of helpfulness, Charles extended us flutes of Moët & Chandon champagne from the half-empty bottle sitting on the Italian glass dining table. Then, noting that it was only 9:46 P.M., he positioned himself at the piano and the pair treated us to a rousing aria from *Carmen*. We were transfixed, and bad feelings evaporated as art and bubbly conquered all.

"I love that music in the house," I remarked tipsily to John, as we made our way downstairs after a couple of encores.

I didn't love it as much the next night, or the next. It turned out that the tenor-baritone had a loose interpretation of time—10 P.M. stretched to 3 A.M. when he had company or was in a postcoital flush.

And there were many such flushes. While Charles tormented me with all-night concerts, he and Vianca tormented each other with multiple lovers. It turned out that they had been sweethearts during his brief heterosexual phase seven years ago, and the unresolved fallout now took the form of seeing who could chalk up more conquests. Charles was way ahead in the competition, and as well as the late-night concerts, we grew accustomed to the noise of piercing orgasms that were a bit theatrical in volume.

Despite the piano and other antics, the singers were immensely charming, and we grew fond of them. The house breathed with music—from the street, from Aidan belting out show tunes in the basement, to the celestial singing above. We didn't lock the doors to our apartment, and the household felt like one extended family, as our various tenants dropped by for visits, often timed right at cocktail hour. Aidan delighted in playing with Anton, and occasionally we'd deploy him as babysitter to catch a few hours alone.

The opera singers' chaotic zest for life was invigorating, and they embraced West Harlem with a freshness that recharged us. Vianca delighted in the family-style restaurants, which reminded her of home. Charles liked shocking people with the revelation that he lived on a street infested with drug dealers. So great was the pair's infatuation with the neighborhood that they acquainted themselves with the local amenities with vigor. They became regulars at the jazz bistro's bar. They bought piles of mangoes on the street. They discovered an obscure Portuguese wine at our seedy liquor store, where one had to wait patiently in line behind the drunks buying tiny airplane bottles of bourbon. Through their eyes, the neighborhood took on a new glow.

Mom was delighted with our choice of tenants. A passionate opera fan, she spent hours discussing performances past with the pair, and impressing them with her knowledge. They sat, enraptured. "Joan Sutherland! Caruso! What were they like?" My mother had season tickets for the Metropolitan Opera and made sure to book seats for productions in which Vianca was singing. Charles took a particular shine to my mother and, like most others who came into her orbit, called her "Mom."

"I'm going to adopt her!" he exclaimed, wrapping his cashmere-adorned arms around her shoulders.

Mom, in turn, wanted to cultivate Vianca when she found out that the young woman was a protégée of the opera star Plácido Domingo. When a short, modest man in thick glasses appeared in the corridor one afternoon bearing a bouquet, I rushed to the phone to call my mother. Was it really him? I checked an old record sleeve. He seemed so much larger in photos but there was the distinctive profile. Yes! Thereafter, Mom spent more time in the house, particularly in the corridor, where she hovered, ever hopeful for a sighting.

Our extended household was a big hit when we held a neighborhood barbecue to celebrate our first anniversary in the house. We had invited people without keeping track of the numbers, and were amazed when Mr. Anderson counted the early arrivals at sixty-five before we even started carving the ham. The gay men doted on Mrs. LaDuke. One stylist who dressed the hair of movie stars offered to do her coif for free. Mrs. LaDuke reserved her best flirting skills for Charles, asking coyly why he left the lights on all night. "I love you!" he crooned, clasping her newly waved crown to his chest. "I want to adopt *you*!"

Mrs. LaDuke assumed the role of party photographer, standing in the middle of the garden taking pictures of guests with disposable cameras as they came down the back stairs from the kitchen. It was our pioneer version of the Pilgrims' first Thanksgiving. Mrs. Campbell made her legendary plantains, others brought various pies, and Mr. Anderson grilled hot dogs. The white lawyer contributed a chilled white Bordeaux. John tried out a recipe that a South African friend dubbed "sodomized chicken." It involved rubbing a hen with chili and then sticking an opened beer can up its posterior before grilling. The beer soaked into the flesh and softened it better than any marinade. The already warped table sagged further under the cornucopia: chocolate cake, ribs, corn bread, salads, soda, corn, and Jamaican jerked chicken. Susan and Rafael couldn't make it—they had some community meetings of their own to attend. But Mom represented the family, milling about with Anton in her arms. Mr. Anderson brought along his attaché case of accolades. Over yellowed clips of his grand tour of Europe, he reminisced with the matriarchs about the good old days when Harlem was still grand.

The dealers were of course on everyone's minds, and the swapping of tales began even before the rum was poured.

"I had to physically push aside those thugs to get in your gate," complained Bailey, the professor. The event turned into an impromptu political rally when Bloodsaw arrived with an entourage of election aides, courteous men in suits and rectangular eyeglasses. Bloodsaw was running for councilman to replace Stan Michels and the talk invariably turned to the campaign. It was a crowded field; nine other Democrats were vying for the seat. Bloodsaw wasn't a front-runner in other parts of the district, but he didn't have to work hard to win votes with this crowd. He was our man, fighting crime.

Neighbors came, left, returned. Still others arrived. The tally rose to eighty-five. Finally at 3 A.M., we not-so-gently suggested that the last stragglers go home and let us sleep. As we hauled dishes into the sink, I counted our many blessings. We had been vindicated in moving here. Everything was lovely, lovely! Mrs. LaDuke had survived. We had wonderful neighbors. Not only was the house done but it was beautiful to boot. We had an adorable child. We had a wonderful life!

Chapter 22

SNORTING ANTHRAX

The election primaries were Tuesday, September 11, and I wanted to get out early to vote for Bloodsaw. He was our man, after all. I kissed John good-bye as he left for the office. Right after 8:45 A.M., I tucked Anton into the shoulder sling and was just putting my registration card in my bag when I heard a curdling shout from upstairs. The opera singers ran down to say that a plane had crashed into the north tower of the World Trade Center. We switched on the television in John's study to see a replay of the scene, staring in amazement at the pillar of smoke and flames. "Unbelievable," Charles kept repeating. "Unbelievable." The newscaster thought an accident was to blame but I had doubts. How could a huge plane swerve into the building by mistake? "Looks like an attack," I pronounced curtly in my best know-it-all tone. After all, I had seen these things before. Well, things somewhat like this, maybe. I tried to phone John but couldn't get through.

Charles worked in the vicinity of the towers, and he left for his office saying that he'd call when he got to the scene, repeating, "Implausible," on his way out the door. Vianca went on her way to a rehearsal. She kissed Anton tenderly good-bye. "Take good care of him," she said over her shoulder.

I was jealous. Why wasn't I, on this, of all days, on the beat? Here was a big story, in the city I grew up in, no less, and for the first time in twenty years I was in no position to cover it. Someone—that would be me—had to stay home with Anton. I took him out of the sling and put him on my lap, and sat, mesmerized, in front of the television screen. I remained in that same position, one hand clamped over my mouth, the other grasping Anton, as a second airplane sliced into the other tower. The newscaster—*this* was unbelievable—speculated that there was a problem at air control. ("Fire that fool," I said to my almost-four-month-old, nearly dropping him.) Smoke billowing like an ominous ostrich boa reminded me that the baritone was heading right toward the inferno, and I tried to call his cell phone to warn him. I also tried to call John, Mom, the babysitter, my sister, my brother-in-law, and my cousin Greg. All I got were busy signals, so I sat dazed in front of the television, mechanically rocking Anton in the wicker chair and feeling powerless. Every third rock the chair creaked, and it seemed a reminder of how alone I felt.

I also felt an unfamiliar mix of anger, fear, and frustration. Was this war? Was there more to come? Who had attacked? What might be hit next? And when? I thought about New York's strategic sites—we were uptown, in an area of poor people of color. We weren't near any obvious targets, except for the George Washington Bridge. Fortunately, that was two miles north, sufficiently far from our house.

While most normal people wanted to be far away from the towers, I felt a pull toward them. That's what I would have done in Bogotá or Johannesburg. That's what I did for a living, or used to. I gently placed Anton on a soft green armchair and packed the usual kit for covering disasters abroad: pens, spare batteries, tape recorder, camera, notebooks, bottles of water, raisin snacks (high energy), press card, driver's license, cash, first-aid supplies, a bandanna for dust. Then I added some new things: baby bottles and diapers. "I've got to get down there," I mumbled like a crazy woman to my innocent baby, as I changed his diaper. Reality took over as I wiped him, and the mother in me said, "You are a terrible person." I couldn't take Anton with me. I couldn't go alone, either. There was no one to leave him with. Anyway, I didn't have spare breast milk in the freezer. And for whom would I write? I wasn't even employed at present.

While reporting on conflicts abroad, I'd often distanced myself with the knowledge that I could always leave wherever I was. Hiding behind a notebook was a convenient survival mechanism for handling the gruesome and keeping uncomfortable reactions at bay. Writing was a way to cope with horrible sights—mass graves, lynchings, slashed corpses—or the guilt of leaving victims behind. But this was my city that was being attacked, and I didn't have work to distract me. I wasn't writing for a newspaper full-time, and my new job, teaching journalism at New York University, hadn't yet begun. Suddenly I had lost my professional shield as trained observer. The realization that I was just another vulnerable citizen, in combination with this new, strange responsibility of motherhood, was making me agitated. Into what kind of world had I brought Anton? We had moved here for a quieter life, and what did we have now? War? *What was going on?* What kind of mother was I? Was I really a mother whose first instinct was to leave her infant at a time like this? And whose second idea was to bring him along?

While I was berating myself for my heartlessness, a call came in from a new acquaintance. (It appeared that I could receive calls from some parts of the city, but not place any.) The caller, Aliza, had just transferred to New York from covering conflict in the Middle East, and, like myself, had just had a baby and was taking a break from work. Her television had not yet been unpacked and she was blithely unaware that the United States had been attacked for the first time since Pearl Harbor.

"What about a playdate?" she asked. I told her the dramatic news. She didn't miss a beat. "I'm getting right down to the Twin Towers."

This only made me more confused. What type of professional was I?

Needing to clear my head, I carried Anton outside. Broadway was deserted, except for emergency vehicles flashing downtown. The corner deli run by Arabs was shuttered, and other storefronts were rolling down their metal gates. The only people on the street were rattled dealers, milling about in confusion as they tried their paralyzed cell phones.

"Coño, no funciona." ("It doesn't work.")

"Llámale." ("Call him.")

"No puedo, coño." ("I can't.")

The problem wasn't just that they couldn't communicate with customers. The clients also couldn't make it over the bridges or through the tunnels, which were closing down. One of the dealers shook his phone as though that would summon the clients. The muchachos gathered around a parked SUV and tuned in to radio reports. They let me join them; we were united in bewilderment, and I found the shared sense of impotence oddly reassuring. "You know anyone down there?" Nose kindly asked. It occurred to me that this was the first time that I'd seen the muchachos listen to news rather than dance music. This wasn't a group that normally tuned in to NPR, but now the guys flicked from station to station seeking updates, even if they could find only English-language broadcasts. One fellow asked me to translate. I had a flashback to Africa, where dozens of people frequently crowded around a single radio as the only source of information. I, too, often relied on battery-powered radios for news while abroad. That's how I heard about the start of the first Gulf War and impeachment proceedings against Clinton. But huddling on a street corner to catch the headlines wasn't normal in media-saturated Manhattan.

Without working phones, people emerged from their houses like bears running from a forest fire, to seek news and company. Mrs. Campbell's grandson dropped by "just to say hi." Mackenzie went up to the roof of his building, saw the smoke from afar, and promptly went back inside and switched on the BBC. People spoke of stockpiling candles, diapers, and canned food. The small bodegas had closed or run out of basics, and a clothing designer from up the road offered to take a carload of people to Fairway for supplies. I placed an order for baby formula. For one of the first times, I thought, "Thank God for this block." Without John to anchor me, I was brought down to earth by the neighbors.

Heartened by this show of solidarity, I carried Anton back into the house with renewed calm. I resumed my seat in front of the television with a sense of motherly purpose. Yes, I was doing the right thing.

The south tower collapsed, and then the north one. In the first aerial shots, the concrete dust spread so widely that it looked like the rubble might have buried Midtown, where John worked. The newscaster speculated that perhaps tens of thousands of people had died. I couldn't reach John, or our tenant, or my brother-in-law, who had meetings downtown. Were they alive? Warplanes streaked above and Anton screamed.

Just when I felt I couldn't take the solitude anymore the doorbell rang and an apparition appeared: Cindy, a colleague who was now living in New York. Cindy hadn't been able to get me, or anyone else, on the phone. She walked the forty-six blocks to my house seeking company, rightly assuming I wouldn't go anywhere. I couldn't think of a better companion for the moment. Cindy was a favored travel mate in Africa, when she worked for *The Washington Post*, and we had experienced several sobering events together, including an endless night in Kinshasa, when we feared that retreating soldiers of the dictator Mobutu Sese Seko would blow up our hotel. Like me, she was taking time off from her former incarnation as a foreign correspondent. At this precise moment she, too, was having some serious second thoughts about that decision.

"Let's go somewhere," Cindy said at the door. "I can't sit still."

We aimlessly walked downtown, Anton snug in the shoulder sling. Broadway was deserted as we passed closed mechanics' shops in the West 130s. Here in West Harlem there was no hint of the horror downtown, aside from a glimpse of a television screen through an apartment window. As we reached Columbia University at 116th Street, the streets again filled up with people. Cindy shot me a look as we passed a woman madly buying postcards of the towers at a newsstand. ("These will be collectors' items one day," the woman was saying.) We ended up at a Mexican restaurant that was popular with students, and as we sat down I felt relief at being part of humanity again. The bar had a television, and passersby stopped and looked at the news bulletins. I gazed at the replays of the falling buildings as though in a trance. It broke when a woman shouted at me, "What are you doing with that baby?" I looked down and realized that Anton was wailing. I nestled him deeper into

the sling, gave him a breast, and returned my gaze to the sight of disori-
ented people covered in ash. What had become of our city?

When I got back to the house a couple of hours later, I was jolted
by the sound of the phone ringing. It was Mom, with a roll call of good
news. Everyone in the family was safe—my husband, Rafael, Susan and
her son, and my cousin Greg. His wife had been trapped in a subway
near the disaster site, but she managed to escape without injury and
walk across the Brooklyn Bridge and onward to Bed-Stuy. On Mom's
urging, John eventually phoned me, something that had not occurred
to him with the sudden, huge workload that had descended on him.
The attacks had galvanized oil markets and the Middle East, which was
the area he covered, and he was also looking after employees who
feared for loved ones at the disaster site. John brusquely assured me
that he was fine, work would detain him well past midnight, and that
his trusty bicycle would get him safely home.

Charles stumbled back in the evening, shaken and coughing from
ash but intact. He had survived the fall of the buildings, thanks to a
subway train that fortuitously reversed, and he had escaped through
the thick dust. That night we huddled in a daze with Vianca over a bottle of wine, unsure whether we were celebrating the safe homecoming
or mourning the dead. Afterward, I lay in bed with the baby waiting for
John to come home, wondering what calamity might follow.

Three days later, a bereaved New York held a citywide vigil for the
dead.

At 7 P.M. sharp, Broadway flickered with lights, as the working people of West Harlem solemnly walked five abreast holding candles. The
sight of all the humble busboys and taxi drivers made me think of those
who had died at Windows on the World. The sharp charred smell of the
inferno had drifted uptown, as a further reminder of the dead. John
and I sat on our stoop holding Anton and candles, and tearfully
watched the procession of soft lights move silently up the avenue. A
cluster of dealers sprawled on the steps of the abandoned house and lit
their own tall candles of red, white, and blue. Nose noticed us and

nudged the others to switch off the bouncy merengue emitting from a Mercedes parked in front. He lifted his white candle at us, as though in a mournful toast.

For one small moment, Nose and I were in perfect synch.

In my dreams. The next morning began with a blast of music. The dealers were out in force, sixteen men shouting into cell phones. Miguel marshaled them right and left. The steps of the wrecked house next door were streaked not just with wax, but also with Hennessy bottles and aluminum chicken containers. The dealers had thrown a nice little party while the rest of New York grieved. Unlike many others in the city, who tried to numb their pain with booze, these guys seemed to have simply used the occasion as an excuse for a good time.

The neighborhood plunged into chaos in the following weeks. Even at their most irritating, I had previously nurtured a bemused tolerance for the dealers. Now I hated them. I hated them for profiting from the city's bereavement. Like the callous opportunists who suddenly jack up food and water prices in war zones, the muchachos were exploiting the tragedy for commercial gain. They cynically hung up American flags and patriotic signs saying: DIOS BENDIGA E.U. (God Bless America) above their trading spots, as a cover in case the cops drove by. They needn't have bothered. Law enforcement in West Harlem had practically vanished, with police officers redeployed downtown to security checkpoints and recovery efforts. If any sirens raced past, they were not in pursuit of dealers. The muchachos took advantage of the vacuum and became more brazen, trading directly in front of people's houses. They harassed women, and the front steps smelled of urine again. One afternoon I came home to find three dealers defiantly sitting on the stoop.

"Call the cops," Penknife taunted, refusing to budge.

I appealed to Miguel, but he said there was little he could do. "They know the police won't come. *Mami,* I can't control them."

I had visions of Anton playing on a nuclear landscape amid scarred trees. His trusting smile was painful. I dreamed of the limbless people whom I couldn't save in Africa. While I struggled to fall asleep, I half expected to hear the bridge blow up. By now al-Qaeda had claimed responsibility for the attacks. Surely the group wouldn't stop at this spectacular triumph. What would happen next? Suicide bombers in the subways?

During the day I moped around the house. My shared grief for strangers who had jumped from the towers only worsened the sleep deprivation of new motherhood, and simple things like attending to Anton's diaper rash seemed overwhelming. Sobbing after a mere glance at the newspaper one morning, I realized just how much I had relied on work as a defense mechanism in the midst of past tragedies. But even if I could have broken my funk to change out of sweatpants, I still didn't have a job to report to. New York University was closed temporarily. I had a written a long article for *The New York Times* on the West Harlem drug scene that was scheduled to run on September 16 under the title "Living at Ground Zero." But it had been delayed indefinitely after the towers were attacked, and for the time being the editor wasn't running copy that didn't directly relate to 9/11.

I moped around the house for days, compulsively watching replayed images of the imploding towers. Every evening Charles knocked on the door, and I'd go upstairs to eat dinner with him and Vianca in front of the television, where we revisited his ordeal. I was grateful for the company, as John was always at the office late. Our depressed little band comforted one another like family.

Because John was so busy with work, he didn't notice that I hadn't gotten out of the house in days. The one evening he came back in time for dinner, which wasn't prepared, he was so horrified by my sloth that he pulled the television plug right out of the wall.

"You've seen worse things abroad," he snapped. "Get a grip."

It was easy for John to say this, with his exciting, diverting job. Besides, how would he react if his hometown, Rotterdam, had been blitzed? Actually, I reflected, it *had* been bombarded during World War II, and John had been weaned on stories about the ordeal. I recalled that the plucky Dutch just picked themselves up and rebuilt the city, as well as their lives. Shamed by this realization, I did a load of laundry and dashed off some new article proposals for the *Times*.

Even this activity didn't lift the gloom, though. I hadn't lost anyone in the tragedy, but people I knew had. When the police barricades were finally removed near the university, I reported to work and faced a classroom full of students traumatized by the attacks. Many had seen people jumping from the World Trade Center windows, a hundred stories up, desperate to escape the flames. I encouraged them to write through their crises. Reading their stories only deepened the heaviness that I felt walking past the makeshift shrine to the dead under the arch at Washington Square Park.

I didn't need my social-worker mother to point out that the tragedy had awakened buried memories of events from my journalistic past. I needed only to see the smoke at the site to recall a mass grave in Rwanda, where the remains of fifteen thousand people had been exhumed and piled on platforms like strips of bacon. I dreamed each night about the South African men I had seen murdered with burning tires around their necks. My route to the university passed the photocopied flyers of the missing tacked up outside St. Vincent's Hospital, and the empty hope of the people who posted the pictures reminded me of refugees elsewhere. On windy days, I thought I smelled a whiff of smoldering corpses, but perhaps I was conjuring up a memory of a place far away.

The activists decided that this was not the moment to make demands on the beleaguered police, and meetings were called off for the time being. Bloodsaw had lost the primary race for councilman, and we felt especially voiceless without our hoped-for advocate to represent us. With the officers searching for the remains of nearly three thousand people, it seemed frivolous to complain about a couple hundred noisy drug dealers. Yet something needed to be done. It was bad enough that al-Qaeda had terrorized the entire city. We didn't need heartless dealers further intimidating it. I decided to fight back privately. Let them pay for their cold-bloodedness, I thought.

I developed my strategy in October, when Anthrax was discovered. One chilly afternoon I sidled over to the dealers, who were standing under a large American flag on the gate next to Salami's house. Then I transmitted a rumor that cocaine and Afghan heroin had been tainted with the deadly powder.

"Anthrax is best absorbed through mucous membranes," I informed Nose, in case he was unaware of the fatal effects. I used a the-atrically whispery voice.

Nose's face paled, which emphasized his red nostrils even more. I tapped my nose in turn. "People could die."

His breath grew shallow. *"Gracias,"* he mumbled.

"My pleasure." It was, to see him squirm.

Within twenty-four hours the streets were empty. They remained deserted for days. John and I didn't share our secret with anyone, not even Clarence. "Something must have spooked them," the super spec-ulated, as he searched in vain for even a candy wrapper to sweep up on the clean pavement.

Eventually, the rumor made it into the Spanish-language press.

"El ántrax afecta a los narcos," the October 25 edition of *El Diario* proclaimed. *"Una fuerte baja en la distribución y venta de cocaína y heroína ha sido el resultado de rumores sobre la posible mezcla de ántrax con aquellos otros 'polvitos blancos.' "*

("Anthrax affects the drug traffickers. Rumors about the possible mixture of anthrax with those other 'white powders' has caused a big drop in the distribution and sale of cocaine and heroin.")

One of the interviewees estimated that business had halved. An-other went so far as to speculate that this was a plot against the poor. It went on to quote some *tipos*—guys—who sounded suspiciously like the characters who loitered outside our front door.

John read the article with bemusement. "This is probably the only time that you've had an impact on an event as a journalist." I chuckled, but upon reflection didn't find it quite so funny.

As fall moved into winter, my gloom deepened. I kept waiting for another catastrophe to strike. What would be next—nerve gas? While President George W. Bush launched his war against terror, we West Harlemites felt under siege by the lack of police presence. It was hardly reassuring that a rash of thefts had occurred on the street, just paces from Nose's big American flag. A burglar slipped through the skylight of our neighbors, the Campbells, and took a pair of diamond studs and a microwave oven. Other people were then robbed farther up the road.

We wondered if Salami was profiting from the heists. He could barely push his stroller because it was stacked so high with televisions and microwaves. I declined his offer to buy but took down the serial numbers in order to report them.

John found a white Sharp microwave stashed in front of the house next door that fit the description of the Campbells' stolen goods. He picked it up with plastic bags wrapped around his hands so as not to leave fingerprints, and jotted down the serial number. But the Campbells didn't want to look at the device; they just wanted to forget the theft. We called the police, who unenthusiastically offered to send someone over to pick it up. However, the last thing we wanted was for a uniformed cop to ring our front bell and then walk out with a stolen good that we had lifted from its stash place. So we waited a couple of weeks until John had time to bring it over to the police precinct, discreetly covered with a black plastic bag. The dealers watched suspiciously as he strapped the unwieldy package onto his bike and wove up Broadway. I hoped they wouldn't tell Salami.

Spirits hit a new low on November 12. I walked into Mercedes's bodega to buy some diapers to hear the sound of a woman keening, "No, no, no." Mercedes was grimly ringing up votive candles with pictures of saints while the men who normally sat in the back room held the wailing woman from collapsing. In the background, a radio announced somberly in Spanish, "American Airlines flight five-eighty-seven . . . heading to the Dominican Republic . . . crashed in Belle Harbor, in Queens . . . two hundred and sixty aboard presumed dead."

The woman let out another cry.

Someone else burst into the shop. "Have you heard from them?"

"My cousin was on board," said one of the men.

"Are you sure?"

"He was on the flight. He took it every year."

Two middle-aged women with wet faces entered the shop. "Anyone have news of Manny?"

Mercedes made the sign of a cross. She held out a candle.

"One of the dealers lost his mother and his baby," a woman said. "I don't like the guy, but you have to feel for him."

"God is punishing them for selling drugs," tartly replied her companion.

Mercedes shook her head. "No, but you have to feel for him."

As I left the bodega, I saw cardboard and wooden shrines with pictures of the dead being set up along Broadway. The muchachos gathered around the one on our corner, looking subdued. No one had a cell phone out.

"You know anyone?" I asked.

"Him," Penknife said, pointing to a photograph on the shrine of a young man with neatly combed hair and the forced smile of a high school yearbook picture. Penknife's eyes filled. "It could have been me. I took that flight twice a year."

Without thinking, I touched his shoulder in sympathy. Then I recoiled, though I managed to hide it.

"I'm sorry." I meant it. The thought crossed my mind that under ordinary circumstances he might have pulled out his switchblade. Just weeks ago I was trying to sabotage his business, but now was not a time to hold a grudge. Penknife smiled wanly back. "This city's getting crazy," he said. "Too many people dying." It was a strange sentiment, I thought, from a merchant of death.

The sense of unyielding grief deepened with the approach of Christmas. Holiday decorations in New York normally cheer me up, but this year the lights had the opposite effect. It was impossible to forget September 11, what with the red, white, and blue bulbs erected on Broadway. Most were in good faith, but one light display on the 140th Street traffic median made me feel like grabbing a hammer and smashing it. The arrangement was of the Twin Towers, with an orange glow depicting where the planes had hit. Next to the towers was a light display of the Statue of Liberty, holding a red, white, and blue torch. She flashed a smile that looked like a smirk.

I took another route to the subway to avoid her mocking grin.

My mood lifted slightly when the police started dribbling back in mid-December. The men were emotionally drained after three months of overtime, and were mourning their comrades. They were pale and somber and tearful. There wasn't the usual banter and foul jokes. But the return of the cops, no matter how exhausted, was a sign that life was returning to normal.

It was deemed appropriate to hold a meeting right before Christmas. The activists agreed that they would not press matters too heavily, and this first gathering in three months served more as a social occasion to express appreciation for all the NYPD had been through. Even the most aggressive moaners among us extended sincere condolences. The cops teared up at the mention of their dead colleagues, and awkward hugs were delivered along with holiday wishes.

Despite their hiatus from West Harlem, law enforcers ended the year 2001 by seizing record amounts of cocaine, Ecstasy, and marijuana worth billions of dollars. We were still number one in narcotics arrests: 5,103.

The guy from the D.A.'s office handed out a report from Bridget Brennan, the tough special narcotics prosecutor for the city. We were amazed to read that she was taking a new tack: working with telecommunications carriers to ensure no "unnecessary obstacles" to gathering evidence to investigate and prosecute drug traffickers. Her office had implemented a digital eavesdropping investigation and presented high-tech wiretap evidence to a state grand jury.

We wondered whether this approach would really have an effect. It seemed so technical and removed. Miguel's boys were still here yakking on their cell phones and throwing garbage on the street. The SUVs were still coming over from New Jersey and keeping us awake with their noise. What was the difference?

The one thing that kept up my spirits after 9/11 was Anton. As my mother constantly reminded me, this small person was dependent on me, and now was no time to wallow in self-indulgent paralysis. After my initial urges to neglect my infant in favor of the biggest media event in the history of New York, it was impossible to ignore the enchantment of this little imp slowly engaging with the world. He had a beguiling tendency to stare deep into my eyes, hold his hand up in what looked like a thumbs-up, and then giggle raucously.

While Anton thrived, our dog deteriorated. Khaya's hind legs had so shriveled with arthritis that he howled with agony when trying to sit down. He became incontinent.

"Dead dog walking," a passerby intoned as we limped past one day, an all-too-apt remark. I made an appointment with the vet that afternoon.

She told us there was nothing she could do, gently suggesting that we were keeping him alive for our sake, not his. "You're not doing him any favors," she said, stroking the silver fur behind his ears. I burst into tears and Khaya, ever the comforter, licked my hand.

The next week, John and I took Khaya on his final walk—to the vet. At the examining table, John held the trusting animal's head as the needle went into his thick fur. He barked, and shuddered into still-ness.

The vet hugged us, and we slowly walked home.

The neighbors, as good neighbors will, checked up on us. Mrs. LaDuke and other dog owners called on us with little pretexts, knowing that we felt bereaved. It was oddly reassuring to go out on the block and see Mrs. Campbell shaking her broom at the muchachos. Even the po-lice meetings felt homey.

A handwritten note from someone I'd never met was slipped through our mail slot a week later. It was from a woman who lived up the hill, who identified herself as "The Lady from the Park." The enve-lope was addressed to Mr. John, Wife, and Little Baby Boy. I didn't know who it was. John said there were a lot of the ladies from the park whom he had met. The woman had heard that our pet had died and wanted to express her condolences. Folded inside the white envelope was a yellowed newspaper clipping from an Ann Landers advice col-umn, about putting a beloved pet to sleep.

The article was maudlin, though the bit about driving the dog to the vet one last time prompted a rush of tears. But what stirred me more was the notion that a stranger had taken the time to deliver the article. Judging from the neat cut of the scissors and brittleness of the paper, the clipping had had great meaning to the woman. She had guarded it carefully for years. It struck me as an act of generous grace to send it to people she barely knew. Uplifted by this thought, I walked toward the playground with Anton, wondering if I would run into the mystery woman. We bumped into Mr. Anderson, who was standing over his window boxes of plastic flowers.

"Isn't it lovely?" he exclaimed. "It's winter and they're still in bloom!"

PART THREE

Chapter 23

ADIÓS, MIGUEL

The real spring that arrived a few months later did not require plastic flowers. Live daffodils that had been a gift from the Netherlands to the city in memory of 9/11 sprouted under the oak trees lining the block. In fact, a gardening craze was under way, unlike any that we had seen in our previous two Aprils in West Harlem. Now, for the first time that anyone remembered, the old ladies were tackling their front yards. A row of bent-over figures sifted through the soil to clear out the crack vials. They reminded me of dentists doing root canals. With the dynamism she had used to shake her broom at the muchachos, Mrs. Campbell now tore out the weeds that clogged her hyacinth buds. "It was pointless to plant here before. The dealers trampled on the flowers," she explained. Mrs. Campbell pulled a particularly lethal shard of glass from the dirt. "Aha! Got it! What was I saying? Oh yes, the block is so much nicer now, so I thought, let's give it a try. Maybe the boys will leave the flowers alone." I went around the block and saw a welder drilling window boxes onto the façade of Mrs. LaDuke's house. She grinned flirtatiously at his back as she directed the work.

The sound of gentrifying repairs accompanied the botanical pursuits. The seasonal beacons of *bachata* and whacked baseballs were joined by new ones—the clunk of scaffolding planks, the whine of electric drills, the *tap-tap* of hammers. One morning I jolted awake at five o'clock to the clatter of a truck removing a Dumpster of construction debris from one of the crack houses. As much as I wanted to sleep, I felt excited as the vehicle thumped by. Every piece of rubbish inside it was a sign of momentum and change. The block had a turned a corner, so to speak.

Further vindicating our decision to move here was the sale of the last three crack houses on the street, including Salami's former domain. The eccentric owner finally parted with her hulk when the bank threatened to seize it through foreclosure. She proved herself a master of brinksmanship, signing the building away just a day before the repossession team came. The lucky winner was an architect with two young children, who paid what the owner could have gotten six months before. Salami found a place to live around the corner. A respectable elderly lady took him in, much to the annoyance of her relatives, who shared the brownstone. The woman saw it as her mission to save Salami's soul, but her family was more interested in protecting their silverware and other valuables. The good Samaritan installed Salami in the basement, where he stored his electronic junk. It was a symbiotic relationship; the lady gave Salami shelter and he did odd jobs for her, including, he said, providing "protection." The other two crack houses up the street went to some minor celebrities who upped the 'hood's cachet considerably: the Dominican writer Junot Díaz, and a hair stylist who did the tresses of Sarah Jessica Parker. Díaz had won a following as the literary voice of Dominican York prose, and he had graduated from writing about crack houses to buying and renovating one. Even cynical Clarence was impressed, in his fashion.

"Who would have thought one of them buildings would go for more than half a million dollars?" he said one morning, marveling at the arrival of another Dumpster. "Anything could happen here. All these bad things happening in the world. Suppose there would be an earthquake? They say it's our last days. Tell me about it. We never used to have so many earthquakes and hurricanes."

On other streets, middle-class families were settling in in noticeable numbers, so many that yellow cabs, spotting new business opportunities, began to cruise with regularity on Broadway.

"They're back!" Mr. Anderson exclaimed about the vehicles, as though talking about the swallows returning to Capistrano.

With so many abandoned houses now filled with young families, we had a gold mine of playmates for Anton, or rather potential future playmates. Less than a year old, he was still new even to the concept of parallel play. Our son replaced the dog as the family diplomat in terms of making new acquaintances on the street, and we benefited from his engaging smile. He had widened his seductive power beyond the mezzo upstairs, and the oddity of his auburn curls and milky skin attracted much attention. Typical of mothers starved of social company at home, I struck up conversations with anyone in proximity to another small human body.

This being New York, I found others as culturally adrift as my husband and me, and we gradually amassed a new social life that was rich with roots in the Southern Hemisphere. Encounters by the sandbox gave us a sense of the latest immigration trends: Mexicans, Albanians, Surinamese, Ecuadorians, and, of course, Dominicans. At the playground, the familiar lilt of Swahili opened a particularly warm acquaintance with Bilal, an electrician from Tanzania, with a doll-faced little daughter. A serendipitously slow red light gave reason to meet Rose, a Haitian painter with a green-eyed baby, Unico, named after a favored wine. Through them, we met Ghelila, who was just as beautiful as her Ethiopian mother.

While cultivating friendships on the street, we also felt we had won an ally at the NYPD, in none other than the new police commissioner himself. After taking office in January, Mayor Bloomberg appointed Raymond W. Kelly, who seemed even more receptive to the West Harlem activists than his predecessor had been. There was no reason to doubt Kelly's sincerity. In a previous incarnation at the Treasury Department in 1997, Kelly had cracked down on the money laundering of

Dominican traffickers. Under his urgings, the federal government imposed stricter reporting requirements on electronic cash transfers to the Dominican Republic. The sums sent back to the island by small wiring parlors on Broadway had gone down dramatically. Now Kelly was determined to get to the heart of the narcotics trading floor itself. He drew up a plan with narcotics chief William Taylor and the commander of the 30th Precinct, Captain Cody. In April they launched their crackdown—surprisingly named "Operation Crackdown." It was a multi-pronged attack, deploying scores of extra forces, among them the best men of the five boroughs.

A huge police trailer was installed on the corner of Broadway, within full view of our house. The cops flooded the zone with every sort of unit: foot, bicycle, and horseback patrols and vans and unmarked cars. Twenty more uniformed officers were deployed temporarily to help out the precinct's 189 beleaguered members. Another 100 undercover narcotics operatives saturated the area.

The area was so drenched in law enforcement that the cops struggled to keep track of who was on what side. Undercovers approached one another to do deals, and two police cars crashed into each other on Broadway.

In one particularly memorable instance, traffic police ticketed a car that belonged to undercovers who were conducting a raid inside of Clarence's building. The lawn-chair ladies who did lookout duty for the dealers—whose apartment was being searched—doubled over with laughter. The joke was too good to keep quiet.

"Yo," one portly mama called out to the traffic cop. "Leave that car alone. It's one of yours."

The cop didn't believe her. "Mind your own business." He stuck the paper under the windshield wiper and stalked away.

I myself was amazed that any dealer would sell to anyone these days, seeing that the streets were teeming with undercovers. But sell they did. And every day we watched men hauled away in handcuffs, or pushed up against cars, whole groups of up to twenty of them.

The operation bore fruit. By June 2002, the NYPD claimed three hundred more narcotics arrests than the previous year. I calculated that that was about as many men who would hang out within a few blocks of my house on a given day. Quality-of-life-violation citations ballooned by 138 percent, as irate citizens grew louder about reporting drug nuisances. More than half of the detainees faced heavy sentences that carried twenty-five years or more. At a community meeting, Captain Cody was more cheerful than I had ever seen him, as though he didn't quite believe it was happening. The bags under his eyes had lightened and he smiled readily.

"What matters isn't necessarily the numbers. What matters is getting the key guys," Cody said giddily, explaining that the police were targeting more big fish for offenses like conspiracy. "I'm really excited about what's happening," he confided, adding that this was an open-ended campaign. For the first time, the city wasn't going to cut off funding or manpower by a predetermined date.

The old-timers were thrilled, too, especially given that this was less than a year after 9/11. At a time when police resources were stretched by increased vigilance against terrorism, Operation Crackdown was surely a sign of commitment to West Harlem. "They really seem to mean business," commented Bloodsaw.

Part of the NYPD assault involved new targets, and the cops were casting their nets past the SUV-driving "give me ten kilos" Latino wholesalers. One of the officers' favorite trawling grounds was the parking space in front of the church next door, and their zealousness was such that they would pounce on cars with New Jersey license plates even before the drivers shut off the ignition.

Although the cops would never admit it, racial profiling was in effect. The new quarry was what could be described as the white artsy type, prone to thrift-shop chic and looking for a party-night gram. The police went for cigarette smokers who were too thin, and red-eyed people who clearly hadn't slept much the night before.

In other words: our basement tenant. Aidan was having a lot of late nights these days, and no amount of Clinique aftershave or crisp shirts could change the fact that he fit the suspect description. The police spared no opportunity to drape the unfortunate kid and his friends over car hoods, or stop them for document checks. Aidan reported that even an innocent trip to Broadway to pick up a pizza resulted in a full body search.

While other residents of the block—including the lookout ladies who were working in cahoots with Miguel—were allowed to cross the wooden barricades when a raid was under way, Aidan would have to wait until the operation was over to enter his apartment. As raids sometimes lasted four hours, this was a huge inconvenience for a guy who had run home just to change clothes before an audition or club hopping.

The cops were also sabotaging Aidan's social life. On hot nights, fifteen of his closest friends might gather in his apartment to enjoy its turbo air-conditioning. Now they refused to visit for fear of being detained.

I had wondered if Aidan's complaints were exaggerated: He wanted to be an actor, after all, so drama was his specialty. But then I happened to walk by one evening as he was shoved, spread-eagled, against a police car by a muscular cop muttering, "Explain it, bud." The officer gripped Aidan's Banana Republic wallet in his right hand. Apparently, the Colorado license of our tenant had prompted suspicion—the police were targeting out-of-state drivers—but it was hard for him to explain matters with his mouth pressed against the car hood. The cop wasn't much older than Aidan; he probably was one of those newly graduated rookies who were notorious for their zeal to get collars. I thought I saw Aidan smile as the officer's hands moved to the inside of his thighs, but then he grimaced as the frisking went higher and rougher.

I bounced over, perky as a cheerleader. "Hi, Aidan! *There* you are!"

The cop glanced up grumpily from his half nelson. "You know this guy?"

"Sure do!" I chirped. "He's our tenant. Hey, Aidan, how's it going?"

The policeman appeared annoyed at being interrupted. He reluctantly handed over Aidan's wallet.

"Go, scram!" he said, as though to a cat.

Aidan straightened up and hurried back to the house without even waiting for me.

We got the situation slightly under control after I complained to Commander Cody. As per his instructions, I issued Aidan a letter that essentially served as a visa to enter the street. The document stated that our tenant was an upstanding citizen who lived in the building. I told

"Whom It May Concern" that Commander Cody had granted him right of passage and should be called in case of doubts.

As the operation continued, police became constant fixtures on our block. Even more undercovers came over to chat as they awaited vans to take the detainees to jail. One particular dark-haired guy made a habit of leaning on the gate and discussing the real estate market; his brother had paid off the mortgage on his house in Queens and was looking for a good investment elsewhere. It was unseemly for me to be seen fraternizing with the enemy, but the muchachos were headed to Rikers Island and besides, there's no proper etiquette for asking an armed officer to buzz off, as many times as I had tried in Africa.

While Anton snoozed in the stroller one evening, this undercover, Franco, recounted for me the Method acting techniques that got him into character. He smoothed down his greasy goatee and gave his shoulders a shake.

"I never was into acting in high school but I take it very seriously now. You have to prepare the role and practice your lines carefully," he explained earnestly. "I develop a character down to whether he drinks coffee. I'm half Puerto Rican but I grew up in an Italian neighborhood, so I can play anything from a Mafia tough guy to a Hispanic drug dealer." Franco squinted meanly to fit the part. "I have a good story. I give them names of relatives back on the island, if they want to know whom I'm dealing with. These are real names, but there's no way that they could check it out."

His other trick was to mine his inner shyness.

"It helps to act low-key. The thing about cops, they can be too aggressive. If a suspect asks for a hundred thousand dollars, the undercover might offer a hundred and five thousand just to seal the deal. That arouses suspicions because that's not the way people do business. A real businessman wants to get the product for cheaper, so he'd offer ninety-five thousand and then walk away until they called him back to negotiate. So I say, 'Forget it,' and walk away. That way, they trust me."

Franco had lots of opportunity to develop his character. The average investigation in this neighborhood lasted about ten months for a midlevel gang that moved a kilo every two weeks. One of his favorite parts of the job was following a suspect.

"We always do 'a day in the life.' There will be eight team members in solo cars. I'll never forget one guy we followed. It went like this: He gets up, has breakfast, visits his mother, hangs out with his friends, does some transactions, goes to the video arcade, sees his wife, picks up the kids from school, goes to Jersey. All the time he's on the cell phone doing transactions. Then he spends three hours with his girl-friend, then he goes to 42nd Street and Eleventh Avenue and gets sex from a he-she in his car. I remember, it was a black Nissan Maxima. Then he goes to 181st and Amsterdam, hangs out with some friends, they meet three woman friends, and get motel rooms in Lodi, New Jersey. They check in, we stay the whole night until they leave."

It sounded like a ton of fun for the guy they were following, but highly dangerous. Wasn't Franco frightened?

"Nah. Maybe I'm deluding myself, but I don't think I'm going to be blown away. I've had people put guns in my face. I've been hospitalized seventeen times, hit by a car, beaten. But never stabbed or shot. One guy put out a fifty-thousand-dollar contract on me once. He offered a hundred thousand if they killed me in front of my family. Did I hide my wife and son in another country when it first happened? Yes. But I'm not scared now."

Suddenly one of the lawn-chair ladies came out of Clarence's building. She stood by the van and watched us with ill-disguised hostility. The undercover considered her thoughtfully. "The females are the most difficult ones. The guys, maybe it's a macho thing, they just do the deal and don't make much small talk. But the females look at you, and they ask questions like, 'Where are you from?' You have to be careful with the females."

The woman continued to stare suspiciously. I had a vision of her storming over and demanding, "Where are you from?" This hobnobbing with New York's Finest in front of her would not do. I suggested that maybe, just perhaps, of course only if he wanted to, Franco might want to join his colleagues across the street.

· · ·

By June, the swarm of cops and the big mobile police office on the corner had put a damper on the activities of Miguel and Company. The muchachos continued to sit on the steps of the formerly abandoned house next door, refusing to move an inch even when the new owner and her contractor came to inspect the property. Still, the boys seemed on edge, and tended to spend more time inside El Floridita than on the open street. Perhaps it was my imagination, but Miguel seemed less friendly to me, and avoided eye contact.

I wondered if he was behind a new campaign to move the police van. According to Commander Cody, several Dominican merchants believed to be sympathetic to the dealers had complained to the Civilian Complaint Review Board that the police presence was scaring off business.

"We'll have to move the van," Cody said apologetically at a community meeting. He suggested that the residents who approved of the van write to the board to say so. Yet again, a petition campaign was mobilized, and the old ladies went door to door to collect signatures. The van stayed.

Eventually the law caught up with the muchachos. I came home on the balmy afternoon of June 18—two years after we had bought the house—to find thirty-six of the usual suspects squatting uncomfortably on the corner, wrists handcuffed behind their backs. Miguel was among them. He managed to look dignified in that humiliating position, and even succeeded in straightening his trouser leg without using his hands, a feat that impressed me to no end. As the police rifled through his wallet to look for identity documents, Miguel calmly rolled his neck as though he were merely taking a break from a computer screen. He looked remarkably relaxed for a man who could be facing twenty-five years in jail. Our eyes met. I asked: "You?" He shrugged, a calm shrug. I wanted to say something but couldn't find the words. Lacking appropriate language, I went to the stoop, and watched for what felt like a slow half hour. Miguel continued to remain stylishly calm in that squatting position. Eventually, the police led him to a marked van, and Miguel looked out the back window expressionlessly, as the vehicle pulled away.

As I contemplated the empty corner, I felt surprised by my ambivalence over Miguel's arrest. I wouldn't go so far as to say that he was a friend, but I did sort of miss him already. It was a relief to see the guys off the street, but who would replace them? Miguel was relatively benign for the head of a street drug crew, and we had had a decent, respectful working relationship for two years. He was the devil that we knew, and a gentlemanly devil at that. Who would follow Miguel? Would it be someone mean like Penknife? That would erase all the stability we had so carefully negotiated.

Miguel was arraigned two days later under the name Miguel Pérez Pérez. That made me smile: It was a common name, the Dominican equivalent of John Smith. At last count, the D.A.'s office had 102 Miguel Pérezes in its books. Also arrested were men identified as Albert Rincón, Emiliano Alvarez, and José Sánchez. The D.A.'s office wasn't sure if these were their real names, as dealers, especially those in the country illegally, often used aliases or fake identification.

Wanting to know more about this mystery man who, for better or worse, had been such a fixture on the street, I asked a contact at the D.A.'s office to read me the court docket. It described Miguel as thirty-seven years old, birthplace unknown, current residence in the Kingsbridge section of the Bronx. I took a taxi to check out the street—it was quiet and leafy with two-story white clapboard houses of the type common in working-class areas of outer boroughs. The neighborhood used to be heavily Irish, but was seeing an increase in Latinos, and it struck me as the perfect place to maintain a low profile. The undercovers had told me it was not uncommon for dealers to live far from their place of business, in quiet residential areas not known for narcotics activity. Miguel's address—or rather what he claimed was his abode when arrested—was the sole apartment building on the block, a yellowish brick property. The only hint of possible dubious activity was a couple of muscled guys in do-rags loitering outside.

Court records said Miguel had prior criminal records in other states. This time he was arrested for multiple sales of cocaine, including three counts in excess of two ounces and selling near school grounds. The coke had been stashed in brown paper lunch bags and clear plastic ones. The offense could get him up to twenty-five years in prison and bail was set for $72,000. A bondsman paid the minimum $15,000 in cash.

I never saw Miguel again. Nor did anyone else in West Harlem, from what I gathered. Miguel jumped bail, and knew better than to come back.

Two tabby cats appeared in our backyard. Perhaps they were drawn by the rats dislodged into the block's gardens by the demolition of the crack houses. The felines snoozed on the garden table that we had bought from Leticia, leaving striped hairs on the batik tablecloth that I had brought from Kenya. The cats were sufficiently tame; we could even touch them, although they were too skittish to pick up. We named them Lola and Bloomberg: the first after the Kinks' song about a transvestite because we were unsure of its sex. The second cat was an interloper who strutted in and established himself as the alpha. This reminded us of businessman Michael Bloomberg, who had upset the front-runners in his race for mayor the previous year and had changed the city—and especially our neighborhood—in such large and generally positive ways.

We added seafood Meow Mix to the weekend grocery runs, but fed the cats only small dishes so as not to ruin their appetites for live rodents. After one misguided incident when I invited Lola into the kitchen—he revealed his true gender by pungently marking the walls— I promised John that I wouldn't try to domesticate these felines. At least, not as long as Mrs. LaDuke had a killer dog just beyond our backyard.

The human occupants left the crack houses as well. They came back to the street only occasionally to score, running their hands behind the garbage cans and on car tires hoping to find a stray package left behind. Mackenzie said one couple from up the street had gone to a city shelter. The female of the pair was pregnant and didn't want to squat in a crack house in her delicate state. Other addicts moved to the homeless colony by the river. Salami rarely appeared on our street anymore, and

Mackenzie said he was still living with the old lady around the corner. The hunched-over guy from our block took up residence on the A train. Sometimes our paths crossed, and we'd nod hello as he panhandled from car to car. I wasn't sure if he could place me out of context. He gave me a vague look, as though he recognized me from somewhere.

About twenty-five hundred drug suspects had been arrested by mid-August. As Operation Crackdown continued, the remaining guys on the street made themselves scarce. I didn't see Nose or Penknife, and guessed that they had been picked up or had fled to the Dominican Republic. Mackenzie, too, kept a low profile and spent long periods in the cellar "reading and resting."

He reflected on his own close calls. "The dumb risks because of addiction and opportunity. I could have gotten twenty-five years to life for taking two kilos from here to 143rd Street on a dolly filled with rocks and debris. They paid me fifty bucks to go past a slew of cops and then wait ten minutes for someone to open the door." He shook his head. "I wouldn't do that again."

So many muchachos had been arrested that the corner was often empty. The replacements flown in from the Dominican Republic were a rudderless bunch. I didn't expect any reaction from them when I published an article about the drug trade for *The New York Times*. Surely they didn't read the *Times*, I thought.

I was probably right. However, I didn't think about the newspaper of choice of their rich white lawyers.

In a bad version of the game Telephone, word went out on *Radio Bemba* that I had referred to all Dominicans as criminals. The coke salesmen apparently also took offense at my assertion that their business robbed legitimate residents of parking spaces. Later in the afternoon, a clutch of dealers glared as I strolled by with Anton after buying milk at Mercedes's. I nodded hello, but one guy shook a can of orange spray paint and ostentatiously painted our house address in big letters on the asphalt next to the curb.

"This is your parking spot," he spat. "Now *everyone* will know where you live."

The sound of the shaking ball in the can attracted Anton's attention and he looked with intent curiosity at the orange letters.

I smiled. First, the graffiti artist had gotten the wrong house; he had written my address in front of Salami's old hovel. Second, I wondered out loud, what was the point of the exercise? "Everyone but you knows where I live."

The painter considered this, with much annoyance. His confederates laughed.

Jokes aside, the incident was unsettling. Had I gone too far with my article? My sister and her Puerto Rican husband were angry at me; they felt I had written insensitively about an issue that was a sore point with many Dominicans. Rattled, I ran the story by Manuel and Raul, who were Dominican. They thought I had reported in an impartial way, although Manuel noted that I was pretty dumb not to have anticipated a backlash from the dealers. He was right: I was so much in the foreign-correspondent mentality, where one writes for a distant readership, that I didn't consider the dangers of reporting on my own neighborhood. The police crackdown had made me feel cocky enough to write about what I saw, but with my usual lack of foresight I hadn't contemplated possible consequences. Without Miguel I had lost a safety net, however thin. Miguel would never have spray-painted in front of the house. He would have taken me aside with his soft hand and told me in silky terms that he was upset. Who knew what these guys would do? I shared my misgivings with John, who predictably didn't see cause for worry. "They're not going to hurt a white reporter," he said dismissively. "They know the wrath of law enforcement would descend."

John's nonchalance about our welfare was not shared by the chairman of our community board, Mr. Goodwill, who dropped by one morning to give Anton a plastic gingerbread man tree ornament that he had meant to deliver at Christmas. A melodramatic rotund fellow given to wearing long scarves, the chairman slammed his teacup on the kitchen table when I told him about the dealers' reaction.

"No harm shall befall you!" Mr. Goodwill thundered, waving his arms in an expansive V. He reminded me of Sylvester Stallone in the movie *Rocky* after he knocked out an opponent. I hoped Mr. Goodwill wouldn't hit anybody. His scarf slipped, and he swung it over his shoulder with a dramatic flourish. Anton put down the ornament, which he'd been gnawing on, watching the chairman in wonder.

Just to alarm the good man further, I shared the contents of an e-mail from a Listserv of Dominican-American professionals. One member of the group, a lawyer, urged the others to storm our house. She felt that I had denigrated the community by suggesting that some Dominicans tolerated the dealers, and she argued that, as a homeowner, I was clearly motivated by greed to protect my property value. (This logic escaped me. If I wanted top dollar for the house, why would I broadcast to the world that this was a lawless corner overrun by thugs?)

I recounted all this to the chairman, whose large eyes angrily bulged at the thought that a constituent had been threatened.

"Measures will be taken," Mr. Goodwill proclaimed loudly, sweeping Anton into his arms for a good-bye hug. "No one will hurt this innocent child!"

My stomach knotted as he charged out the door. What was he up to? Would Mr. Goodwill deliver on his name? Or would he inflict more mischief?

Days passed without undue drama. In any case, I had other matters with which to occupy myself: the visit of the Dutch in-laws. John's older brother, Carel, and his wife were social anthropologists who specialized in apes, and they had spent years in the jungles of Sumatra intrepidly tracking orangutans. However, a visit to New York was an unnerving prospect for these gentle travelers, who felt more comfortable in rain forests than among skyscrapers. We didn't see them often and I wanted them to feel relaxed with us. The pair was particularly protective of their shy ten-year-old daughter, Johanna, who was intimidated by this big city.

Despite his dislike of urban spaces, Carel was intrigued by the goings-on on the block and leaped out of the house at the sound of a crowd. A definite highlight of his visit was when the cops hauled off another load of muchachos to Rikers Island, and he eagerly went outside to observe the aggressive mob that was shouting abuse at the police.

His daughter was less enthusiastic about the excitement of West Harlem. Accustomed to country living, she was upset by the police cars racing up our street the wrong way. We repeatedly assured her that she was safe.

Our words, however, rang hollow when Carel and his family returned from a pleasant day at the Bronx Zoo. In front of our door a uniformed cop stood guard. The guy looked uncomfortable—either because of the stares he was getting from the muchachos or because his uniform included Bermuda shorts. He looked more like an English schoolboy than a protector of the peace. I had an idea why he had been assigned to our door.

We knew from experience in Africa that there's nothing like an armed man to provoke another armed man. This was like sending out a beacon to the block that we were in cahoots with the police. Even more worrying was John's explosive reaction. He was puffing up like a rooster spoiling for a fight.

"You'll have to move," John ordered the man in shorts.

The cop looked longingly at the freedom of Broadway—so close, yet so far. "Can't. Orders," he said regretfully.

"Whose orders?" John's voice dropped an octave.

The policeman put his hand on his holster for greater authority. "The commander of Manhattan North, Díaz. He says you need protection."

Fearing that we might soon have a dead cop on our doorstep, I dashed in to dial the commander. As I suspected, Mr. Goodwill had put out the word that we needed a twenty-four-hour guard. Commander Díaz seemed a bit surprised that we didn't want a uniformed cop announcing to the dealers that we were cooperating with law enforcement. He agreed to "sort it out."

His idea of defusing the situation was to send a second uniformed officer to the house, to make sure that we truly felt uncomfortable having the first cop around.

"Nice woodwork," the lieutenant commented admiringly upon entering the hallway, after ordering the cop in Boy Scout shorts to remain in place. "Is that oak or mahogany?"

The lieutenant understandably preferred our air-conditioned house to patrolling in ninety-degree heat, and was in no hurry to venture back outside. He invited himself in, settling down on our living room couch for a prolonged chat about real estate.

"I've always wanted to see the inside of one of these brownstones," he said. "How much did you pay?"

He inquired about electrical overhaul and roof. After about an hour of this pleasant company—he had some terrific suggestions for landscaping the garden—we politely suggested that perhaps he should protect the good citizens of West Harlem. He reluctantly picked up his hat and headed out the door.

He turned. "That was one hell of a good buy." Then he tapped the officer melting from the heat in front of the house and told him he could go.

We thought we were done with our personal guard, and felt more relaxed in the company of the muchachos. No longer would they think we were handing them over to Rikers Island. But unbeknownst to us, the police had so many spare undercovers running around the neighborhood that they instructed whoever was on the beat to keep an eye on the house. In the weeks to come, the drug crowds thinned remarkably.

By the end of the summer, all the familiar faces on the street were gone. We heard from Mackenzie that some of them went back to the Dominican Republic. New imports appeared on the corner, but they kept to the safety of Broadway and rarely strayed onto our side street.

Any doubt that the tide was turning was erased when I consulted the crime anthropologist Ric Curtis. Stephanie Herman, one of his disciples who had studied the sales crews on 136th Street, joined us.

The report from the academic front lines was that the dealing was on the decline. Some of Herman's subjects were talking about leaving the pavement to take computer courses. Others considered taking advantage of their stylish looks to pursue modeling.

"They are always asking if I can get them a job," she said. "One even asked me for help in writing a résumé."

Chapter 24

A SON OF THE *CALLE*

There was no doubt: Anton was a true son of the *calle*. While the other middle-class kids were playing with wooden blocks, his favorite games were "Cops and Dealers" and "Triple Parking." These were enactments of scenes he had witnessed from our window. The tableau involved lining up his little plastic men in formation on a mock street, where cars were parked in three parallel lines. Then, when a toy police car approached, they scattered, shouting what sounded like *"¡Coño!"* Occasionally he'd vary the scene, with a miniature ambulance frantically trying to get past.

While amusing, this game was discomfiting. What else might he pick up? Would his stuffed koala buy mock drugs from the teddy bear? And what about when he was older?

Something else was peculiar. We had read in child development books that awareness of racial identity came later in life, certainly not at twenty months. However, Anton not only seemed to be conscious of ethnicity and race, but he thought he was the wrong one.

It was true. Our son didn't realize he was white. We gave him both white and brown dolls, but he would point to the coffee-colored ones and say, "Anton!" Just in case my eyes betrayed me, I asked him which was Mama. Anton picked up the white one and held it up. My son's sense of skewed identity was a mirror image of the 1940s test by psychologists Kenneth and Mamie Clark, in which children with dark complexions preferred white dolls. The same kids colored in outlined figures white or yellow when asked to choose hues the same as themselves. Clark said his test proved that segregation had a damaging effect on personality development. Had we unwittingly fostered the same self-hatred in our young son by immersing him in Latino culture?

That wasn't all. From an uncommonly early age, Anton developed a fashion sense that veered toward bling. Children generally like sparkles, but our son gravitated excessively to flash. He liked to drape himself with the emeralds and gold chains and bangles that Miryam's husband had bought her in Colombia. He looked like a tiny white Ja Rule, minus the tattoos and muscles. From age one onward, Anton insisted on putting on shades before leaving the house, regardless of whether it was sunny or not. The child development books told us that small kids often copy their parents, but we had no idea where he got the sunglass mania. We never wore them. It could only be the coke dealers.

Strangers were taken aback by this red-haired *gringo*. Anton had learned to dance salsa and the *cumbia* from Miryam, and he would break into an impressive swivel any time he heard the beats on Broadway. More than once we heard someone exclaim, "Where did that kid learn to dance?"

All this was cute, but not the fact that Anton spoke only Spanish. Being multilingual ourselves, we were thrilled that Anton spoke another language, except that it was his *only* language. We were confounded by his complete lack of mastery of the two parental tongues. The pediatrician speculated that this was because Spanish was the easiest of the three languages to master. I suspected that it was because Miryam was a better pedagogue than we were. Anton's only word that sounded remotely like English was "cuck," an amalgam of *car* and *truck*. Nothing was uttered in Dutch. I read to him two hours a day, enunciating as precisely as Eliza Doolittle, but Anton trained his hazel gaze upon me and asked in puzzlement, *"¿Qué, Mami?"* Our son's command of English was so poor that he qualified for a state program that provided free speech therapy three times a week. Dyslexia and speech troubles ran in the family—I had struggled to speak properly and read when young—but the caseworker doubted that an organic problem had caused Anton's handicap. "It's his environment," she concluded and suggested that he work with a bilingual speech therapist to enhance the learning process. She also recommended that we enroll Anton in a private preschool where he could have contact with English-speaking kids.

The latter suggestion required some getting used to. We learned to our amazement that New York City did not have free nursery schools. John and I were products of public education, and the notion that we would have to fork out $4,500 to give our toddler the privilege of playing with plastic dinosaurs in English seemed a bit excessive.

"This is what I hate about American society," John grumbled. "You have to pay for what's a human right. Learning should be free. That's how we Dutch do it."

Nonetheless, we both warmed to the idea of exclusive education after I inspected a grim day-care center in the neighborhood where irritable adults barked at listless, crying children. And we did want Anton to learn English.

We applied to a school conveniently situated across the street from Columbia University, where I now taught. John could easily take Anton by bicycle on the mornings that I was not reporting to work. This school had come recommended by colleagues with whom we had worked in Africa and Russia. Their kids seemed happy and spoke good English. Aside from the nurturing environment, a major draw was that the school was still taking applications, unlike the other ten that we had contacted. Having lived abroad for so long, I hadn't realized that Manhattan preschools were harder to get into than Harvard, and that the application procedure closed in some places as early as November. I had started looking months later, in February, and had just made it under the wire with this place.

The school claimed a large proportion of European families, and our European colleagues assured us that we—or at least John—would fit right in. The school, however, could not have been more different from Anton's home environment. The community was Episcopalian, socially conservative, and overwhelmingly moneyed. We—a Jewess, a socialist Dutchman, and a child who thought he was Latino—did not seem an ideal fit. But we pinned hopes on the admissions director, who appeared to have an appreciation for all things European. During our tour of the school, she threw in French phrases and enthused about our global wanderings.

"*C'est très magnifique*," she said, while presenting the magnificent library.

"Yeah," I replied.

We took as a good sign that, when showing off the art room, she threw John a pointed look as she made a comparison with the northern light of Flemish Renaissance painters. (Afterward, John asked me: "What the hell was she talking about?")

I felt compelled to make a good impression on the day of Anton's "interview," with assimilation in mind. Since he couldn't speak English, I wanted him at least to look the part of someone who could. My plan was to deemphasize the street flair and go heavy on European chic, and I chose a jaunty olive-green jersey that sported the words TOUR DU MONDE, sent by a friend from Paris. I thought that this would convey that our boy was *cosmopolitain*. (If anyone commented, I would say, oh so casually, "Yes, it was a present from our friend Michel, who writes for *Le Monde*.") The effect, however, was spoiled by Anton's own sartorial preferences. He grabbed his shades and neck chain from the corridor table on the way out, and turned his baseball cap backward. I sighed but didn't fuss; I couldn't risk a tantrum on the Big Day.

I nervously escorted my son into the cheery interview room of blocks and toys to find three other sets of equally nervous parents sitting uncomfortably at toddler-height tables, rubbing their backs. We shot looks of competitive hatred at one another above forced smiles. The other children were kitted out in lovely ensembles from the French apparel company Petit Bateau. No bling in sight. A handsome woman with a large bosom presented herself as the observing teacher.

Anton observed her in turn, climbed into her lap, and said, "Ciao, baby," as he snuggled into her chest.

He then squirmed vigorously in her lap, waved his police car at groin level, and exclaimed: "Cuck!"

The teacher looked uneasily at me. I smiled weakly. "That's his word for vehicles. You know, like an amalgam of *truck* and *car.*"

She didn't say anything.

"His father is European," I said lamely.

One purposeful little boy headed straight to the easel and began painting a Cubist masterpiece. "Just like Kandinsky!" exclaimed the admissions director. We all agreed it was terrific.

A budding mathematician on the other side of the room counted to ten in English and then in Chinese. Then he did it backward. "He's only two!" the admissions director marveled. "Incredible!" I enthused, wanting to seem like a good sport.

The admissions director looked at Anton, searching for something nice to say. She frowned as she thought, and then came up with something. "What beautiful coloring he has!" she said.

"Yes, I don't know where that red hair came from," I replied.

She looked taken aback.

Oh, boy—there I went again. "I mean, of course I know who the father is. It's my husband. But he doesn't have red hair. I'm not a real redhead. My color is fake. I read something about recessive genes—you just never know what's going to pop up in later generations," I prattled on.

The admissions director looked away, at my son. With dismay, I noticed that he continued to nestle atop the buxom lady and had not explored the play area like a normal intellectually gifted child. I pointed animatedly to a basket of toy vehicles. "Look, Anton! Look! Nice toys!" Anton obediently climbed off his voluptuous nesting spot and set up a game of Cops and Dealers. He made a convincing "woo, woo" of a siren as the police cars careened into the passenger cars and knocked them over. This awakened the admissions woman's interest.

"What are you doing, honey?"

"Cuck. *Policía.*"

I felt that translations were in order and in my nervousness spoke without thinking. "Art imitating life, " I said, anxious to show that my son had an active brain underneath those Titian curls. "Drug dealers work on our street. He's re-creating a police raid. He watches from the front window and then acts it out, with embellishments. He has a vivid imagination."

"Oh." The admission director's Dior-lined lips twitched at a loss for words.

I couldn't think of anything else to say, having obviously put my foot in my mouth yet again. I watched as my son created a traffic pileup on the imaginary street. The dealers exacted their revenge on the police, who were run over by the triple-parked cars.

As we left the building, I resigned myself to rejection, and went online to read about home schooling. I would have to accept that Anton would not learn English until kindergarten. Worse things could happen, I thought. I called John to report on our fiasco.

"At least we'll save money," he said. "I really don't like the idea of paying for education."

Two weeks later, an envelope from the school arrived. I waited a long while before opening it. What was the point of confronting this humiliation? We were fated to be outsiders wherever we went. I prepared myself for the negative response as I unfolded the letter, citing as my mantra, "We'll save money, we'll save money." I had so prepared myself for a rebuff that I needed to readjust my thinking when I finally read the letter. Anton had been accepted and the school said it was delighted.

In early 2003, Salami got new front teeth.

What's more, Salami assured me that he had entered a drug rehab program. "I'm clean, Mama. Those days are behind me," he insisted.

I wasn't convinced. Salami often gave off an unwashed smell, and he still had moments of manic highs when he'd scurry up and down the block shouting, "Love is in the air!" Still, I was willing to give him the benefit of the doubt. He had dropped all claims on our house. After three years, he had not hurt us. I wanted to believe that the neighborhood, its denizens included, had become a calm place where one might feel comfortable bringing up a kid. I asked if Salami missed the drugs.

"Miss being miserable? Mama, you gotta be kidding."

One day, as I escorted Anton down the steps on the way to school, Salami was sweeping up broken glass in front of our house. I didn't quite trust his motives, but Salami made a big fuss about the public service he was performing. For the first time that I had known him, he didn't try to hit me up for money.

"You gave me money when I was starving. Now it's my turn to look out for you," Salami explained. "Besides, it won't do for the Gerber baby to step on glass."

It wasn't just Salami's attitude that had changed. Something strange happened one night as we sat under the dogwood tree in the garden, watching the fireflies. The light switched on next door! A light-bulb! We needed no more proof: Someone lived next door, a person who paid electricity bills and didn't smoke crack. Before, I only reluctantly joined John outside after dark; I never felt completely safe in our yard after sundown, knowing the adjoining houses on both sides were abandoned. This one flick of a switch erased three years of apprehension.

The buyer of Salami's old house had quickly rebuilt it. The first thing she did was air out the stench. Then she tore off the psychedelic wallpaper, stripped the wood, and restored the 1950s bathrooms. I felt like I was watching a once-delinquent child graduate from Yale. Even Salami was impressed with the workmanship, though he differed with the way she designed her new kitchen, with stainless-steel appliances. ("They should have hired me. I got a good eye.") I asked if Salami regretted seeing his former abode inhabited by others. "Nah, it's better this way. I wish all these dealers would go away. Then I wouldn't be tempted." He looked unusually thoughtful.

The new owner also knocked down the pernicious mulberry tree that had so sullied our yard. She planted wildflowers that attracted white butterflies. We in turn enhanced our garden with new crabapple and holly trees. With the help of a new bird book and binoculars—which Anton generally held upside down—we identified fifteen different types of migrating birds passing through our yard. A mockingbird sang on warm nights.

So many other middle-class families had now moved into West

Harlem that the impetus grew to improve the local public schools, which were among the worst in the city. The small parents' group now numbered about eighty people on the e-mail list, and a critical mass had been reached to open a public alternative elementary school nearby. This in turn attracted more middle-class families. Real estate maven Willie Suggs reported that West Harlem had crossed a Rubicon: A house had sold for more than $1 million.

The flip side of these nicely rising values was that Harlem was suddenly attracting just the sort of people whom we didn't want as neighbors: greedy property developers who desired top dollar for square footage regardless of aesthetics. Without Landmark Commission protection, our street was suddenly fair game for any rich person who wanted to demolish a historic building and replace it with an ugly tower.

Unfortunately for us, the Christian Science church next door was vulnerable. Heretofore it had been largely unused except as a parking space for Salami's baby carriage, or drug customers who idled their engines in front awaiting packages. Wagering that the church—which was a double brownstone—could fetch well over $1 million now, the four remaining members of the congregation decided that it was better to take the money and run. The church was attractive to developers, as the ten thousand square feet could be built up and back into the garden, owing to a fluke in zoning.

The block association managed to thwart a succession of potential neighbors, including a man who wanted to erect a twelve-story tower, a theater excited about using the backyard as a stage, and a noisy Pentecostal church that would have placed loudspeakers in front to mobilize the unfaithful. The usual activists mobilized a petition and picketing campaign. Donna the actress recited an eloquent and dramatic monologue to plead the case to the Community Board. Mrs. LaDuke wrote letters about her need for quiet in her twilight years. Borough President C. Virginia Fields was emphatically reminded that she was a daughter of Harlem, too.

The church's various plans were blocked by various city authorities, including the Planning and Building departments. We had won! Victory was sweet, yet we had merely bought time. The end result of sabotaging the church's plans was that members of the congregation no longer kept us informed about future plans. The irony did not escape me that now that the street had grown more peaceful, developers might come and spoil it.

And it was quiet, indeed, in front. The drug presence had decreased to such an extent that barely anyone attended police meetings. When they did, the complaints were often about minor nuisances such as littering. After listening to one homeowner's tirade about dog excrement, the narcotics detective with the big scar shifted in his chair and said dryly, "I guess my services aren't needed anymore." Amazing! Could the drugs be gone completely?

Not completely, it appeared. The commander of the precinct explained that drug activity was merely more "discreet" now. Most of the narcotics business had moved inside and off the streets. Likewise, the police were shifting methods, to long-term investigations whose fruits were announced with much fanfare in press communiqués. In one of the more notable takedowns, thirty-eight men were arrested on 146th Street on April 10 and charged with a hundred counts of sales and possession of cocaine and conspiracy to distribute illegal narcotics. The official yearly estimate for that gang was sales of ninety kilos of crack per year, earning $3 million annually.

Then, in a separate case, on July 25, Police Commissioner Kelly announced that a five-month operation had borne fruit, with the indictments of seventeen men on multiple counts of high-level felony sales. One of the storefronts used for drug business was a pizzeria just around the corner from our house, where dealers would grab a slice on their way to the back room to negotiate and weigh the product on digital scales.

With so many guys going behind bars, much of the homeowners' anger shifted away from the dealers to insensitive gentrifiers. These heartless interlopers did gut jobs without work permits and cracked their neighbors' walls as they drilled. Their Dumpsters monopolized valuable parking spaces, and they didn't pick up the high-fiber poop of their poodles.

Mr. Anderson, ever so tolerant of the dealers, was good-tempered no more. He was particularly enraged by the black hair stylist who had moved in next door. The man's extensive renovation job was noisy and messy. Worse, the hairdresser ruined Mr. Anderson's pansies when he refurbished his own brownstone steps, splashing chemicals on the flower boxes.

"Look at this," Mr. Anderson said, his gloved hands balling into fists as he surveyed the wreckage. "They're dead."

The blossoms were wilted indeed. But how could that be? I thought they were plastic.

"How can plastic die?" I asked.

"They were real!" Mr. Anderson shook with fury. It was scary seeing this gentle man so riled. "The neighborhood got better. So I planted live flowers."

Chapter 25

LIGHTS OUT!

On August 14, 2003, I found myself in a hotel bar in Midtown ordering a white-wine spritzer. I didn't usually drink in the afternoon, but I was about to meet my friend Nick and there was cause for celebration. We had last seen each other in Chechnya during that fateful trip in 2000 when I lost the baby, and now I reflected on the last three and a half years as I waited for him. So much had happened. John and I had survived the house construction. We had made peace on the street and had had Anton.

Suddenly the lights and air-conditioning went out. "Must have been overload," the waiter said, as he set a votive candle on the table to provide illumination. But no, the hotel staff checked the fuses and the problem was wider. I called Nick on my cell phone; he worked at the Associated Press and probably could fill me in. He did: It was a citywide blackout.

We agreed to meet another time: Nick had to report on the crisis and I faced a long walk home, as the trains were stalled. I gulped down my drink, worrying about Anton. He had spent the day with the babysitter visiting friends in Brooklyn and they were probably heading home when the electrical system crashed. I had an image of them trapped in a stifling subway car, Anton wailing from fear of the dark. I tried to telephone Miryam or John, but the cell-phone network had jammed by now. I left money on the table and bolted out of the bar.

As I began my five-mile trek uptown, memories flooded back of the blackout of July 13, 1977, and ensuing rampage in Harlem. I recalled news clips of plunderers, running with televisions in their arms amid the flames. What awaited us now? Needless to say, I couldn't get into the festive spirit of the inordinately merry crowd that was heading uptown. The couple next to me were quipping about making babies in the dark and took turns directing traffic at the intersections. Contemplating the mayhem that lay ahead in Harlem, I resentfully watched a jolly blond foursome plunk themselves down at a sidewalk bistro table on 84th Street and gaily order the last two bottles of chilled pinot grigio. "We wouldn't want it to go bad," joked one woman, slipping off her Jimmy Choos.

The well-heeled trekkers had peeled off by the time the Gap stores yielded to bodegas above 96th Street. Those of us who remained anxiously plowed toward 125th Street, that invisible Berlin Wall that separates white affluence from Harlem. Who knew what we would find when we crossed that line? Practically the only people working were gypsy cab drivers, and they sped through the intersections with double the legal number of passengers. Whereas cafés downtown were handing out free quiche to weary walkers, most shop owners here had pulled down their metal gates and gone home in case all hell broke out. The same thought must have occurred to law enforcers. National Guardsmen wearing camouflage and brandishing assault weapons patrolled Broadway.

The sight of heavily armed men made me nervous. What did they know that I didn't? Were mobs ransacking Mercedes's? Had anyone been shot? Dread melted into relief as I rushed toward my street. As it was downtown, it was a party in West Harlem; men had set up grills in-stead of breaking shop windows. It was like any other warm night here, except that cell phones weren't chirping and the dealers had knocked off work earlier than usual. A great air of hilarity infused the atmos-phere. For many first-generation Dominicans, a blackout was no big deal. Electricity cuts occurred all the time back on the island.

At my street, the familiar lopsided figure of Salami directed traf-fic. He clearly savored his newfound power, waving on some cars and holding up others at whim. A police car nudged forward, and a devilish smile flooded Salami's face as he firmly told the occupants that they couldn't pass. "Sorry, it's the law," Salami chortled maniacally, plant-ing himself in front of the vehicle. About twenty people gathered at the corner, teasing the cops, "You can't go. There's no green light."

The officers played along for a couple of minutes, but then they gunned the engine and stormed through the frozen lights, almost knocking down Salami.

"I'm going to arrest you!" he screamed at the taillights.

This made me chuckle momentarily, but despite the amusing sideshow I fretted about Anton and picked up my pace toward the house. The lawn-chair ladies must have spotted my apprehension as I rounded the corner, and they called out: *"Llegó, el niño llegó"* ("The child got home.") Indeed, there was my beloved son with Miryam on the stoop, observing the triple-parked traffic as though it were a nor-mal day. I swept them into a tight hug that was far more emotional than the situation called for, causing Anton to yelp, *"¡Ay! ¡Mami! ¡Déjame!"* ("Mom, let me go!") Miryam tried to extract herself from my embrace to grab the gypsy cab awaiting her on the street, in order to reach home before authorities closed the bridge to Queens.

Blackouts had been plentiful during our Third World life, and out of habit we had stored candles, flashlights, and kerosene lamps here in our new house. What we were missing was cold beer, and figuring that it would be a long night, I went to Mercedes's, Anton in tow, where about thirty other people had had exactly the same idea. It took nearly as long to get to the head of line as it had to trek those four miles home. But Anton was remarkably patient, moving up and down the line in his sunglasses, exclaiming, "Black! Black!" After finally getting our stash—a bag of ice and thirty-six bottles of assorted Dominican and Mexican beers—we emerged onto Broadway to hear the familiar *cling cling* of a bell. It was John on his trusty bicycle, with another neighbor, Andrew, sitting behind on the fender.

John was surprisingly cool in manner, if not in temperature—his shirt was so drenched with sweat that it looked as if he had just come out of the shower. He had pedaled a collective 340 pounds 110 blocks. My thirsty husband and his passenger inspected my package approvingly.

Once at the house, we took stock of our food supplies. We had a huge deep freezer in the basement, a legacy of life and food shortages in Moscow. That we had imported the habit of hoarding meat in the cellar was a source of mirth to American friends, who reminded us that long lines at grocery shops here were more likely to be for a sale on cured Iberian ham. Indeed, our frozen cornucopia was creating problems today—it included $187 worth of chicken, quite a few steaks, and gallons of ice cream that would spoil as the freezer defrosted. Not wanting the plenty to go to waste, we ventured into the street to recruit a dozen neighbors to share the feast. They obligingly streamed into the backyard, where we readied Russian icon candles for when the natural light dimmed. I called across the garden fence to invite Mrs. LaDuke to the impromptu feast, but she demurred with obvious regret about missing another party. "Hon, I'm going to sit on my steps with flashlights and wait for the tenants to get home. My brother will escort them up," she said. "I don't want them to trip."

As I unwrapped the meat, I realized that the food was so deeply frozen that it would have retained its permafrost characteristics for another three days without power, but now I had to feed all those hungry people sitting in the garden, so defrost I did. While Anton distracted the guests in the garden, showing off his sunglasses despite the blackout, I heated a huge vat of water on the gas stove to thaw the meat.

Now to face the next entertainment challenge. Despite having lived for six years in Johannesburg, one of the world's capitals of barbecuing, neither John nor I was proficient at the grill.

Just as John opened the lighter fluid, with the expression of the doomed facing a speeding truck, in walked Douglas, a new neighbor from across the street, whom we were always pleased to see. He was a brawny, heavy-lidded journalist from Zimbabwe with a zest for parties, particularly at other people's houses, where he didn't have to clean up. He was also one of the great masters of the South African *braai*, or barbecue. Douglas even arrived with his own marinating sauce and sausages. He pushed everyone aside with a manly air, opened a Presidente beer with his keys, and started up the flames with his filterless Camel cigarette. He flipped the steaks as though the tongs were an extension of his calloused hands. Douglas was not just capable; he was inventive, too. He stuffed the green peppers with Havarti cheese and soaked the chicken breasts with a Mozambican sauce containing chilies that he had crushed himself. The mighty chef prepared garlic bread without singeing the crust. He sprinkled the pyramids of broccoli, corn, and mushrooms with oil and garlic and salt, and roasted them to perfection. Douglas even baked dessert on the grill, by pasting blueberry jam on Brie wrapped in tinfoil.

The crowd oohed and ahed. I boiled water to defrost more provisions. John savored his role as gracious host. The adults spoiled Anton with unwavering attention.

We could just make out the silhouette of Bloomberg the cat atop the cinder-block wall. He mewed shrilly for scraps. Sandals crunched in the gravel, under the Indian lanterns hanging from the dogwood tree. The sounds of festivity rose from the street, which had filled up with braziers and diners. For once, I thought, there was confluence between the front and the back of the house. The aroma of lighter fluid and charcoaled chicken was seamlessly the same. After three long years we had finally achieved harmony with the *calle*.

I was jolted out of this reverie by Mackenzie, who came in to join us after putting out the night's trash. As I looked out on Broadway, phosphorus flares illuminated every intersection. Emergency vehicles of every type—contractor vans, police vans, and utility trucks—were parked at intervals, flashing their emergency lights as though to warn, "We are here."

Mackenzie was annoyed that he couldn't watch his nightly BBC news. Our lavish spread only seemed to further irritate him.

"You folks are soft," he said, as he approached the bulging worktable that served as the night's buffet. "Look at all that food. I've gone months squatting in buildings without electricity. You have one night without it and you act like the apocalypse is coming. Didn't you say you lived in Africa?"

This sentiment did not deter Mackenzie from heaping his plate with chicken and corn. He helped himself to one of Douglas's Camels. Then he got into a passionate discussion about Zimbabwe's land-reform policy.

"I don't get what Mugabe is doing," Mackenzie told Douglas. "He says he's a revolutionary but he's starving the little man."

"I'm with you, bro—it doesn't make sense," Douglas said pleasantly, as he flipped another chicken breast. "He's hurting the blacks as much as the whites."

Sated and sluggish with meat, we stirred the embers as Anton found a lap to sit on. His choice was John's friend Andrew, who it turned out knew quite a lot about the constellations. Without the normal electric glare of city lights, we could easily see the stars, and Andrew pointed to an especially bright spot. "There's Venus." I doubted that Anton could see anything behind his sunglasses, but he nodded vigorously. Then he gestured around us. *"¡Planeta Nueva York!"*

We heard Mrs. LaDuke across the cinder-block wall. Her voice made me reflect on our hodgepodge of friends here. The soft evening, and no doubt the several glasses of shiraz, unleashed a profound sentimentality. Eyes teary with emotion, I considered the assortment of eccentrics who formed our surrogate family. Just like our cobbled-together meal, we had amassed a community of misfits like ourselves, who were all oddballs yet managed to complement one another. One doesn't have the luxury of choosing blood relatives, and likewise we had ended up on this block without prior thoughts about neighbors. Yet how fortunate we were. I studied the silhouettes around the grill and thought about the mishmash. We were all outsiders: the stubborn old-timers who stayed on in the neighborhood way after their friends left; a Dominican karate master who had resisted the drug tide; a bookish crack addict from Jamaica; a Zimbabwean writer who feared prison back home. The drug dealers—not that we considered them friends, but they were neighbors in a fashion—were also marginalized, living in this foreign country outside the law. And who could be more out of place than my husband, John, this solid Dutchman, who'd moved to Africa and then

Russia and now here, and our little imp with the perfect Spanish. Yet we all somehow fit in.

As I poured another plastic cup of wine, I reflected that a house does not stop at four walls. By becoming part of something larger on this block, I had regained, somewhat, the sense of mission that I had lost by giving up foreign reporting. We were living a smaller life but in many ways a much deeper one.

I gazed at my two men. What a wonderful family! I was blessed! I startled John with a big smack on the lips and then took Anton from his astrological perch and hugged him tightly. Oh, my beloved, healthy son! My treasure!

Anton struggled to wiggle free. *"Mami, ow!"*

As the cookout drew to a close, we walked our guests to the door and bade a soft goodnight. The flare at the intersection of Broadway illuminated the clusters of lawn chairs on the pavement. Other homeowners waved from their stoops. People were mellow and folks had put on gentle *bachatas*. We sat for a long time, watching the glowing grills and candles, and listening to the murmur of conversation.

EPILOGUE

The blackout marked a turning point. After that night, the street assumed a greater level of civility. Raids became rarer and we no longer kept a six-pack on hand for the dramas in front of our stoop. One evening, as I brought in the chairs from the garden and locked the back door, I realized that it had been months since I'd heard a surveillance helicopter.

Even the services changed. The Asian manicurists who had colonized the rest of Manhattan discovered West Harlem, and suddenly it was obvious that the old salons that had truly been drug fronts were just that. New possibilities arose on the culinary front, too. A wave of Mexicans moved to the neighborhood and opened restaurants, posing competition for the tamale lady outside the subway station.

As we busily explored our new eating options, law enforcement nabbed more suspects. The police busted a gang that had terrorized two buildings on 146th Street and then closed down a string of shops that had served as drug fronts—bodegas, communications stores, restaurants, and beauty salons. Broadway from 140th to 144th Streets was a sea of yellow police ribbons, after the cops hauled away forty-eight traffickers who supplied narcotics to at least twelve states, from Ohio to the Carolinas.

Then developers bought the two drug hubs across the street. The dealers moved out before the new management got the keys to their apartments. Just months later, the cops confirmed that much of the cocaine business had moved farther uptown or to the Bronx and New Jersey.

I still attended occasional police meetings, which served more as an opportunity to catch up with old friends than to gripe about crime. The main issue was the incessant noise—apparently West Harlem residents lodged more of these complaints than anyone else in the city. After one such meeting, I greeted one of the undercovers. He had some startling news: Drugs had been essentially eradicated from our street.

I was flabbergasted. Could things have changed so quickly? "No more drugs?" I asked incredulously. "If the dealers are gone, then what's that activity on the corner?"

The cop looked as me as though I were dim. "Lady, where you been? Didn't you know? We have Mexican brothels now!"

Naturally, the drug trade never fully stopped. Even the Darwinian forces of New York real estate could not completely cleanse the area. Clumps of men still stand out on Broadway in below-freezing weather. Occasionally a small-time dealer, unaware that the neighborhood has changed, will stash a five-gram bag in the front yard of Salami's former house. A number of the suspiciously empty sneaker boutiques still manage to pay $10,000 a month in rent. And two crack dens remain around the corner from us.

Of course I'm a white gentrifier, but I have yet to see the evil in driving the dealers out. For the first time in years, elevators in the apartment buildings across the street are scrubbed of piss, and residents can walk in the corridors without running into men packing handguns. The new owners Sheetrocked over the peeling lead paint and installed proper lighting in the lobbies. The major criticism of gentrification is that it elevates rents and in the process drives out low-income tenants. Yet, on our street, these apartments are rent-stabilized and the poorer families remain.

Mackenzie has certainly thrived from the change. At first, things didn't look good when the new management evicted him the moment it took over. For a few tense months he squatted around the corner in a brownstone populated by angry heroin addicts. Then he charmed his way into a bona fide position as super in another apartment building across the street from us. A perk of the job is a free basement room—with a working toilet, his first in years. Mackenzie has a sideline, "valet parking," or moving the cars of richer residents on alternate-side parking days. At last count he claimed seven clients. Our literary friend can often be seen seated behind the wheel of a well-polished Mercedes, reading novels. As if that weren't lucky enough, Mackenzie beat prostate cancer right before his sixtieth birthday.

Salami has profited, too. He's still living with the old lady around the corner and has developed the midsection flab of the well fed, although he apparently lost his new dentures. Who knows how they went astray, or why he couldn't replace them—I know better than to initiate a discussion on such intimate matters.

Clarence, however, didn't fare well. He was fired by the new building management and moved to an old-age home about twenty-five blocks away, but he periodically came back to sun himself on the meridian bench on Broadway. His routine began by absorbing his daily Vitamin D via the carbon monoxide from the six lanes of traffic. Then he would ring our bell to request orange juice, always grumbling that it wasn't organic.

Suddenly, in December 2005, he disappeared. Mackenzie heard that Clarence was in Harlem Hospital following a stroke. Thinking that he would welcome visitors—Clarence had no family that we knew of—I went to the clinic bearing a jar of wheat germ. I imagined a recuperating Clarence scowling about the poorly conceived dietary plan of the hospital nutritionists. However, the man at the front desk reported no sign of our friend. It was the same story with the police, and at the old-age home. *Nada.* Clarence had vanished. Gone. Which I feared meant dead.

This didn't seem possible. How could someone with such a large personality and presence simply evaporate? I was devastated to think we'd never again hear that mumble "It is what it is." Although gruff, Clarence seemed to have liked us in his bah-humbug sort of way, and he had been my first buddy on the block. I miss him.

Lots of new people have moved in, but we don't know them as well. Perhaps it takes uniting under truly difficult circumstances to forge those kinds of bonds. We have grown close, though, to the Corsican who bought the church next door, converting it into a ten-thousand-square-foot bachelor's pad shared with eight cockatiels that fly uncaged in the gigantic space.

A Corsican who uses Rollerblades in his own house is a sign of changing times, but no gentrification is complete without a Thai restaurant. We're still waiting. Starbucks and the Sugar Hill Bistro closed a couple of years ago owing to a dearth of latte drinkers. New establishments have opened in their place but they are struggling. We find it promising that the corner liquor store has begun offering wine tasting on Fridays, although other gentrifiers are put off by the cheap Gallo served beside the cashier's bulletproof glass. Word has it that the desolate warehouses by the Hudson River will become Manhattan's latest restaurant row, now that the city is rebuilding the piers for a waterfront park. Real estate agents eager to convey a "loft-style" Soho cool renamed the district ViVa—Viaduct Valley. The centerpiece is the triangular brick building that used to house the homeless colony. Presumably diners in this future gourmet emporium will be unaware that the cocktail patio used to swarm with unwashed addicts.

El Floridita on Broadway wasn't ready for the switch. After the busts of 2003, new management took over and posted a big sign in the window declaring drugs verboten. The café was empty without the coke merchants, and we enjoyed many a romantic meal uninterrupted by chirping cell phones. Sadly, our patronage was not enough business, and the owners eventually removed the NO DRUGS sign to woo back the old clientele. This desperate measure came too late, and the restaurant folded in mid-2006 because of unpaid rent.

Unlike El Floridita, Raul continued to steer clear of *narcotrafi-*

cando. At the first winter frost his enthusiasm for street vending withered and he switched to busing tables indoors at an Italian restaurant in Midtown. He still comes to the house now and again, to teach us karate and work off the fat from the free pasta.

Someone else returned—Esmeralda, the nubile teenager from the corner who had requested the "attack" services of our late dog, Khaya. Her mother had sent her to live with relatives in the Caribbean for a couple of years, to keep her out of trouble. Now she is back—a confident young woman who doesn't need a canine escort to walk to the bodega. The last time I saw her, she was smacking the face of a muchacho who had dared to comment on her butt.

The old guard is also going strong, especially Mr. Anderson and his live pansies. Mrs. LaDuke, at eighty-eight, talks about passing on—"Oh, I'm bad! I'll never make it up there to heaven!"—but shows no sign of ebbing, aside from an azure hint of cataracts on her eyes. Age is catching up with Mrs. Campbell, who has confused days but still stands on the stoop to monitor proceedings on the street.

Mom has not let up, either. Despite a hip replacement, a broken shoulder, and botched back surgery, she continues to drive and refuses to entertain the notion of moving in with us. Grandma's ashes remain in Mom's garage. It's something I must attend to one day—but somehow, like Mom, I can't seem to find the right time to do it or the ideal place to take them.

Recently I made a trip to the Dominican Republic, where I looked around a bit for Miguel, who, according to American law enforcement, was still on the lam. I didn't try very hard. What would I have said if I saw him? "Fancy meeting you here"? Would he brandish a gun, thinking that I was after him? A cursory glance at the national phone book revealed several listings for Miguel Pérez Pérez, not that I expected a savvy fugitive from justice to register himself. Who even knows if that was his real name? Naturally, I didn't call.

My work took me to Miguel's hometown, San Francisco de Macorís, which, although the distinction is not listed in tourist brochures, is the capital of Dominican drug trafficking. By the looks of it, much of the proceeds have gone into the garish architecture ringing the city.

The style is known locally as Narco Deco—stucco villas with cherub fountains and enormous satellite dishes. I doubted that a small-time thug like Miguel could afford one of these *arriviste* monstrosities, or the chauffeur-driven fleets parked behind the fortified walls, but naturally I didn't make any inquiries.

A market city that bakes on a flat plateau may seem an odd place to park a fortune considering the 773 miles of coastline or mountain estates in which to reside. But many cocaine traffickers hail from San Francisco, and, being a clannish bunch, they bring their money home. Locals pointed me toward the so-called gangster cemetery, where *narcotraficantes* rest in temple-size mausoleums. No sign of Miguel here, or in the more modest cemetery for ordinary folks. I felt oddly relieved. No matter how he made his living, Miguel had behaved like a gentleman.

The next day I visited a tiny fishing town named Miches, where unstable wooden vessels called *yolas* take off for American territory on moonlit nights. The cargo comprises humans and narcotics, which, if they make it across the shark-infested currents of the Mona Canal, are delivered to deserted beaches in western Puerto Rico. From there, passengers who have not drowned make their way through the mountains to a connection that will provide false documents and a plane ticket to New York. This type of journey is called *ir con machete*, or "going by machete," since in the old days, passport pictures were cut out with sharp knives and replaced with false ones. With the increased border scrutiny after 9/11, these desperate travelers are now more likely to "rent" someone else's documents.

For a major departure point of contraband, Miches is a surprisingly dozy village of pastel cottages, with nary a policeman in sight. The palm-fringed beaches—minus the pigs munching coconut husks—are of Bacardi ad perfection but there's barely any tourism. The main sources of income are fishing and the boats leaving for *allá*, or "there."

A local schoolteacher told me that the number of trips was rising. The previous week alone, twenty had left for Puerto Rico. I thought about the ultimate destination for some travelers: our street. What a shock it must be to leave this pastoral setting, where everyone knows one another, to harsh winters in cramped apartments. A vision of our house drifted into my head, and, standing on the beach in Miches, I reflected on home. What an amazing time it had been. It really was quite something. We had fallen into a pit and climbed out intact. Everyone had said we were mad, and we probably were, but all had worked out in the end. Now, even Salami's deranged threats were but a quaint memory. Over the past seven years, the house project and becoming a parent had injected a long-needed mellowness into my life. I had learned to slow down, and see the mystery in the mundane, such as Anton's first words. Stamping out aphids in a garden is not as meaningful as exposing corruption, but simple pleasures do have their own rewards.

While some of the more recent gentrifiers are uncomfortable about raising kids in this neighborhood, we appreciate the variety of perspectives it has to offer. Yes, Anton did attend a fancy private school downtown, but uptown he had his own *apodo*, "El Gringo," as the only white kid on his Dominican baseball team.

Still, we had been growing restless. John traveled increasingly for work, and I was beginning to do the same. Just little reporting trips, three weeks at most, to old haunts like Angola. The world was a very big place, and John reminded me that we had never been to Australia or Antarctica. Lately he had been mumbling about moving "somewhere else." With nostalgia, he recalled the stone grange in Portugal that no doubt someone had bought by now. Just the other week I spotted the well-worn atlas and what looked like sketches of a barn on his desk.

I looked at my watch, as I stood in the softening Caribbean sun. It was late afternoon—time to leave Miches if I wanted to reach the capital before dark. Once on the reddish dirt road, the car swerved to avoid a goat, and I caught a glimpse of the mountain tumbling down to the ocean. On the left was a cute wooden house of cerulean blue. Red-plumed roosters strutted through the fecund garden of bananas and bougainvillea. My practiced eye spotted a hand-painted sign in front: SE VENDE (FOR SALE).

I mentally measured the property and calculated what the price might be. Purely out of curiosity, of course.

ACKNOWLEDGMENTS

The book resulted from a happy chain of encounters. It all began when Connie Rosenblum commissioned a piece about the neighborhood for *The New York Times*. Michela Wrong happened to be visiting at the time and ordered me to convert the article into a book. She put me in touch with Clive Priddle, who refined the idea and introduced me to the wondrous agent Joy Harris. One couldn't hope for a fiercer, and sweeter, advocate. I'm blessed that Joy delivered me to the peerless Jennifer Hershey and Laura Ford at Random House. More dedicated and wise editors cannot exist. Gratitude goes to copy editors Amy Edelman and Evan Camfield for catching silly blunders, and to Avideh Bashirrad for her marketing inspirations.

True friends neglected their own writing to look at mine.

Tony Wende, Aliza Marcus, and Eve Conant steered me in the right direction at the start. Louisa Campbell made sure I finished the book. Her trusty blue pencil improved some truly awful passages and her enthusiasm kept me going when I was stuck. I can't praise her enough.

Others urged me on and helped brainstorm an appropriate title. For this I thank Bruce Porter, Diane Solway, David Resnicow, Cyd Harris, Steve and Claudia Malley, Alissa Quart, Andrej Gustinic, Andrew McCarthy, Bruce Ellerstein, Doug Raboy, Yadwa Yawand-Wossen, Marla Joel, Rob Urban, and Lerone Wilson.

Adalgiza Almonte Lopez de Anderson, José Antonio Rosario, and Jon Anderson served as wonderful guides in Quisqueya. Michele Wucker and Dan Schulman extended vital research tips that filled gaps. Crystal Vidal and Dolores, Axel, and Guillermo served as extended family when I abandoned my own to work. A fellowship at the Hoover Institution at Stanford University supplied a quiet corner to write.

Profound gratitude goes to my ever-tolerant family—Susan, Larry, Saul, and Hildy. They may grit their teeth but they never fail to support me, no matter how ridiculous the endeavor. Above all, I must mention Anton Syril and John, my beloved son and husband. They put up with my antics and absences and inspire me in so many ways. *Mijn lieve schatten.*

ABOUT THE AUTHOR

JUDITH MATLOFF is a contributing editor of the *Columbia Journalism Review* and teaches at Columbia University's Graduate School of Journalism. She was a foreign correspondent for twenty years, last as the Africa and then Moscow bureau chief for *The Christian Science Monitor*. Her articles have appeared in numerous publications, including *The New York Times*, *The Economist*, *Newsweek*, and *The Dallas Morning News*, and she is the recipient of a MacArthur Foundation grant, a Fulbright fellowship, and the Godsell, the *Monitor*'s highest accolade for a correspondent. Matloff still lives in Harlem with her husband and son.